P9-ECO-252

SET FOR THE HOLIDAYS

with

ANNA OLSON

Recipes to Bring

Comfort and Joy

appetite

by RANDOM HOUSE

Appetite by Random House® and colophon are registered trademarks of Penguin Random House LLC.

Library and Archives of Canada Cataloguing in Publication is available upon request.
ISBN: 978-0-14-753081-3
eBook ISBN: 978-0-14-753082-0

Book and cover design: Scott Richardson with Rachel Cooper
Cover design: Rachel Cooper
Photography: Janis Nicolay
Prop styling: Catherine Therrien
Endpaper ornaments: Pepin Press—*Graphic Ornaments*
Printed and bound in China.

Published in Canada by Appetite by Random House®,
a division of Penguin Random House Canada Limited.

www.penguinrandomhouse.ca

10 9 8 7 6 5 4 3 2 1

appetite
by RANDOM HOUSE | Penguin
Random House
Canada

To Michael, thank you for bringing comfort and joy to every single day.

Contents

Happy Holidays   i

MENUS & MEALS FOR THE HOLIDAYS
(AND ALMOST EVERY DAY)

BAKING FOR THE HOLIDAYS
(AND ALMOST EVERY DAY)

Happy Holidays

When does your holiday season begin? Mine starts with the first pumpkin pie I bake. I don't bake a pumpkin pie on a regular Tuesday night when it's just Michael and me at home, so the aroma of pumpkin and cinnamon drifting through the house means the weather is crisp and cool and we have guests coming over.

I look forward to Thanksgiving, Christmas and New Year's with the same eagerness and excitement as I did when I was a child, but my focus has changed from receiving gifts to giving them. And these days that means making the extra effort to connect with friends and family in a way that is different than at any other time of the year.

When we host at holiday time, I take extra care when planning the menu, decorating the table (and the house) and thinking about what will please our guests the most. But what really brings "sparkle" to the holidays is the authentic joy that arises when everyone is relaxed and enjoying each other's company over good food and good conversation. And isn't that the spirit of the holiday season?

In this book, I'm sharing my joy with you—and since my joy is expressed through what comes from my kitchen, it is the recipes along with the helpful hints, stories and good memories that help my holiday season sparkle. You can't have sparkle if you have stress, so I've provided lots of tips for planning and making things ahead, ensuring that your food is delicious and beautifully presented, and that you can focus on being with your guests.

Part one of the book is organized by occasion, with menus included for almost every event during the festive season. With holiday entertaining, I tend to book the date and confirm the guests first, then plan the menu. The occasion dictates the shape of that menu (be it a cozy dinner with friends, or a big family feast, or an open house, or something in between), so instead of sending you willy-nilly through the book to piece a meal together from the different chapters, I have neatly organized each chapter by the occasion itself. There are also recipes for the in-between moments when you need a break from the feasting and the frenzy, as well as new ideas for how to reinvent your leftovers.

Naturally, a great deal of this book also covers holiday baking. No wonder I love this time of year! In part two there are recipes for cookies and cakes, of course, but also for breads, savoury bakes, chocolates and confections, and gifts from the kitchen. Homemade gifts show thought and commitment—and many of these recipes are perfect for making in large batches to share with family and friends.

Throughout the book, you'll see a few different symbols to help you quickly spot key features of a recipe. Those that are particularly giftable have this 🎁 icon; and those recipes that are Vegetarian Ⓥ, Vegan Ⓥe and Gluten-free ⒼⒻ are also noted, so you can plan inclusive dishes and meals for everyone you love this holiday season.

My true holiday wish for you is to find your "sparkle." If mistakes happen, just move on, knowing that your friends and family will forgive you. Find joy in the kitchen, express your love through the dishes you make and have a delicious festive season!

Anna

Menus & Meals
for the Holidays
(AND ALMOST EVERY DAY)

Holiday Cooking Basics

Hosting family and friends is a key part of the holiday season, but with so much tradition and expectation woven into festive meals, it can be a stressful time for cooks. To help take the pressure off food planning, I've presented the chapters in this first half of the book as themed menus. Whether you're making a classic holiday meal such as a Thanksgiving or Christmas turkey dinner or preparing little bites and shareable items to entertain friends, I've got you covered. Follow the whole menu or pick and choose individual dishes, combining them as you like.

Before you start cooking, here are some essential tips, tools and ingredients to have at hand over the entertaining season to help make it more manageable.

PREPARATION

WRITING LISTS—Writing a shopping list, followed by a prep list, gets me organized and in the spirit to host my event. I set up my *shopping list* by the key areas in the grocery store: produce, proteins, dairy and dry goods. Then I comb through my recipes and write the needed items and their quantities under each heading. This way I'm not zig-zagging around the store. I arrange my *prep list* by time: what I can prepare ahead and freeze, what to do one to two days ahead and what to prepare the day of the event. Even little tasks like chopping parsley make the list (because, once I cross them off the list, I feel a sense of accomplishment).

BLANCHING—Green vegetables such as broccoli and green beans take no time to cook, but they can take up space on the stove and require your undivided attention when you are at your busiest, trying to get everything to the table on time. For that reason, I often blanch green vegetables a day or a few hours ahead of time.

To do this, bring a large saucepan of salted water to a boil over high heat, drop in the washed and trimmed green veggies and cook until al dente, or just under your desired doneness. Immediately drain the vegetables in a colander and run cold tap water over them until cooled

to stop the cooking and to set the green colour. Drain, allow to air-dry completely and store in a resealable bag or airtight container in the fridge. To reheat, toss them in a saucepan with a little butter over medium heat for a minute or two before serving.

REHEATING—When I create my holiday menus, I think about how to ensure all my dishes will be ready when I need them, and how to avoid the issue of too many pans and not enough burners, or a lack of space in the oven. A key part of this is making parts of the meal ahead of time and reheating them at the last minute. In each recipe, I've provided instructions on what to make ahead and when and how to reheat it, if applicable.

SEASONING—Savoury cooking involves a lot of seasoning, but when a recipe says "season to taste," what does that mean? Salt maximizes flavour. For example, with just the right amount of salt, a cooked carrot tastes more like a carrot than an unsalted one—but it should never taste salty. I recommend using a coarse sea salt and adding it a pinch at a time, tasting until you are happy with the result. Black pepper heightens flavour and adds contrast. For example, adding pepper to the Roasted Squash and Tomato Bowl with White Beans, Spinach and Olives (page 140) brings out the natural sweetness of the squash, which balances the saltiness of the olives and the acidity of the tomatoes. Use a pepper mill to grind it right into your dishes, a little at a time.

The golden rule when it comes to seasoning is to taste the dish before it goes to the table.

STORAGE

Real estate for food storage is at a premium around holiday time, so storing raw and prepared foods takes a little organization.

FRIDGE—For food safety, always store cooked foods (especially those to be served cold) above raw, and vegetables above meats, wherever you can. I empty one of my crisper drawers and store my turkey in it, away from other food and right at the bottom of the fridge. I just pull out the drawer and give it a good wash after the bird has gone into the oven.

Keep dips and spreads in resealable containers and blanched vegetables in resealable bags that can be wiggled into small spaces. Be sure you don't block the vent toward the back of the fridge—it lets air flow throughout your fridge, so the entire fridge stays cold and items at the back don't freeze.

FREEZER—Wrap your foods well in resealable freezer bags or in plastic, or other freezer-safe containers, and try to store baked goods and delicate items away from more aromatic ones. Even in the freezer, a garlic kielbasa will transmit its garlicky taste and smell to everything around it—especially to baked goods, which absorb odours very quickly. Remember to label and date all your packages, and include reheating or cooking instructions if you can so you don't have to dig up your recipe later.

PANTRY—I transfer packaged dried goods such as rice and beans to mason jars once they are opened, which keeps the food airtight but also visible. I also trim specific cooking instructions from the package label and drop them into the jar.

TOOLS

These tools sit at the ready in my kitchen, for whenever I get the urge to cook, and are particularly handy when I'm prepping for the festive season.

BOX GRATER—I use a basic model with large holes, small holes and a slicer for grating cheese and vegetables and even for grating cold butter when making a crumble or scone recipe. Use the grater attachment on your food processor, if you prefer.

KITCHEN TIMER—This tool is a definite MUST, whether it's an app on your phone or an old-fashioned wind-up or digital clock. When baking cookies and cakes, I always set my timer for a few minutes *before* the stated time for doneness, just so I can check on their progress. I also set my timer when I know I want a deadline to stop working

in the kitchen so I can tidy up, set the table or change out of my yoga pants before my guests arrive.

OVEN-TO-TABLE SERVING DISHES—Many wintry and holiday dishes (such as Roasted Carrots and Parsnips, page 106, or Croque Monsieur Bake, page 133) can go right from the oven to the table, which means fewer dishes to wash! Ceramic bakeware makes this job easy, so I keep a few of these presentable dishes on hand. Glazed dishes need just a quick soak and most will wipe clean without a problem.

PEN, PAPER AND STICKY NOTES—Even with hundreds of apps and digital devices available, I still prefer sticky notes for writing lists, labelling bowls and storage containers in the fridge, and assigning each recipe to its platter or dish before a dinner party so I don't forget anything.

RASP—When a box grater is too big for the job, this slender file with fine cutting points is what you need. It's ideal for finely grating garlic cloves, grating ginger or citrus zest, or making a fine snow from Parmesan cheese. And unlike a garlic press, it's a snap to wash.

ROASTING PAN—If you're in charge of the Big Feast, you'll likely need a roasting pan. Be sure that it fits in your oven with enough room for air to flow around it. I like a heavy steel or enamel roasting pan without a lid. If you can, avoid using a disposable aluminum foil roasting pan—it can collapse under the weight of a turkey and you can't make the gravy in it on the stovetop after the bird comes out of the oven. If you must use disposables, double or even triple the foil pans to give them more strength and structure.

SCALE—Just like in baking, weighing your ingredients for cooking will give you more consistent results than measuring them by volume. I provide measurements for both weight and volume, and though savoury cooking is generally more forgiving than baking, I invite you to give weighing a try—it's a tidy and more precise way to measure. I favour a digital scale because its small, flat shape stores easily in my kitchen; it is also easy to read and reset to zero (tare) with each new ingredient addition. A spring scale has the benefit of never needing batteries, but it can be more difficult to read and takes up more space.

SHARP KNIVES—A set of sharp knives makes slicing, dicing and carving easier—and you'll be doing lots of all of these around the holidays. A good chef's knife is best for dicing vegetables and preparing basic meats, a serrated knife is perfect for cutting bread and fragile cakes, and a slender carving knife is ideal for slicing roasted turkey, ham or beef. A paring knife is perfect for cutting foods in your hand, and a vegetable peeler is indispensable for removing thick skins. It's a myth that having your knives professionally sharpened will damage them. In fact, you're more likely to damage them—or hurt yourself—if you use them when they're dull. I never put my knives in the dishwasher—to avoid harsh detergents and them being damaged—but wash and dry them by hand instead, and put them away as soon as I'm done (and remember never to drop a knife into a sink of soapy water).

STORAGE CONTAINERS—I use stackable glass containers for prepared foods because they last a long time (compared to plastic) and, quite simply, I can see through them, so I know what's there. Most are made with tempered glass, so they are sturdy, but even so I prefer not to keep them in the freezer.

TEMPERATURE PROBE THERMOMETER—An instant-read probe thermometer is a display screen atop a slender skewer and is considered more reliable than other kinds of meat thermometers. You can move it to different parts of the roast to check them for doneness (which is especially important when cooking turkey), and unlike larger thermometers, they don't leave large holes in the meat from which flavourful juices can leak out.

TRIVETS AND COOLING RACKS—With all of the hot pots and pans on the go around the holidays, you need a place to put them. Wire cooling racks offer a sturdy base for your roasting pan when there is no room on the stove, and a few table-friendly trivets come in handy when you need to set a casserole dish onto a buffet or dining room table.

WINE TOOLS—Depending on your level of wine appreciation, you might need just a few basic wine tools, or maybe a few extras. A rabbit-ear corkscrew is the easiest to use because it requires little leverage to extract a wine cork from the bottle. A waiter's corkscrew (my

preference) is the most compact, but it takes a little practice to use. Aged wines can sometimes benefit from decanting, but in general, red wines rarely require it and white wines never need decanting.

Two other items I like to have on hand are foil wine pourers, which, when rolled and inserted into the wine bottle, prevent any drips, and a Champagne bottle stopper, to keep the sparkles in our sparkling wine for a day or two after opening.

INGREDIENTS

APPLES—Apple varieties will vary according to the time of year and where you live. Try to stick to local apples, wherever you are—you'll be happier with the taste and texture. In this book, I specify an apple variety when it makes a difference; otherwise, the choice is yours.

BUTTER—When I bake, which generally requires a lot more butter than cooking, I prefer to use unsalted butter (see page 164); that way I can be in charge of the salt (since the amount of salt in salted butter varies by brand). I also find that unsalted tends to be fresher and sweeter tasting, ideal for baking. For cooking, for example when sautéing vegetables or starting a savoury dish in a pan, I use unsalted or salted interchangeably.

CHEESE—For a full lesson in building a cheese board, check out page 35. For "cooking" cheese, I try to keep a few on hand: medium and old Cheddar, Gruyère, Asiago and Parmesan.

CRANBERRIES—Fresh cranberries keep for quite a long time, so you may find them in your grocery store until Christmas. That said, frozen cranberries are as easy to work with and produce exactly the same results as fresh. For frozen cranberries, measure them straight from the container and thaw by letting them sit on the counter for an hour—they won't let out too much juice, and if they do just drain before using.

HERBS—Certain herbs dominate the winter season. Thyme is one of my favourites, as it builds flavour for so many soups, stews and sauces. Rosemary is also common, and sage is the herb we identify with classic holiday dishes such as stuffing and gravy. The key is to cook them into your dishes—you would never serve them raw, sprinkled on food as a garnish at this time of year. I prefer to use fresh herbs, even in the winter, because I find their flavour brighter than dried. The one exception I allow myself is oregano. There is something pleasing and familiar about dried oregano in certain dishes.

MAPLE SYRUP—Maple syrup adds a subtle sweetness and shine when just a hint of sweetness is needed in savoury dishes. Honey has a specific flavour—which I like for a few of my recipes (such as my Hazelnut Orange Panforte, page 248)—but in many cases its flavour can be overwhelming or its texture too sticky, and I prefer to leave granulated sugar to my baking. So maple syrup feels just right. And it's vegan! You can substitute maple syrup for honey in an otherwise vegan dish.

MILK—I use 2% milk in most of my cooking and baking. Whole milk is a treat but, honestly, I always have 2% in the fridge because that's what I like in my coffee and tea. 2% milk can be swapped with 1% for similar results, but please avoid using skim, especially in baking. The little extra milk fat in 2% adds more than you might imagine, including moisture, so that cookies and cakes don't crumble.

OILS AND VINEGARS—A decent extra virgin olive oil is essential for drizzling and finishing dishes, and as with wine, you may have your preferences by taste or country of origin. Generally, the farther south the source of the olive oil (Greece, southern Italy), the more intensely peppery the oil. An inexpensive extra virgin olive oil is sufficient for cooking.

A white wine, red wine and decent balsamic vinegar will all provide acidity for vinaigrettes. I also like to have rice vinegar on hand, not just because it is perfect for my Asian dishes but also because it is not as intensely sour as wine vinegars. It is suited to more delicate recipes, like my Avocado Yogurt Dressing and Dip (page 149). Having said that, if you only want to stock one vinegar, choose white wine vinegar for its clarity and mild acidity.

ONIONS—In most cases, a regular cooking onion is all that is needed in any dish where it will be cooked. For a milder flavour, shallots and leeks are more delicate.

Onions and shallots should be stored in a cool, dark and dry place (never under the sink), and leeks and green onions should be refrigerated.

POTATOES—In my recipes, I specify which type of potato will work best. Russet potatoes contain less starch, and so they are wonderful for roasting and mashing. New potatoes have more starch, so they are best for boiling. Yukon Golds are ideal all-purpose potatoes—they are lovely boiled, chopped into salads, or served mashed or roasted. As with onions, store potatoes in a cool, dark, dry place.

ROOT VEGETABLES—We inherently understand that root vegetables are a part of winter menus, because they store so well over the season. Their natural sweetness and complexity round out a winter meal. Unless you have a root cellar, refrigerate your carrots, parsnips, beets and celeriac (celery root). A waxed turnip can be stored with your potatoes until you cut into it—then refrigerate it.

SALAD GREENS—In the winter, traditional lettuces—which are either grown in a greenhouse or imported from abroad—can be expensive or taste flat. Instead, I am drawn to winter greens—leaves with a little more structure and substance but with a hint of bitterness. Think frisée, radicchio, Belgian or curly endive and, if I'm buying hothouse greens, spinach or oak leaf (feuille de chêne). In my recipes, I balance the full-bodied taste of these greens with a bit of sweetness from fruit.

SALT—When I bake, or need to measure a precise amount of salt, I use fine sea salt. When I am seasoning to taste or dressing a salad, I prefer flaked sea salt because it's easier to pick up with my fingers for just a pinch. When I'm salting water for cooking pasta, vegetables or potatoes, I use a less expensive coarse pickling salt.

SPICES AND SPICE BLENDS—As in baking, spices have an important place in savoury cooking. Spice blends such as Chinese five-spice or ras el hanout add complexity and sometimes even a kick of heat to roasted root vegetables, for example, and the warmth from chili powder and cayenne heightens their sweetness.

FESTIVE BRUNCH

HOSTING A BRUNCH CELEBRATION is one of my favourite ways to entertain at holiday time. With a little extra time off, guests are alert and energetic (and I am as well), and there's something just a little bit decadent about eating a large, celebratory meal in the morning or at midday. Plus you can have the dishes done and your feet up on the couch (leftover ham sandwich in hand) while it's still light out!

Because you're hosting earlier in the day, what is really important is a little bit of planning. Part of enjoying your brunch is *not* getting up at 5 am to start preparing, so write a list of everything you can make the day before and keep the morning for last-minute necessities only.

WINTER SUNSHINE SMOOTHIES 13

VIRTUOUSLY RICH HOT CHOCOLATE 15

MULLED APPLE CIDER
& MULLED RED WINE 16

SPICED HOLIDAY GRANOLA 19

MONTEBELLO BAKED MAPLE
BUCKWHEAT CRÊPES 21

BAKED HAM WITH ROASTED
APPLESAUCE & HORSERADISH CREAM
23

POTATO AND EGG SALAD WITH
SNAP PEAS 24

OAK LEAF SALAD WITH TOASTED
BUCKWHEAT KASHA, GRAPES AND
BLUE CHEESE 27

served with (your choice of)

BLUEBERRY WHITE CHOCOLATE
SCONES (TO START) 176

RASPBERRY JAM DANISH WREATH
(TO START) 179

PANETTONE OR BUTTERY SOFT DINNER
ROLLS (WITH THE HAM) 182 *or* 99

LEMON CRUMBLE LOAF CAKE
(TO FINISH) 172

AN ASSORTMENT OF COOKIES
(TO FINISH) 193 *to* 221

CHOCOLATE BARKS (TO FINISH) 240

PECAN BUTTER TART CHEESECAKE
(TO FINISH) 268

CHOCOLATE ORANGE BUNDT
FRUITCAKE
(TO FINISH) 283

Opposite: Raspberry Jam Danish Wreath (page 179); Oak Leaf Salad (page 27); Roasted Applesauce (page 152); Montebello Baked Maple Buckwheat Crêpes (page 21); Baked Ham (page 23); Blueberry White Chocolate Scones (page 176); Potato and Egg Salad (page 24)

While I love cooking and baking with local, seasonal ingredients, tropical fruits are at their peak in mid-winter, so craving a taste of sunshine is not unreasonable. Bananas, mangoes, pineapple and citrus all have fantastic flavour and blend healthfully into a smoothie that brightens any wintry morning!

WINTER SUNSHINE SMOOTHIES

GF

V

SERVES 4 AS BREAKFAST, 6 TO 8 AS A START TO BRUNCH • PREP: 5 MINUTES

MAKE AHEAD

This smoothie recipe can be made and refrigerated a few hours before serving (any longer than that and the banana will start turning brown), although the ice or frozen fruit will thaw, so stir it to return to its smooth state.

2 cups (500 mL) plain yogurt (fat-free is OK)
2 medium bananas, diced
1 cup (150 g) diced fresh or frozen pineapple
1 cup (150 g) diced fresh or frozen mango
2 navel oranges
3 Tbsp (45 g) almond butter
1 tsp pure vanilla extract
Pinch of ground cinnamon
Ice cubes (optional)

1. Place the yogurt, bananas, pineapple and mango in a blender and squeeze the juice from the oranges overtop.

2. Add the almond butter, vanilla and cinnamon. If using fresh pineapple and mango, you may want to add a cupful of ice cubes to cool everything down.

3. Purée on high speed until smooth and serve within a few hours.

HELPFUL HINTS

Almond butter is a tasty way to add flavour and a little extra protein to your smoothies. It does mute the sunshine yellow colour, but it's a worthy compromise. Or add half an avocado for a healthy, rich and creamy option.

I find that the banana sweetens this smoothie enough that I don't need to add honey or sugar. And I do prefer regular yogurt in this—Greek yogurt is just too thick.

ADD SPARKLE

Add a splash of coconut milk for a piña colada flavour.

Skim milk powder is the secret ingredient to making a thick and creamy
hot chocolate without the added fat. To serve more than one person, simply
multiply the quantities by the number of guests.

VIRTUOUSLY RICH HOT CHOCOLATE

SERVES 1 • PREP: 5 MINUTES • COOK: 10 MINUTES

MAKE AHEAD
The dry ingredients for this recipe can
easily be made in larger batches and
stored in an airtight container for up
to 3 months.

2 Tbsp (30 mL) instant skim milk
   powder
1 ½ Tbsp (12 g) good-quality cocoa
   powder (regular or Dutch process)
1 ½ Tbsp (18 g) granulated sugar
1 ½ cups (375 mL) 2% milk
Snowflake Marshmallow (page 250),
   for garnish

1. Stir the milk powder, cocoa powder and sugar together in a small
   dish. Whisk in ¼ cup (60 mL) of the cold milk to blend.

2. Pour the remaining milk plus the cocoa mixture into a small saucepan
   and slowly bring to a gentle simmer over medium heat, stirring often.
   Cook for 1 to 2 minutes, until the mixture thickens a little. Ladle into
   a mug and serve topped with a snowflake marshmallow.

HELPFUL HINT
Batches of the dry ingredients work wonderfully for gifting, wrapped in a cellophane bag or a mason jar
tied with a ribbon. Make sure to package the mixture in multiples of 5 Tbsp (75 mL) and tell the recipient to
mix 5 Tbsp (75 mL) for every 1 ½ cups (375 mL) of milk.

So many scented candles try to replicate this smell of apples, citrus and spices, but to no avail. And why rely on artificial scents when you can so easily create the real thing while mulling cider in your own kitchen? Better yet, you'll have a warming beverage to share with family and friends. (A candle can't do that!)

GF

Ve

MULLED APPLE CIDER & MULLED RED WINE

SERVES 6 TO 8 (CIDER) & 8 TO 12 (WINE) · PREP: 5 MINUTES · COOK: 20 MINUTES

1. Pour either the apple cider or the wine, brandy and sugar into a large saucepan and add the citrus rounds. Drop in the cinnamon sticks, cloves and cardamom pods. Bring to just below a simmer over low/medium heat, uncovered, and warm through, letting the spices and citrus infuse into the cider or wine.

2. Before serving, remove and discard the spices. Ladle the cider or wine into glasses or mugs and place a slice of citrus in each glass as a garnish (and for nibbling). The cider and wine can be kept warm over low heat on the stove throughout the brunch.

MAKE AHEAD
Although you can make mulled cider or wine ahead of time, there is no real time saving as you will want to reheat it before serving—and, truly, it's all about the aroma as it steeps. I chill any leftovers to enjoy the next day. The chilling mutes the spices a little, so it's a bit milder tasting.

CIDER
8 cups (2 L) fresh unsweetened apple cider

WINE
2 bottles (each 750 mL) red wine— any type
2 oz (60 mL) brandy
¼ cup (50 g) granulated sugar

1 navel orange, unpeeled and cut into rounds
1 mandarin or clementine orange, unpeeled and cut into rounds
3 cinnamon sticks
6 whole cloves
4 green cardamom pods

HELPFUL HINT
Be sure to use fresh apple cider rather than clear apple cider or apple juice in this recipe. The cloudy, brown mire really does make a difference to the flavour. Look for fresh apple cider in the produce fridge of your grocery store or at a local farmers' market. Need to upgrade this cider to a more adult version? Pour a little spiced rum into the grownups' mugs and get back to opening those gifts!

A good homemade granola should not be limited to the holidays, but the combination of spices and the addition of crunchy cocoa nibs in this version make it feel festive. Better yet, it has no refined sugar and less fat than commercial brands—two reasons I prefer to make my own granola. Serve it with plain yogurt for breakfast or a snack.

SPICED HOLIDAY GRANOLA

MAKES 7 CUPS (1.75 L) • PREP: 10 MINUTES • COOK: 25 MINUTES

MAKE AHEAD
You can store the baked granola in an airtight container at room temperature for up to 1 month.

2 cups (200 g) regular rolled oats (not instant)
1 ½ cups (150 g) sliced almonds
½ cup (50 g) unsweetened, flaked or shredded coconut
½ cup (65 g) cocoa nibs
½ tsp ground cinnamon
½ tsp ground ginger
¼ tsp ground nutmeg
5 Tbsp (75 mL) pure maple syrup
¼ cup (60 g) virgin coconut oil, melted
¾ cup (100 g) dried cranberries
½ cup (50 g) diced dried mango

1. Preheat the oven to 325°F (160°C) and line a baking tray with parchment paper.

2. Toss the oats, sliced almonds, coconut, cocoa nibs, cinnamon, ginger and nutmeg in a large bowl. Add the maple syrup and oil and stir well to coat evenly. Spread this mixture in an even layer on the baking tray and bake for about 25 minutes, stirring twice during cooking, until the almonds are toasted and light brown.

3. While the granola is still warm, stir in the dried cranberries and mango and let the granola cool on the tray on a wire rack.

4. Pour the cooled granola into an airtight container. For gift-giving, package it in cellophane bags of at least 1 ½-cup (375 mL) capacity tied with a ribbon, or scoop it into mason jars.

HELPFUL HINT
Switch up the nuts and dried fruits with your family favourites. Chopped hazelnuts in place of the almonds are decadent, and raisins and dried apricots in place of the cranberries and mango are colourful and tasty. You could even stir chocolate chips or other candied chocolate pieces into the cooled granola (and serve it more like a movie-time snack than a breakfast food).

ADD SPARKLE
The crunch and flavour of this granola make it perfect for coating a goat cheese log for a cheese board, sprinkling on top of a salad or garnishing a soup, like Leek, Potato and Celeriac Soup (page 88).

Years ago, one late November weekend, Michael and I visited Château Montebello, a large log-cabin resort on the Ottawa River near Papineauville, Quebec. We were guest chefs for a special event and we stayed afterwards to rest and take in the hotel. I remember most fondly the spectacular breakfast spread, which included buckwheat crêpes. The earthy crêpes were rolled and baked in a sea of maple syrup so that their edges were crispy but their centre was soft and sweet. Friends who've been more recently tell me that dish is still on the menu, and that it is just as memorable.

MONTEBELLO BAKED MAPLE BUCKWHEAT CRÊPES

V

MAKES 6 EXTRA-LARGE (10-INCH/25 CM) OR 12 REGULAR (6-INCH/15 CM) CRÊPES •
SERVES 6 TO 12 • PREP: 20 MINUTES, PLUS CHILLING • COOK: 45 MINUTES

MAKE AHEAD

I prefer to make the crêpes the day before my brunch, then baste and bake them the morning of. You can even roll and baste the crêpes with butter in the baking dish a day ahead as well, but save pouring the maple syrup over them until they are about to go in the oven. If you'd prefer to make them well ahead of time, stack the cooked and cooled crêpes, wrap well and freeze for up to 3 months. Thaw at room temperature before using. Never refrigerate crêpes—they will dry out and crack when you try to roll them.

CRÊPES
½ cup (75 g) buckwheat flour (light or dark)
⅓ cup (50 g) all-purpose flour
1 cup (250 mL) 2% milk
2 large eggs
¼ cup (60 g) unsalted butter, melted, plus extra for the pan
2 Tbsp (30 mL) vegetable oil
½ cup (125 mL) sparkling apple cider (or beer or club soda)

ASSEMBLY
¼ cup (60 g) unsalted butter, melted
1 cup (250 mL) pure maple syrup

1. For the crêpes, whisk the buckwheat and all-purpose flours together and then whisk in the milk, followed by the eggs, melted butter and oil, until smooth. Chill the batter, covered, for at least 2 hours.

2. Line a baking tray with parchment paper. Right before making the crêpes, whisk the apple cider (or beer or club soda) into the batter. Heat a crêpe pan or other non-stick pan on medium-high heat and brush it with a little melted butter.

3. Ladle about ¼ cup (60 mL) of the crêpe batter for extra-large crêpes (half this for small) into the centre of the pan and lift the pan, swirling to coat it thinly and evenly. Cook until the edges of the crêpe begin to brown and the surface of the crêpe loses its shine, about 90 seconds.

Recipe continues ▶

HELPFUL HINT
Buckwheat is a naturally gluten-free seed, and the buckwheat flour makes these crêpes tender and délicate. Light buckwheat flour has a mild flavour whereas dark buckwheat flour has an earthy nuttiness to it—making it a perfect companion to maple syrup.

4. Use a spatula to flip the crêpe over and cook for 10 more seconds before transferring it to the prepared baking tray. Repeat with the remaining batter.

5. Stack the cooled crêpes on top of each other (no need for parchment between them).

6. Preheat the oven to 375°F (190°C). To assemble the crêpes, brush the base and sides of a casserole dish (wide enough to fit all the crêpes) with a generous amount of the melted butter. Roll up the crêpes individually and nestle them closely in the dish side by side. Brush the tops with any remaining melted butter and then pour the maple syrup overtop.

7. Bake the crêpes, uncovered, for 25 to 35 minutes, basting with the syrup in the dish occasionally, until the edges become browned and crisp. Let cool for 15 minutes before serving.

ADD SPARKLE
Sprinkle a little cinnamon on top or toss a sliced apple in the maple syrup and bake it on the crêpes to make them more of a dessert.

BEYOND THE HOLIDAYS
Use buckwheat crêpes (also called galettes) to make a savoury breakfast. After spreading your crêpe batter in your crêpe pan, crack an egg in the centre and break the yolk, spreading the egg around so it cooks at the same rate as the crêpe. Add a little ham and a sprinkle of grated Swiss cheese, fold the crêpe into a square *et voilà*: galette complète!

When I was growing up, the ham went into the oven earlier on Christmas morning than I would get up to open gifts. It was likely the smell of the ham baking that coaxed me out of bed, rather than the thought of getting the gifts I had asked for. These days, I bake a whole ham for the leftovers. Once I've had as many sandwiches as I can manage, the rest gets diced up and frozen in small containers—it's a great staple ingredient for many meals (see When It's All Over, pages 125 to 145).

BAKED HAM WITH ROASTED APPLESAUCE & HORSERADISH CREAM

GF

SERVES 16 TO 20 (OR 8 TO 10, PLUS LEFTOVERS) • PREP: 10 MINUTES • COOK: 4 HOURS

MAKE AHEAD

The recipe itself is a make ahead dish, since the 4 hours the ham spends in the oven leaves you free to take care of your other festive duties. (And technically the butcher who cures, smokes and cooks the ham is taking care of the heavy lifting.)

6.6 to 8.8 lb (3 to 4 kg) bone-in smoked ham or picnic pork shoulder (see note below)
½ cup (125 mL) fresh apple juice or apple cider
½ cup (125 mL) water
Grainy mustard (gluten-free, if needed), for serving (optional)
1 recipe Horseradish cream (page 154), for serving (optional)
1 recipe Roasted Applesauce (page 152), for serving

1. Preheat the oven to 300°F (150°C).

2. Remove and discard any netting on the ham before placing it in a roasting pan. Score the top of the ham (parallel lines or criss-cross, if you wish), right through the fat. Pour the apple juice (or cider) and water into the bottom of the pan and bake the ham, uncovered and basting occasionally with the juice, for about 4 hours, until it reads 170°F (77°C) on a meat thermometer. Set aside.

3. Transfer the ham to a cutting board and carve slices across the grain. Serve with a dollop of the horseradish cream and/or grainy mustard (if using) and my delicious Roasted Applesauce.

Photo on page 25

23
—
FESTIVE

BRUNCH

HELPFUL HINTS

If you're in charge of making the main meat dish for Christmas and you've never roasted beef or turkey, offer to make a ham—all of the work goes into a ham before you put it into your grocery cart. However, do buy a good one, and if you are cooking for someone with gluten intolerance, be sure to check that the ham is gluten-free (some cured meats are not), and check that the mustard you use is as well.

A hot potato dish can seem heavy and stuffy at brunch, whereas a potato salad is the perfect fit. This creamy potato salad perfectly balances with the texture of the ham (the same way hot scalloped potatoes do) and the green of the dressing and the peas complements the ham's pink colour. The addition of hard-boiled eggs makes it even "brunch-ier."

POTATO AND EGG SALAD WITH SNAP PEAS

GF

V

SERVES 8 TO 10 · PREP: 20 MINUTES, PLUS CHILLING · COOK: 20 MINUTES, PLUS RESTING

1. Cut the potatoes in half (lengthwise, if using fingerlings), place them in a saucepan and cover with cold water. Add a generous pinch of salt and bring to a rolling boil, uncovered, over high heat. Reduce the heat to medium-high and cook until the potatoes are fork-tender, about 15 minutes.

2. Drain the potatoes and transfer them to a large bowl. Sprinkle with the rice vinegar and a little salt and pepper, toss and then let cool completely. Place the cooled potatoes, uncovered, in the fridge to chill.

3. Place the eggs, in their shells, in a single layer in a saucepan and cover with cold water. Bring to a boil over high heat and boil for 4 minutes. Remove the pan from the heat, cover immediately and let the eggs sit for 25 minutes in the hot water. Run the eggs under cold water for a minute then drain and refrigerate.

4. To blanch the snap peas, bring a saucepan of salted water to a boil over high heat. Add the snap peas for 2 minutes, then drain and rinse them under cold water to stop the cooking. (Frozen peas do not need to be blanched after thawing.)

5. To assemble, toss the chilled potatoes with the Avocado Dressing, snap peas (or thawed garden peas) and green onions and season lightly with salt and pepper, if needed. Spoon the salad onto a serving platter. Peel the eggs, cut in half and arrange over the salad. Sprinkle salt and pepper over the salad (and eggs) and serve.

MAKE AHEAD

This salad holds up best when it's assembled pretty close to when you want to serve it, simply because it is so prettily arranged. You can boil the potatoes and the eggs and make the dressing 1 day ahead and refrigerate them in separate airtight containers for last-minute assembly. Of course, left-over assembled salad still tastes just as good as fresh.

3 lb (1.5 kg) fingerling or other miniature potatoes

2 Tbsp (30 mL) rice vinegar

Salt and black pepper

8 large eggs

2 ½ cups (250 g) sugar snap peas, trimmed (or 2 cups/280 g frozen garden peas, thawed)

1 recipe Avocado Yogurt Dressing and Dip (page 149), chilled

4 green onions, thinly sliced

24
—
SET FOR
THE
HOLIDAYS

BEYOND THE HOLIDAYS

This salad is a year-round staple for me, and I even enjoy it as a quick lunch all on its own: protein from the eggs, carbs from the potatoes, green vegetables in the peas and a healthy dressing . . . check!

Baked Ham served with Potato and Egg Salad (page 24) and Applesauce (page 152)

Oak leaf (feuille de chêne) is a hothouse variety of lettuce that looks pretty on a Christmas brunch table, especially alongside a little radicchio. The hint of bitterness from the greens, the touch of sweetness from the grapes, the salt and creaminess from the blue cheese and the crunch from the toasted kasha all add up to a beautifully balanced salad.

OAK LEAF SALAD WITH TOASTED BUCKWHEAT KASHA, GRAPES AND BLUE CHEESE

GF

V

SERVES 8 · PREP: 10 MINUTES

MAKE AHEAD

When making a salad to serve at any party, I always wash and trim my greens beforehand. They refrigerate well in a resealable bag or a bowl with a lid, with a damp paper towel placed in the bag or on top to keep everything crisp.

1 head oak leaf lettuce, trimmed, washed and dried
1 cup (250 mL) chopped radicchio leaves
1 ½ cups (375 mL) seedless red and/or green grapes, cut in half
4 oz (120 g) crumbly blue cheese
⅓ cup (80 mL) French Vinaigrette (page 147)
½ cup (125 mL) Toasted Buckwheat Kasha (page 158)
Salt and black pepper

1. Arrange the oak leaf and radicchio leaves on a serving platter or individual plates.

2. Top the greens with the grapes and crumble the blue cheese overtop. Spoon the dressing over the salad and then sprinkle it with the toasted buckwheat kasha. Finish with a little salt and pepper to serve.

HELPFUL HINT
If you can't find oak leaf lettuce, a 50/50 blend of Boston and romaine, plus the radicchio, makes a balanced and colourful alternative.

BEYOND THE HOLIDAYS
Turn this salad into a tasty Cobb salad by topping it with diced leftover cooked turkey, a little crumbled bacon and some sliced avocado—a fantastic main course for lunch or dinner.

ENTERTAINING A CROWD
(HORS D'OEUVRES, SNACKS AND SHARED PLATES)

CELEBRATING THE HOLIDAY entertaining season from Thanksgiving through New Year's, and even beyond, is all about the snacks, the nibbles and the starters—which is why this is the biggest chapter in the book. It's always easy to make your favourite recipes over and over, especially when time is tight, but why not try something new and different?

Whether you're having a few friends drop by or you're hosting a seasonal open house (page 30), here is a wide range of options to cover any occasion. I've also included a few ideas for savoury baked goods (pages 41 to 47) you can give as gifts, plus a menu for a Sunday get-together for sports fans (page 30). Get snacking!

Opposite: Crispy Baked Chicken Wings (page 64); Michael's Signature Caesars (page 38); Winter Crudités with Dips (page 48); Chicken Carnitas (page 65)

Entertaining a Crowd

If you are hosting a group of friends for a holiday open house, or a gang is coming by for an afternoon of watching sports, you want the right combination of snacks and treats on hand. Here are my tips for those types of gatherings and two sample menus to get you started (one a little bit fancy and festive, the other more dive-in casual). Don't feel that the suggested items are mutually exclusive though; I love a good crispy chicken wing, and would happily serve them at my open house (wearing a sparkling outfit, and with extra napkins on hand, of course).

HOLIDAY OPEN HOUSE

PLAN A MIX OF ITEMS. People will be arriving at different times, so choose a mix of dishes, including many that can sit out at room temperature (such as Bacon and Parmesan Gougères, page 45), some that can come straight from the oven in small batches (Mini Tourtières, page 53) and others that are served cold and can be re-stocked from the fridge as needed (Avocado Yogurt Dressing and Dip, page 149).

MAKE AND BAKE AHEAD. Prepare as much of the food ahead of time as you can. I've provided make-ahead tips for all the recipes in this book, so you're not running in circles on party day.

ESTIMATE QUANTITIES. Professional caterers count on three pieces per person, for every hour they will be at a cocktail party, so I use the same guide.

LABEL POTENTIAL ALLERGENS. Place a tag listing the name of the recipe and its ingredients beside each dish in case you are not on hand to answer questions.

GO BUFFET-STYLE. Letting guests serve themselves allows you easily to circulate and refill platters as needed. This open house menu includes Platters, which can be put out and remain out in accessible locations, and Plates, which should be assembled (either with a single item or a mix) and passed once around the room before being placed in a convenient spot. Set out bowls of pickles and pickled chili peppers so people can add them to their plates.

SATISFY A SWEET TOOTH. Set out a few sweets to start, for those guests who pop in early and leave early, but bring out all your treats a third to halfway through the party (to make sure kids—and all guests, really—have something savoury before they get to the sweets).

Check out Set a Stunning Dessert Table (page 266) and Build a Butter Tart Buffet (page 228) for fun ideas to have guests help themselves to a sweet treat.

SPORTS SUNDAY

BRING THE SNACKS OUT IN STAGES. If you put everything out at once, it will all be devoured before the end of the first quarter. I put out one or two small-bite items, and then bring out the larger items as the "main course" at halftime.

HAVE EXTRA CONDIMENTS ON HAND. Mustard, hot sauce, pickles, chili peppers and sour cream are all appreciated with this sort of food.

AND OF COURSE . . . PROVIDE LOTS OF NAPKINS!

Sausage Dressing Square (page 58); Spinach, Mushroom and Parmesan Squares (page 55); Lobster Mac 'N' Cheese Squares (page 56)

Menu

❧

Holiday Open House

PLATTERS

CHEESE BOARD WITH CLASSIC OAT CRACKERS, page 35 and 41

BACON AND PARMESAN GOUGÈRES, page 45

and/or PUMPKIN SEED MULTIGRAIN BREAD, page 73

WINTER CRUDITÉS WITH DIPS, page 48

PLATES

BBQ TURKEY BAO, page 63

MINI CHICKEN SCHNITZEL SLIDERS, page 61

LOBSTER MAC 'N' CHEESE SQUARES, page 56

MINI TOURTIÈRES, page 53

SAUSAGE DRESSING SQUARES, page 58

SPINACH, MUSHROOM AND PARMESAN SQUARES, page 55

SWEETS

LEMON CRUMBLE LOAF CAKE, page 172

ASSORTMENT OF COOKIES (ESPECIALLY LEMON TWINKLES, GINGERBREAD CRINKLES,

CHOCOLATE CRINKLES), pages 193 to 221

ASSORTMENT OF BARS AND SQUARES, pages 227 to 237

EARL GREY TIRAMISU TRIFLE, page 289

CHOCOLATE-GLAZED BAKED PUMPKIN DOUGHNUTS, page 301

Menu

Sports Sunday

ANNA'S FAVOURITE CEREAL SNACK MIX, page 50

WINTER CRUDITÉS WITH DIPS, page 48

CRISPY BAKED CHICKEN WINGS, page 64

PICKLED HOT AND SWEET PEPPERS, page 157

MICHAEL'S SUPER MEATBALLS, page 67

(WITH MINI BUTTERY SOFT DINNER ROLLS, page 99, TO MAKE SANDWICHES)

CHICKEN CARNITAS, page 65

SPICED SWEET POTATO WEDGES, page 104

BUTTER TART BUFFET, page 228

Cheese Board 101

A cheese board is now such a common way to start a gathering that it can feel like a challenge to make yours stand out. These tips will help you build a cheese platter that has everyone talking—and diving in for more.

SELECTION

- An odd number of cheeses looks best on display. Choose 3 types for a small gathering (4 people), 5 for a medium-sized group (6 to 8) and 7 for a large party (10 to 16).

- Balance your flavours and textures first and then see if you can sneak in some colour variance (colour variety looks good but it's not as important as taste and texture contrast). This means including a few styles and ages of cheese, and some different milk types (goat, sheep, cow) for variety. The basic types to include in the mix are:

TYPE	EXAMPLES	BUYING AND STORING TIPS	SERVING SUGGESTIONS
FRESH	Bocconcini Buffalo mozzarella Chèvre Cream cheese Ricotta	• Store well wrapped and away from other, strong cheeses (fresh cheeses pick up odours easily) • Abide by the expiry date on the package	• Serve topped or rolled in fresh herbs or cracked black pepper • Present in a beautiful bowl or dish with a spreading knife or a small spoon • Drizzle with a little honey
BLOOMY RIND	Brie Brillat-Savarin Camembert Château de Bourgogne Triple crème Brie	• If purchasing a whole wheel, press the centre gently—if it gives, then it is ripe and ready to cut • Avoid portions that appear to have a white, chalky centre—they have been cut too soon (and will not ripen further) • The bloomy rind is an edible type of mold (not harmful); trim it away if it spreads to the exposed part of the cheese as it sits in the fridge • Many whole wheels come wrapped in a lined paper wrapper. Save this to re-wrap the cheese, placing the paper directly onto the exposed interior of any leftover cheese.	• Do not portion into bite-sized pieces • Place a wedge, or a quarter of a small wheel, on a platter with a small knife so guests can help themselves • When helping yourself to a piece from a wedge, do not cut the tip away; instead, cut a slice parallel to all or some of the long side of the triangle

TYPE	EXAMPLES	BUYING AND STORING TIPS	SERVING SUGGESTIONS
WASHED RIND	Chaumes Morbier Oka Reblochon Sauvagine Taleggio	• Purchase portions that have an even colour tone and even shape (pieces that are discoloured at the edges or misshapen were probably sliced a while ago) • Store well wrapped, and if aged and "fragrant," store them in a resealable bag so the odour doesn't haunt your fridge	• Eat the rind on most washed rind cheeses (they have a wonderfully complex flavour of mushrooms or walnuts and a texture ranging from slightly sandy to smooth) • When displaying, cut 1 or 2 slices to show that the rind can be eaten
HARD	Cheddar Gouda Gruyère Manchego Mimolette Parmesan	• Regardless of their firmness, store these cheeses in the fridge (the firmer/drier the cheese, the longer it will last . . . up to a year for an aged Parmesan!)	• Do not eat the rinds on most of these cheeses (they are often too hard to cut through and enjoy) • Place wedges, with the rind on, on a serving platter with a sharp knife • Serve Parmesan with a fork (the tines break through the cheese easily, so you get lovely little nuggets) • Do not eat the wax coating on cheeses • Present waxed cheeses by peeling the wax away from 1 side to give guests a place to cut
BLUE	Bleu Benedictin Gorgonzola Roquefort St. Agur	• Choose blue cheeses with any shade of blue or even green mold, but if you see pink mold, do not buy or eat • Store blue cheese in aluminum foil to allow it to breathe • Wrap blue cheeses separately from other cheeses (otherwise the mold spores will spread onto the other cheeses)	• Pick a serving knife (or spoon) that matches the texture of the cheese (some blues are crumbly while others are more creamy)
FLAVOURED AND HYBRID CHEESES	Applewood smoked Cheddar Boursin Cambozola Gouda with cumin Guinness-washed Cheddar White Stilton with cranberries	• Look for lots of flavoured and specialty cheese choices at holiday time • Taste before you buy (some can be surprisingly wonderful, and others, well, just surprising) • Depending on its type (fresh, blue, etc.), purchase and store as recommended above	• Try to limit flavoured cheese choices to 1 or 2 on a mixed cheese board, so as not to confuse your palate when tasting

SERVING

- Except for fresh types (which should be served chilled), all cheeses are at their best at room temperature. Pull your cheeses out of the fridge 1 hour before you plan to serve them.
- Give each cheese its own knife. If a knife with blue cheese on it touches another type of cheese, it could spread the blue mold from one to another. This isn't harmful, but it doesn't look appealing.
- Label the cheeses to guide your guests if you are not around to ask. You can keep it simple by listing only the name, or you can show your cheese acumen by listing the type of milk (goat, cow, sheep) and the place of origin.

- Give the cheeses space! Arrange the cheeses on various platters so they have room to breathe and so that your guests can get to them more easily. Set condiments and accompaniments near, but not smothering, the cheeses.
- Present crackers or bread on a separate dish or plate, or if on the board, not touching the cheeses. The moisture from the cheeses will soften the crackers.
- Enjoy cheese with neutral-flavoured bread and crackers (like Classic Oat Crackers, page 41) that won't detract from its flavour.

ACCOMPANIMENTS

- Choose some of these classic add-ons for your cheese board: raisins, Medjool dates, dried cranberries, dried apricots and fresh or roasted nuts.

- Playing on these flavours, consider adding Maple Toasted Pecans (page 321), Cranberry Sauce (page 147) or Roasted Applesauce (page 152). Foods with a subtle sweetness balance the salt in most cheeses.

WINE PAIRINGS

- Choose a wine that complements the cheeses you are serving. Try the following pairings:

WINE	CHEESE
Sparkling	Blue cheeses
Light, fruit white wines (Pinot Grigio, Sauvignon Blanc)	Fresh cheeses
Slightly sweet white wines (Riesling or Gewürztraminer)	Aged washed rind and hard cheeses and blue cheeses
Heavier white wines (Chardonnay)	Most cheeses (a good choice if you are having a wine and cheese party or a tasting)
Light-bodied reds (Gamay and Pinot Noir)	Most cheeses (a good choice if you are having a wine and cheese party or a tasting)
Heavier reds (Cabernet Sauvignon and Syrah)	Intensely flavoured or aged cheeses
Sweet wines (icewine, sweet Sherry and Port)	Intensely flavoured cheeses

5. INNOVATIVE IDEAS

- Try topping a whole, small wheel of Brie with a layer of Festive Red Berry Compote (page 320) and baking it in a dish at 350°F (180°C) for 10 minutes.
- Cheese and chocolate? These make a fantastic match. Try grating good-quality dark chocolate over a wedge of triple crème Brie and letting it sit

for 30 minutes. The complexity of the chocolate against the rich, salty creaminess of the Brie is stupendous.
- Toss mini bocconcini with Raspberry Olive Tapenade (page 151) and serve in a dish with toothpicks. Just watch . . . no one can stop at just 1!

Flavouring your vodka with crudité-style vegetables serves
two functions. The vegetables flavour the vodka, giving your Caesar a fresher
taste, and the veggies absorb the vodka, making a perfect (and potent!)
crunchy garnish to the drink.

MICHAEL'S SIGNATURE CAESARS

SERVES 1 • PREP: UNDER 5 MINUTES

1. Dip the rim of a 12 oz (360 mL) glass in water and then in the celery salt rimmer. Fill the glass with ice cubes and add the vodka, horseradish and Worcestershire and Tabasco sauces. Pour in the Caesar mix to fill the glass, add a swizzle stick and garnish with the jardinière vegetables and pickles, skewered or on the side.

MAKE AHEAD
Make the vodka at least 2 to 3 days (and up to 2 weeks) ahead to allow the flavours to meld, and the vegetables to still be crunchy (and potent). The vegetables can remain in the vodka for up to 2 weeks, and then discarded (they lose their flavour after that).

Celery salt rimmer
Ice cubes
1 oz (30 mL) jardinière vodka
    (see recipe below)
1 to 2 tsp Prepared
    Horseradish, page 154
2 to 3 dashes Worcestershire
    sauce

1 to 2 dashes Tabasco hot
    sauce
1 cup (250 mL) good-quality
    Caesar mix (seasoned
    tomato juice with clam juice)
Pickled Hot and Sweet
    Peppers, page 157, for
    garnish (optional)

JARDINIÈRE VODKA

MAKES 2 CUPS (500 ML) FLAVOURED VODKA •
PREP: 15 MINUTES, PLUS 2 TO 3 DAYS CURING

1. Have ready a 4-cup (1 L) mason jar with a sealable lid.

2. Arrange the vegetables (and jalapeño and garlic, if using) in the mason jar and add the thyme and peppercorns. Pour in the vodka, seal the jar and chill for 2 to 3 days.

4 cups (1 L) loosely packed fresh
    vegetables: cherry or grape
    tomatoes, julienned celery, carrots,
    zucchini, red bell peppers
1 jalapeño pepper (optional)
1 clove garlic (optional)
3 sprigs fresh thyme
6 whole black peppercorns
2 cups (500 mL) vodka

So, I'm a bit of a cracker fiend. Seriously, I could sit with a dish full of crackers and be perfectly content with them as a snack. These oat crackers are ideal companions for cheese because they add texture, hold a nice portion and don't compromise the flavour of the cheese by being overly seasoned. If you are cooking for guests with gluten intolerance, be sure to choose certified gluten-free oats and oat bran.

CLASSIC OAT CRACKERS

MAKES ABOUT 3 DOZEN CRACKERS • PREP: 20 MINUTES, PLUS COOLING •
COOK: 25 MINUTES

MAKE AHEAD
You can store the baked crackers in an airtight container for up to 2 weeks. Do not freeze or refrigerate.

1 ¼ cups (125 g) regular rolled oats
   (not instant)
1 ¼ cups (125 g) oat bran
½ tsp salt
1 cup (250 mL) boiling water
¼ cup (60 mL) vegetable oil

1. Measure the oats, oat bran and salt into the bowl of a food processor and pulse until the rolled oats are finely ground. Add the boiling water and oil and pulse until smooth (the mixture will look like thick porridge, which is truly what it is). Transfer to a bowl, cover with plastic wrap and let cool to room temperature—it will thicken up as it cools.

2. Preheat the oven to 375°F (190°C) and line 2 baking trays with parchment paper.

3. Turn the dough out onto a work surface (no need to flour it, although rolling on a wooden cutting board is best) and roll to just under ¼ inch (0.5 cm) thick. Use a 2 ½-inch (7.5 cm) round cookie cutter to cut out crackers. Lift them onto the prepared trays with a palette knife, ½ inch (1 cm) apart.

4. Roll and re-roll the dough as many times as needed (oats do not contain gluten and therefore you are not compromising the tenderness of the dough) until you have cut all the crackers.

5. Bake for about 25 minutes, until the crackers just begin to brown at the edges. Cool on the tray. If gifting, stack the crackers and pack them snugly in a box or tin, or wrap in a cellophane bag tied with a ribbon.

HELPFUL HINT
Ensure these crackers are crisp before you serve them. Hot out of the oven, it's too hard to tell, but if they aren't crisp enough when cool, you can always pop them back in the oven for a few more minutes.

> These delightfully tender savoury shortbreads are great with a bowl of soup or stew, as a base for an hors d'oeuvre or on their own with a little pepper jelly. They also make a fantastic homemade host gift.

CHEDDAR AND CHIVE SHORTBREADS

MAKES ABOUT 4 DOZEN SHORTBREADS • PREP: 15 MINUTES, PLUS CHILLING • COOK: 20 MINUTES

1. Place the flour, sugar and pepper in the bowl of a food processor with the butter and pulse until the mixture is rough and crumbly and no bits of butter are visible. Add the Cheddar and pulse until evenly combined. Add the egg yolks and pulse again until the dough shapes itself into a ball.

2. Turn the dough out onto a work surface and knead in the chives by hand (if you add them in the food processor, the dough will turn green). Shape the dough into 2 logs about 1 ½ inches (3.5 cm) across, wrap in plastic and chill until firm, at least 1 hour.

3. Preheat the oven to 350°F (180°C) and line 2 baking trays with parchment paper. Place the sesame seeds on a large flat plate.

4. Unwrap the dough, brush the logs with the egg white and then roll in the sesame seeds to coat fully. Slice coins about ¼ inch (0.5 cm) thick and arrange them on the trays, about ½ inch (1 cm) apart.

5. Bake for 18 to 20 minutes, until lightly browned on the bottom. Let cool completely on the trays. If gifting, stack the cookies and pack them snugly in a box or tin, or wrap in a cellophane bag tied with a ribbon.

MAKE AHEAD

You can store baked shortbread in an airtight container at room temperature for up to 1 week. Or make the shortbread dough and freeze it, well wrapped, for up to 3 months. Thaw it overnight in the fridge before slicing to bake.

1 ½ cups (225 g) all-purpose flour

1 Tbsp (12 g) granulated sugar

¼ tsp black pepper

½ cup (115 g) cold unsalted butter, cut into pieces

6 oz (180 g) coarsely grated old Cheddar cheese (about 2 cups/500 mL)

2 large egg yolks

2 Tbsp (30 mL) chopped fresh chives

½ cup (60 g) sesame seeds

1 egg white, lightly whisked, for brushing

HELPFUL HINT

My friend Lisa shared a great trick for ensuring logs of dough keep their shape in the fridge. Shape the dough into a log just a touch smaller in diameter than an empty paper towel roll. Wrap the dough in plastic wrap, slip it into the cardboard roll and chill or freeze. The cardboard protects it from denting or flattening on the side it is resting on while it sits in the fridge.

A few stacks of these shortbreads add sparkle to a charcuterie plate. Slices of prosciutto or other cured meats are a tasty complement to these buttery cheese coins. To make an hors d'oeuvre that can be passed around on platters, ruffle a thin slice of prosciutto over each shortbread.

BLUE CHEESE, WALNUT AND DRIED APRICOT SHORTBREADS

MAKES ABOUT 4 DOZEN SHORTBREADS • PREP: 15 MINUTES, PLUS CHILLING • COOK TIME: 22 MINUTES

MAKE AHEAD
You can store baked shortbread in an airtight container at room temperature for up to 1 week. Or make the shortbread dough and freeze it, well wrapped, for up to 3 months. Thaw it overnight in the fridge before slicing to bake.

1 ½ cups (225 g) all-purpose flour
1 Tbsp (12 g) packed light brown sugar
¾ cup (75 g) walnut pieces
6 Tbsp (90 g) cold unsalted butter, cut into pieces
4 oz (120 g) blue cheese, crumbled
¼ cup (35 g) sliced dried apricots
2 Tbsp (10 g) sliced candied ginger
½ cup (75 g) poppy seeds
1 large egg white

1. Place the flour, brown sugar and walnut pieces in the bowl of a food processor and pulse until the walnuts are finely ground. Add the butter and pulse until no longer visible, then add the blue cheese and pulse until the dough forms a ball. Add the apricots and candied ginger and pulse in briefly, just to combine, but so that the pieces are still visible.

2. Shape the dough into 2 logs about 1 ½ inches (3.5 cm) across, wrap in plastic and chill until firm, at least 1 hour.

3. Preheat the oven to 350°F (180°C) and line 2 baking trays with parchment paper. Place the poppy seeds on a large flat plate.

4. Unwrap the dough, brush the logs with egg white and roll in the poppy seeds to coat fully. Slice coins about ¼ inch (0.5 cm) thick and arrange them on the trays, about ½ inch (1 cm) apart.

5. Bake for 20 to 22 minutes, until lightly browned on the bottom. Let cool completely on the tray. If gifting, stack the cookies and pack them snugly in a box or tin, or wrap in a cellophane bag tied with a ribbon.

HELPFUL HINT
A decent-quality, but not too expensive, crumbly style of blue cheese works here, like the type you would crumble onto a salad. If it's too creamy, like St. Agur or Gorgonzola, the shortbread won't hold its shape when baked.

Step 4

Step 6

Step 7

These cheese puffs, known as gougères in French cuisine, are made using a classic pastry called choux paste (the same dough used to make éclairs and profiteroles). They're a great holiday staple because they can be made ahead and frozen, and used in a number of ways: as a base for a piped cheese or smoked salmon hors d'oeuvre, as a bun for a slider, as a substitute for croutons on a salad, as a garnish on a bowl of soup or simply as a nibble on their own.

BACON AND PARMESAN GOUGÈRES

MAKES 4 DOZEN PUFFS • PREP: 15 MINUTES • COOK: 30 MINUTES

MAKE AHEAD

These puffs need to be piped and baked while the dough is still fresh and warm, but once baked, they freeze incredibly well. You can freeze them, well wrapped, for up to 3 months, and then re-warm on a tray in a 325°F (160°C) oven for 12 to 15 minutes. You can store baked puffs in an airtight container at room temperature for 1 to 2 days. Do not refrigerate them or they will dry out.

6 slices cooked smoked bacon, well drained
1 cup (250 mL) 1% milk
¼ cup (60 g) unsalted butter
1¼ cups (185 g) all-purpose flour
4 large eggs
1 cup (110 g) coarsely grated Gruyère cheese
½ cup (50 g) finely grated Parmesan cheese
½ tsp chili powder
1 egg yolk whisked with 1 Tbsp (15 mL) cool water, for egg wash

1. Preheat the oven to 375°F (190°F) and line 2 baking trays with parchment paper.

2. Place the bacon in the bowl of a food processor and pulse until it is the texture of crumbs. Remove and set aside (no need to wash the food processor bowl).

3. In a medium saucepan, bring the milk and butter to a simmer over medium heat. Add the flour all at once and use a wooden spoon to vigorously stir the paste mixture for about 2 minutes, until it pulls away from the pan. Scrape into the food processor bowl and let sit to cool for 5 minutes.

4. Break the eggs into a cup. While pulsing the food processor, add the eggs about 1 at a time, quickly pulsing to incorporate before adding the next. Scrape down the bowl between additions.

5. Add the Gruyère, Parmesan, chili powder and cooked bacon and pulse well until the cheese is blended into the paste. Spoon this mixture (it will still be warm) into a piping bag fitted with a large plain tip, or use a small ice cream scoop.

6. Pipe or scoop the batter into 1½-inch (3.5 cm) rounds on the prepared baking trays, 1½ inches (3.5 cm) apart. If the rounds have little points from where you lifted up the piping bag, dip your finger in cool water and pat them down.

7. Brush the gougères with the egg wash and then bake for 25 to 30 minutes, until they are a rich golden brown and are light when lifted off the tray. Allow the gougères to cool for at least 10 minutes on the tray before eating. They are best enjoyed warm but can be eaten at room temperature.

Classic madeleines are sweet little cakes baked in shell-shaped molds. These savoury versions are a tender cornbread-style nibble, perfect to serve with cocktails. If you don't have madeleine pans, bake the batter in 24 greased mini-muffin cups instead.

JALAPEÑO CORNBREAD MADELEINES

MAKES 18 MADELEINES (OR 24 MINI MUFFINS) • PREP: 10 MINUTES •
COOK: 12 MINUTES

MAKE AHEAD

Madeleines are best eaten fresh, but toasted day-old madeleines are delicious with soups or salads in place of crostini. You can freeze baked madeleines, well wrapped, for up to 3 months. Thaw them at room temperature, arrange them on a baking tray and re-warm, uncovered, in a 325°F (160°C) oven for about 8 minutes.

⅔ cup (110 g) cornmeal
¼ cup (30 g) cornstarch
2 Tbsp (25 g) granulated sugar
1 tsp chili powder or mild smoked
    paprika
¾ tsp baking powder
½ tsp fine sea salt
⅔ cup (160 mL) buttermilk
2 large eggs
2 Tbsp (30 mL) vegetable oil
1 cup (150 g) frozen corn kernels,
    thawed
1 fresh jalapeño pepper, seeded and
    finely diced (or 6 slices of pickled
    jalapeño, chopped)

1. Preheat the oven to 400°F (200°C). Grease 2 madeleine pans.

2. Stir the cornmeal, cornstarch, sugar, chili powder (or smoked paprika), baking powder and salt together in a medium bowl. In a separate bowl, whisk the buttermilk, eggs and oil together. Add all at once to the dry mixture and whisk until completely smooth. Stir in the corn and jalapeño.

3. Spoon the batter into the madeleine pans, filling them right to the top.

4. Bake for 10 to 12 minutes, until the madeleines begin to brown at the edges. Let the pans cool on a rack for 15 minutes, then tap out the madeleines to serve warm, or let cool to serve at room temperature.

ADD SPARKLE

Whether baked as a madeleine or a mini muffin, these bites make a great base for an hors d'oeuvre. Wrap them in a slice of prosciutto, or split them open to make a mini sandwich or slider.

You can't live on cheese alone at holiday time, so a crudités platter is sometimes a welcome sight. A colourful array of vegetables adds sparkle to a buffet table, and I don't stick exclusively to raw vegetables. Cooked mini potatoes and blanched green beans are accessible *and* tasty in the winter.

WINTER CRUDITÉS WITH DIPS

SERVES 8 TO 12 • PREP: 15 MINUTES • COOK: 12 MINUTES

1. Have ready 2 or 3 dipping bowls, and a platter large enough to hold all the vegetables plus the dipping bowls.

2. Place the mini potatoes in a saucepan of cold, salted water and bring to a boil over high heat, uncovered. Reduce the heat to medium-high and simmer until the potatoes are tender, about 10 minutes. Drain, cool and chill until ready to serve.

3. Bring a second saucepan of cold, salted water to a boil over high heat. Add the beans and blanch for just 2 minutes. Drain and rinse under cold running water to stop the cooking. The beans will be bright green but will still have crunch. Chill until ready to serve.

4. Place the dips in individual bowls and set them in the middle of the platter. Arrange the vegetables around the platter. Chill until ready to serve.

MAKE AHEAD

A platter like this is ideal for preparing ahead. Blanch and cut up all of your vegetables and pack them in resealable bags or airtight containers. I put a damp paper towel directly on the veggies to keep them crisp. All of the dips can be made ahead of time and chilled in airtight containers.

1 lb (450 g) mini potatoes

1 lb (450 g) green beans, trimmed

2 or 3 recipes chosen from Raspberry Olive Tapenade, Michael's Blue Cheese Dressing and Dip, Buttermilk Ranch Dressing and Dip and/or Avocado Yogurt Dressing and Dip (pages 148 to 151)

½ bulb fennel, sliced

1 English cucumber, sliced

1 red, yellow or orange bell pepper, sliced

6 to 8 mini carrots, scrubbed and cut in half (or 2 regular carrots, sliced on the bias)

6 to 8 radishes, cut in half

6 to 8 mini zucchini, cut in half (or 1 large zucchini, sliced on the bias)

½ lb (225 g) button mushrooms (cut in half, if large)

1 pint (275 g) grape tomatoes

HELPFUL HINTS

Cooked potatoes and green beans are a tasty seasonal addition to a holiday crudités platter, and they are budget-friendly too. If the platter is likely to sit out for a while, I add raw green cabbage, which has great crunch and holds up well. I also use small bowls for the creamy dips and top them up every so often, which keeps them fresh and safe to eat.

ADD SPARKLE

For a grown-up crowd, stir a little truffle oil into Michael's Blue Cheese Dressing and Dip (page 148), add some crab meat to the Buttermilk Ranch Dressing and Dip (page 148) or replace the green beans with blanched asparagus.

Raspberry Olive Tapenade (page 151); Avocado Yogurt Dip (page 149); Buttermilk Ranch Dressing (page 148); assorted crudités

If you were to bring me this snack mix as a host gift during the holidays, I would welcome you with open arms. I love receiving cereal snack mixes, and while this recipe is my personal favourite, I do enjoy trying other people's variations. Confession: when I make a batch of this recipe, I always tuck a little away for myself before the rest gets packaged up for gift-giving or putting out for a party.

ANNA'S FAVOURITE CEREAL SNACK MIX

MAKES ABOUT 12 CUPS (3 L) · PREP: 10 MINUTES · COOK: 40 MINUTES

1. Preheat the oven to 300°F (150°C) and line a large baking tray with parchment paper.

2. Melt the butter in a small saucepan over medium-low heat and whisk in the celery salt, chili powder, garlic powder, onion powder, mustard powder, cinnamon, hot sauce powder (or hot sauce) if using, and Worcestershire.

3. Combine the cereals, pretzels, almonds and peanuts in a large mixing bowl and pour the spiced butter overtop. Toss well (using your hands is quickest and most effective) and then spread this mixture on the baking tray.

4. Bake for about 40 minutes, stirring occasionally, until the cereal browns a little. Let the mix cool on the tray on a wire rack. Scoop into an airtight container. If gifting, pack the mix into a cookie tin or a tall mason jar, along with a label and ribbon.

MAKE AHEAD

You can store the baked cereal mix in an airtight container at room temperature for up to 3 weeks (but GOOD LUCK staying away from it that long—put a lock on it!).

½ cup (115 g) unsalted butter
2 tsp celery salt
1 tsp chili powder
1 tsp garlic powder
1 tsp onion powder
1 tsp mustard powder
Pinch of ground cinnamon
1 Tbsp (15 mL) dry hot sauce powder or hot sauce (optional)
4 to 5 dashes Worcestershire sauce
2 cups (100 g) Shreddies
2 cups (50 g) Cheerios
2 cups (50 g) Crispix cereal
2 cups (100 g) pretzel twists or squares
1 cup (160 g) whole almonds
1 cup (150 g) unsalted peanuts

HELPFUL HINT

Vary the cereals depending on your tastes, but I do recommend using 3 types, each with a special feature. In my mix, the Shreddies are hearty and really hold the spice, the Crispix are light and crispy, and the Cheerios fill the corners and round out each bite. You can go nut-free by replacing the almonds and peanuts with more pretzels or a small snacking cracker.

ADD SPARKLE

If you are making this mix for gift-giving, or to have on hand during the holidays, stir a handful of bite-sized chocolate candies (think M&M's or Reese's Pieces) into the cooled mix for a fun touch.

Tourtière at Christmas is a Canadian tradition of French-Canadian origin. In Quebec this meat pie is often served at *réveillon*, a big, lively party among friends and family to welcome in Christmas or the New Year. However, tourtière is now a winter staple beyond the holidays. This recipe makes mini tarts ideal for a cocktail party, but I have also included instructions for a whole tourtière baked in a pie pan (see Helpful Hints). You can use the filling from the Vegetarian Tourtière (page 96) for a vegetarian option.

MINI TOURTIÈRES

MAKES 4 DOZEN MINI TARTS • PREP: 40 MINUTES • COOK: 75 MINUTES

MAKE AHEAD

You can make the filling and pie dough up to 2 days ahead and refrigerate them in separate airtight containers. Or refrigerate baked tarts in an airtight container for up to 3 days, or freeze baked or unbaked tarts (or full-sized pies) for up to 3 months. Thaw overnight in the fridge before baking. Reheat baked tourtières in a 325°F (160°C) oven for 10 minutes or baked full-sized pies for 25 minutes.

FILLING

1 Tbsp (15 mL) vegetable oil
1 ½ lb (675 g) mixed ground veal, pork and beef
1 medium onion, diced
1 medium carrot, peeled and coarsely grated
1 medium russet potato, peeled and coarsely grated
1 apple, peeled and coarsely grated
2 cloves garlic, minced
2 bay leaves
1 tsp celery salt
½ tsp ground allspice
¼ tsp ground cloves
1 ½ cups (375 mL) chicken stock

Dash of Worcestershire sauce
Coarse sea salt and black pepper
1 egg whisked with 2 Tbsp (30 mL) water, for egg wash

ASSEMBLY

1 recipe Basic Pie Dough (page 315), shaped into 2 discs and chilled

1. For the filling, heat a large sauté pan over medium heat and add the oil. Add the ground meat and the onion and stir until the meat has almost cooked through, about 7 minutes.

2. Stir in the carrot, potato, apple, garlic, bay leaves, celery salt, allspice and cloves. Add the stock and Worcestershire sauce and bring to a simmer, still on medium heat. Cook, uncovered, stirring occasionally, until most of the liquid has evaporated, about 30 minutes.

3. Season to taste, remove the pan from the heat and let cool to room temperature.

4. Preheat the oven to 400°F (200°C) and grease your mini-muffin pans.

5. To assemble the pies, lightly dust a work surface with flour. Roll out the first disc of dough into a circle just under ¼ inch (0.5 cm) thick.

6. Using a round cookie cutter, typically 3 inches (7.5 cm), cut out pastry circles large enough to line the bottom and sides of the cups of the mini-muffin pan. Gently press the pastry into the cups.

Recipe continues ▶

53
—
ENTERTAINING
A CROWD

7. Spoon the cool filling into the muffin pans, filling each cup right to the top of the pastry and pressing the meat mixture in firmly.

8. Roll out the second disc of dough to a circle just under ¼ inch (0.5 cm) thick. Use a smaller cookie cutter, typically 2 inches (5 cm), to cut pastry circles that cover the filling completely.

9. Dock each pastry circle once or twice with a fork or make a criss-cross mark with a paring knife, then set it on top of the filling. There is no need to crimp the edges or seal them—just press them gently into place.

10. Brush the tops of the tarts with the egg wash and put them in the oven. Immediately reduce the temperature to 375°F (190°C) and bake for about 30 minutes, until the pastry is a rich golden brown and a paring knife inserted in the centre of the tourtières feels warm to the touch.

11. Let the tarts cool in the pans for 10 minutes and then either serve warm or transfer to a wire rack to cool completely.

HELPFUL HINTS

To make a full-sized tourtière, line a lightly greased 9-inch (23 cm) glass pie plate with 1 disc of rolled-out pie dough. Spoon all the cooled meat filling into the pie, pressing down gently to level it and fill in the gaps. Roll out the second disc of pie dough, cut a hole in the centre for venting and place directly over the filling. Trim and pinch the pastry edges together and brush the top of the tourtière with egg wash. Preheat the oven to 400°F (200°C), put the tourtière in the oven, immediately reduce the temperature to 375°F (190°C) and bake for 45 minutes, until the pastry is a rich golden brown and a paring knife inserted in the centre feels warm to the touch. Let the tourtière cool for at least 30 minutes before slicing.

Some people suggest serving Cranberry Sauce (page 147) with tourtière, others claim ketchup is the only suitable companion and still others prefer a dollop of Dijon mustard. And some people are appalled by the idea of adding any condiment at all. I'll leave that choice up to you.

SPINACH, MUSHROOM AND PARMESAN SQUARES ⓥ

MAKES ONE 8-INCH (20 CM) SQUARE PAN • MAKES 36 BITE-SIZED PORTIONS •
PREP: 15 MINUTES • COOK: 30 MINUTES

MAKE AHEAD

These squares are a real timesaver when you make them ahead and, before cutting them, chill for at least 2 hours or freeze for up to 3 months. Thaw overnight in the fridge, then slice while still cold. Before serving, place on a baking tray and warm in the oven at 325°F (160°C) for about 12 minutes.

1 Tbsp (15 mL) extra virgin olive oil
½ lb (225 g) sliced cremini or button
    mushrooms
½ cup (50 g) finely diced shallot
    (or ½ medium onion)
2 cloves garlic, minced
2 Tbsp (30 mL) dry white vermouth
1 tsp dried oregano
4 oz (125 g) (½ pkg) cream cheese,
    at room temperature, cut in cubes
¾ cup (175 mL) sour cream
¾ cup (75 g) grated Parmesan cheese
½ cup (65 g) dry breadcrumbs
2 large eggs
1 large egg yolk
¼ tsp fine sea salt
¼ tsp black pepper
¼ tsp ground nutmeg
1 pkg (10 oz/300 g) frozen chopped
    spinach, thawed

1. Preheat the oven to 350°F (180°C). Lightly grease and line the bottom and sides of an 8-inch (20 cm) square pan with parchment paper.

2. Heat a medium sauté pan over medium-high heat and add the oil, followed by the mushrooms and shallots (or onions). Sauté until any liquid has evaporated, about 8 minutes. Stir in the garlic, vermouth and oregano and continue to stir until the vermouth has evaporated, about 2 more minutes. Remove from the heat.

3. In a large mixing bowl, beat the cream cheese by hand to soften it and then beat in the sour cream (you can switch to a whisk here to make sure it's completely smooth). Stir in the Parmesan, breadcrumbs, eggs, egg yolk, salt, pepper and nutmeg until evenly combined.

4. Drain the thawed spinach and squeeze out any excess liquid. Add to the cream cheese mixture and stir well, breaking up the spinach to make sure it is well blended (it can be dense after squeezing). Stir in the mushroom mixture and spoon into the prepared pan, spreading to level it.

5. Bake for about 30 minutes, until the centre springs back when gently pressed. Let cool in the pan on a wire rack for at least 20 minutes before slicing to serve. Serve warm or at room temperature.

Photo on page 31

ADD SPARKLE

These squares also make a great base for fancier hors d'oeuvres. Bake them in a 9 × 13-inch (22.5 × 32.5 cm) pan (bake time stays the same) so that they are a little flatter. Once baked, top each square with a cooked shrimp and a little mayo, or some smoked salmon with dill cream cheese, or roasted peppers and a bocconcini, secured with a frilly toothpick.

> These savoury squares are a bit over-the-top, but the holidays totally justify making *and* eating them. A breaded and pan-fried crispy outside yields to a gooey cheesy centre with tidbits of lobster nestled in between the pasta.

LOBSTER MAC 'N' CHEESE SQUARES

MAKES ONE 8-INCH (20 CM) SQUARE PAN · SERVES 24 ·
PREP: 25 MINUTES, PLUS CHILLING · COOK: 35 MINUTES

1. Line the bottom and sides of an 8-inch (20 cm) baking pan with parchment paper.

2. Melt the butter over medium heat in a medium saucepan and stir in the flour with a wooden spoon. Continue to cook, stirring continuously, until the mixture smells slightly nutty but has not changed colour, about 4 minutes.

3. Add the milk in 3 parts, beating well with a whisk and letting the mixture thicken between each addition. Whisk in the Old Bay seasoning and the mustard. Reduce the heat to medium-low and add the cheese in 3 parts, whisking between each addition until the cheese has melted. Whisk in the vermouth and then stir in the cooked pasta, lobster meat and green onions.

4. Spread the mac 'n' cheese into the prepared baking pan. Cover the surface of the pasta directly with plastic wrap and let cool to room temperature before chilling until set, at least 2 hours.

5. For the crust, preheat the oven to 350°F (180°C) and line a baking tray with parchment paper. Arrange the flour, eggs and breadcrumbs in separate bowls for dredging. Turn the pan of chilled mac 'n' cheese out onto a cutting board and cut into 24 portions.

6. Heat a large sauté pan over medium-high heat and add enough oil to coat the bottom of the pan generously and evenly. Dip each square in the flour, coating it fully and shaking off any excess. Dunk into the eggs and then the breadcrumbs and carefully set each square in the sauté pan, about 1 inch (2.5 cm) apart (you may need to work in batches). Fry for about 2 minutes on each side until evenly browned, then transfer to the baking tray and repeat with the remaining squares.

7. Bake for 10 to 15 minutes, to ensure the cheese has melted all the way through. Transfer to a plate and serve immediately.

MAKE AHEAD

You can chill the mac 'n' cheese mixture for up to 1 day or remove it from the pan, wrap well and freeze for up to 3 months. Thaw overnight in the fridge before portioning, breading and pan-frying. You can also bread and pan-fry the squares up to 2 hours ahead of time, chill and then warm through in a 350°F (180°C) oven for 15 to 20 minutes to avoid pan-frying while your guests are there.

SQUARES

2 cups (300 g) tubetti pasta, cooked
   according to package instructions
3 Tbsp (45 g) butter
3 Tbsp (25 g) all-purpose flour
1 ½ cups (375 mL) 2% milk
1 Tbsp (12 g) Old Bay seasoning
   (or 2 tsp celery salt)
1 Tbsp (15 mL) Dijon mustard
4 cups (360 g) coarsely grated old
   Cheddar cheese
2 Tbsp (30 mL) dry vermouth
6 oz (180 g) diced cooked lobster meat
4 thinly sliced green onions

CRUST

1 cup (150 g) all-purpose flour
2 large eggs, lightly whisked
2 ½ cups (200 g) panko
   breadcrumbs
Vegetable oil, for frying

"Dressing" is the term used to describe a stuffing that is not baked inside a turkey or other roast. These squares will remind you of a holiday supper, with sausage, bacon, cranberry and hint of maple. They're always a hit when I serve them.

SAUSAGE DRESSING SQUARES

MAKES ONE 8-INCH (20 CM) SQUARE PAN • MAKES 36 BITE-SIZED PORTIONS •
PREP: 15 MINUTES • COOK: 40 MINUTES, PLUS CHILLING

1. Preheat the oven to 375°F (190°C). Lightly grease and line the bottom and sides of an 8-inch (20 cm) square pan with parchment.

2. Heat a small sauté pan over medium heat and add the oil, followed by the onions and celery. Sauté until the onions are translucent, about 5 minutes. Remove the pan from the heat and allow the vegetables to cool.

3. Meanwhile, cut open the sausage casings (or buy sausage meat without the casings) and place the meat in a large mixing bowl. Discard the casings.

4. Add the eggs, breadcrumbs, cranberries, pistachios, maple syrup, parsley and celery salt and mix well to combine—your hands will make fast work of this task, but you can also use a spoon. Add the cooled onions and celery and mix in well. Spoon into the prepared pan, pressing down to level the mix.

5. Arrange the bacon slices over the sausage, covering it completely. I like to make a bacon weave to top the sausage squares (see opposite).

6. Bake for 30 to 35 minutes, until the bacon has browned and the meat registers 165°F (74°C) on a thermometer. Let cool in the pan on a wire rack to room temperature.

7. Chill for 2 hours (or up to 2 days) before slicing into squares (they slice much better chilled than at room temperature). Before serving, preheat the oven to 325°F (160°C). Arrange the squares on a parchment-lined baking tray, bacon side down, and warm in the oven for about 10 minutes; the bacon will crisp up. Serve hot or at room temperature.

MAKE AHEAD
This recipe reheats brilliantly. You can refrigerate the pan of baked sausage dressing, covered, for up to 2 days, or freeze for up to 3 months. Thaw overnight in the fridge.

1 Tbsp (15 mL) extra virgin olive oil
1 medium onion, finely diced
1 stalk celery, finely diced
1 lb (450 g) uncooked sausages (I like Bratwurst or an Italian-style sausage)
2 large eggs
1 cup (130 g) dry breadcrumbs
½ cup (70 g) dried cranberries
⅓ cup (50 g) coarsely chopped shelled pistachios
¼ cup (60 mL) maple syrup
2 Tbsp (30 mL) chopped Italian parsley
1 ½ tsp celery salt
12 strips bacon

ADDING SPARKLE

To make a bacon weave for the top of these squares: Lay out 6 slices of the bacon side by side on a piece of plastic wrap placed on a cutting board. Peel back 3 alternating slices a little and place a bacon slice across them so that it lies perpendicular. Return the folded bacon slices to their original position (now over the perpendicular slice). Fold back the other 3 slices from the opposite end, lay another slice of bacon across them so that it lies perpendicular and next to the first perpendicular slice. Replace the folded bacon slices to their original position. Repeat with the remaining bacon slices to complete the pattern. Carefully lift up the plastic wrap and invert the bacon weave onto the top of the sausage square. Peel away and discard the plastic wrap.

Unlike their full-sized veal or pork counterparts that hang over the sides of a dinner plate, these daintier mini chicken sliders are easy to eat. They make generous appetizers, or a few together can make a meal. If you prefer a more traditional schnitzel, use thin slices of pork tenderloin instead of chicken.

MINI CHICKEN SCHNITZEL SLIDERS

MAKES 12 TO 15 SLIDERS • PREP: 20 MINUTES • COOK: 8 MINUTES PER BATCH

MAKE AHEAD

You do not want to be pounding, breading and frying the schnitzels as your guests are walking in the door. You can prepare them 1 hour ahead of time and keep them warm on a baking tray in a 300°F (150°C) oven. Or fry them up a few hours or 1 day ahead, chill them in an airtight container and heat them in a single layer on a baking tray in a 325°F (160°C) oven until crisp and warmed through when ready to eat.

1 lb (450 g) boneless, skinless chicken breasts
1 cup (150 g) all-purpose flour
1 large egg whisked with 2 Tbsp (30 mL) 2% milk
2 cups (160 g) panko breadcrumbs, dry breadcrumbs or cornflake crumbs
Coarse sea salt and black pepper
Canola oil and butter, for frying
12 to 15 Buttery Soft Dinner Rolls (page 99)
½ recipe Buttermilk Ranch Dressing and Dip (page 148)
A few drops of your favourite hot sauce (optional)
Lettuce leaves

1. Slice the chicken into 12 to 15 thin pieces and flatten them by placing them 1 at a time in a resealable bag and pounding them with the flat side of a meat mallet.

2. Ready your breading station by placing the flour, egg mixture and breadcrumbs in separate dishes. Season each dish with a little salt and pepper.

3. Heat a large sauté pan over medium-high heat and add enough oil and butter to coat the pan evenly. Let the butter foam. Once it subsides, dip a piece of chicken first in the flour, then in the egg and finally in the breadcrumbs. Ensure the chicken is fully coated, but shake off any excess.

4. Place the chicken pieces in the pan, without crowding (cook the chicken in batches, if necessary, keeping the cooked pieces warm on a plate in a 300°F/150°C oven and adding more oil and butter to the pan for each batch). Cook for about 4 minutes on each side.

5. To serve, slice open the dinner rolls and spread a little dressing on each side. (If you prefer spicy, mix the hot sauce into the ranch dressing first.) Place a chicken schnitzel on the bottom half of the bun, garnish with a lettuce leaf and add the top half of the bun. Serve immediately.

BEYOND THE HOLIDAYS

Schnitzel sandwiches are a regular winter treat for us. I make 2 large schnitzels by slicing 2 chicken breasts in half lengthwise, being careful not to cut all the way through, folding them out and then pounding them thin. Prepared the same way—but cooked for about 6 minutes per side—and served on a kaiser roll, these make a great weekday supper.

These steamed buns filled with BBQ turkey are soft and satisfying, and as part of a tray of sandwiches, they offer a lovely soft contrast to the crunchy Mini Chicken Schnitzel Sliders (page 61). Use any leftover turkey you may have on hand, or make them with chicken instead.

BBQ TURKEY BAO

MAKES 8 STEAMED BUNS • PREP: 35 MINUTES, PLUS RISING AND RESTING • COOK: 15 MINUTES

MAKE AHEAD

Bao are best served warm, but you can freeze the cooled, steamed buns in a resealable bag for up to 3 months. Thaw at room temperature and then warm them in a steamer for a few minutes before serving.

BAO

2 cups (300 g) all-purpose flour
¼ cup (30 g) cornstarch
2 Tbsp (25 g) granulated sugar
1 pkg (2 ¼ tsp/8 g) instant dry yeast
1 tsp baking powder
½ tsp fine salt
⅔ cup (160 mL) skim or 1% milk, warmed to just above body temperature
1 tsp white vinegar
Vegetable oil, for brushing

BBQ TURKEY

½ cup (125 mL) favourite BBQ sauce
2 tsp soy sauce
1 tsp sesame oil
1 tsp finely grated fresh ginger
8 to 12 oz (240 to 360 g) sliced cooked turkey or chicken breast (not deli meat)
Thinly sliced cucumber, for assembly

1. For the bao, sift the flour, cornstarch and sugar into a large mixing bowl. Stir in the yeast, baking powder and salt by hand. Add the milk, stir for a moment, and then stir in the vinegar until the dough just comes together.

2. Turn out the dough onto an unfloured work surface and knead by hand until elastic, about 4 minutes. Place in an ungreased bowl, cover with plastic wrap and let rise on the counter until doubled in size, about 1 hour.

3. Cut out eight 4-inch (10 cm) squares of parchment paper (to place the buns on). Turn out the dough (you shouldn't need to flour your surface) and cut it into 8 equal pieces.

4. Roll each piece into an oval about 5 × 3 ½ inches (12 cm × 9 cm). Brush the top of each oval with a little oil and fold in half to create a half-moon shape. Place each bun on a square of parchment and then on a platter or tray. Cover with plastic wrap and let rest on the counter for 20 minutes.

5. Set a large bamboo steamer over a wok or a saucepan of water (be sure the water does not touch the bottom of the steamer). Bring to a full boil over high heat, arrange 3 or 4 bao in the steamer, cover and steam on high heat for 5 minutes.

6. Use tongs to carefully transfer the bao to a platter or tray.

7. For the turkey, stir the BBQ sauce, soy sauce, sesame oil and ginger together in a small saucepan over medium heat, until bubbling. Add the sliced turkey and gently stir to coat and warm through.

8. To assemble the bao, gently open the buns along the fold (do not break them—the dough will be quite flexible). Arrange a few cucumber slices inside the bun and top with a few turkey slices (and extra sauce if you wish). Serve immediately.

Sharing a bowl of crispy, spicy wings is a great icebreaker to start any party. Since Michael and I live so close to Buffalo, New York, where chicken wings as a finger food got their start, we finish ours Buffalo-style, with Frank's hot sauce and melted butter.

CRISPY BAKED CHICKEN WINGS

GF

SERVES 6 • PREP: 15 MINUTES, PLUS CHILLING • COOK: 90 MINUTES

1. Stir the salt and baking powder together in a large bowl. Add the chicken wings and toss well to coat. Cover and chill the wings for 2 hours, to let the salt seep in.

2. Preheat the oven to 350°F (180°C). Rub a wire rack with oil (to prevent the wings from sticking) and place it over a baking tray lined with aluminum foil.

3. Spread the wings in an even layer on the rack and bake, uncovered, for 75 to 90 minutes, until crisp and cooked through. The wings won't brown too much, but they will be very crisp.

4. Stir together the melted butter and hot sauce in a clean bowl and add the wings, tossing quickly. Pour the blue cheese dip into a bowl and arrange on a platter with the carrots and celery sticks. Serve the wings immediately with the vegetables and blue cheese dip.

MAKE AHEAD

There is no benefit to cooking the wings ahead of time: you truly do want them hot and fresh from the oven. Since the chicken takes 75 to 90 minutes to cook, you have time to take care of other tasks (such as making the dip) before your guests arrive, or to socialize with your guests if you prefer to serve the wings a bit later in the evening (set a timer so you remember to take them out of the oven!).

1 Tbsp (15 g) fine sea salt
1 tsp baking powder, gluten-free if required
3 lb (1.5 kg) chicken wings, cut into drumettes and flats
2 Tbsp (30 g) unsalted butter, melted
Frank's hot sauce, to taste
1 recipe Michael's Blue Cheese Dressing and Dip (page 148)
Carrot and celery sticks, for serving

HELPFUL HINT

The combination of salt and baking powder breaks down the cells of the chicken wing skin, so that the wings release water and fat as they bake, crisping up wonderfully. This salt blend, which Michael calls "skin salt," also works well on pork belly to make a super-crisp and crunchy layer.

ADD SPARKLE

Since the sauce is added to the wings right before serving, you can really customize the flavours as you wish. Maple syrup and garlic make a nice twist on honey garlic, BBQ sauce is always a good one for kids, or you can test your hot sauce limits by using that bottle of 7-alarm hot sauce you got in your Christmas stocking.

These handheld tacos are a finger-food feast! A Mexican classic traditionally made with braised pork, this chicken version is tasty and rather sophisticated thanks to the pumpkin seeds and orange in the braising mixture. Having an assortment of sides so that guests can dress their own tacos is key to keeping this dish fun—and is perfect when kids are part of the party.

CHICKEN CARNITAS

SERVES 12 AS A STARTER, 6 AS A MEAL • PREP: 30 MINUTES • COOK: 20 MINUTES

MAKE AHEAD
You can combine the chicken and the rest of the ingredients for the carnitas in an airtight container and refrigerate for up to 1 day.

CARNITAS
4 cups (450 g) cooked shredded chicken
¾ cup (175 mL) fresh orange juice
½ cup (60 g) unsalted shelled pumpkin seeds
1 small onion, sliced
2 cloves garlic, minced
1 fresh jalapeño pepper, seeded and finely diced
1 Tbsp (10 g) chili powder
1 ½ tsp dried oregano
Coarse sea salt and black pepper

BLACK BEAN SALSA
1 cup (250 mL) drained and rinsed canned black beans,
1 mango, peeled and diced
1 ripe tomato, diced
4 green onions, thinly sliced
⅓ cup (80 mL) chopped fresh cilantro
¼ cup (60 mL) diced pickled jalapeño peppers
Juice of 1 lime or 2 Tbsp (30 mL) hot pickled pepper juice
Coarse sea salt and black pepper

GUACAMOLE
2 ripe avocados
1 clove garlic, minced
Juice of 1 lime
3 Tbsp (45 mL) chopped fresh cilantro
Salt, black pepper and hot sauce

QUICK CABBAGE SLAW
6 cups (1.5 L) shredded green cabbage
3 Tbsp (45 mL) white vinegar
Pinch of chili powder
Salt and black pepper

18 to 24 6-inch/15 cm flour and/or corn tortillas, warmed

1. For the carnitas, place all of the ingredients in a sealable container and shake to blend and coat the chicken evenly. Pour the mixture into a medium saucepan over medium heat and cook, uncovered and stirring often, until most of the liquid has evaporated, about 20 minutes. Season to taste with salt and pepper.

2. For the black bean salsa, toss the black beans, mango and tomato with the green onions, cilantro, pickled jalapeños and lime juice (or hot pepper juice) and season to taste with salt and pepper. Cover and chill until ready to serve.

3. For the guacamole, cut the avocados in half and scoop out the flesh. Use a fork to mash the avocado roughly and work in the garlic, lime juice and cilantro and season to taste with salt, pepper and hot sauce. Cover and chill until ready to serve.

4. For the slaw, toss the cabbage with the vinegar and chili powder and season lightly with salt and pepper. Cover and chill until ready to serve.

5. To serve, arrange the hot carnitas, salsa, guacamole and slaw in individual bowls and set them on the table with a platter of tortillas. Provide small plates and encourage guests to build their own taco, layering on the chicken and whatever toppings they like. Have hot sauce handy on the side for those who want it.

Photo on page 28

Michael loves making a pan of meatballs when we're having a crowd over. It's a simple dish to make, and people know what to do when they see the pan of meatballs and a dish of frilly toothpicks or appetizer forks next to it. Have cocktail napkins ready, or a basket of Buttery Soft Dinner Rolls (page 99) to make quick little meatball sandwiches.

MICHAEL'S SUPER MEATBALLS

MAKES 3 DOZEN MEATBALLS • PREP: 15 MINUTES • COOK: 30 MINUTES

MAKE AHEAD

Meatballs are an ideal make-ahead dish. You can refrigerate baked meatballs in their sauce in an airtight container for up to 3 days, or freeze them for up to 3 months. Thaw frozen meatballs overnight in the fridge and then gently reheat them in their sauce in a saucepan over medium-low heat until warmed through, about 20 minutes.

3 cups (750 mL) good-quality tomato sauce

2 lb (900 g) fresh ground pork, veal and beef mix

1 cup (130 g) dry breadcrumbs

½ cup (50 g) finely grated Parmesan cheese

2 large eggs

1 clove fresh garlic, minced

1 Tbsp (15 mL) chopped Italian parsley

1 tsp fine sea salt

1 tsp black pepper

1. Preheat the oven to 350°F (180°C).

2. Pour the tomato sauce into a large ovenproof sauté pan or other ovenproof pan with a lid. Bring to a simmer over medium heat, uncovered, while you prepare the meatballs.

3. Combine the ground meat, breadcrumbs, cheese, eggs, garlic, parsley, salt and pepper until well blended (using your hands is easiest). Use a small ice cream scoop or spoon to shape the mix into 36 meatballs, shaping them between your palms. Drop them into the gently simmering tomato sauce (they will only be partially submerged), spoon the sauce over to baste them and cover the pan.

4. Bake for 25 to 30 minutes, until fully cooked, basting again halfway through cooking. Serve warm.

❧

BEYOND THE HOLIDAYS

For a hearty winter supper, serve the meatballs and sauce over spaghetti, or make them into hot meatball sandwiches by stuffing them into crusty rolls.

COZY SUPPER WITH FRIENDS

——————————— ❧ ———————————

HOLIDAY ENTERTAINING IS far more than just the main event
meals at Thanksgiving, Christmas and New Year's. I love using the holidays
as an excuse to have friends over, and Michael and I prefer a more relaxed
meal, with dishes that we can make ahead of time so that we have more
time to spend visiting, eating and laughing.

HORSERADISH SHRIMP COCKTAIL ON GOAT CHEESE CRÈMES   71

PUMPKIN SEED MULTIGRAIN BREAD   73

～

BELGIAN BEEF CARBONNADE   75

～

WINTER SALAD WITH ROASTED PEAR, FETA AND HAZELNUT DRESSING   77

～

"THE JASPER" FANCY COFFEE   79

HOMEMADE IRISH CREAM LIQUEUR   80

～

served with

INDIVIDUAL APPLE POUDINGS CHÔMEUR   307 *or*

CHOCOLATE AND IRISH CREAM MARQUISE   303 *or*

PANETTONE BREAD PUDDINGS   308 *or*

STICKY TOFFEE PUDDINGS   310

HELPFUL HINT

Shrimp are sold by size. The number on the package tells you how many shrimp there are per pound. So 21/30 shrimp means that there are between 21 and 30 shrimp per pound, which means they are smaller than 16/20 shrimp.

ADD SPARKLE

Combining a can of drained cocktail shrimp with this creamy horseradish dressing makes a nice shrimp salad that can be used as part of an hors d'oeuvre. For instance, use it to top Spinach, Mushroom and Parmesan Squares (page 55).

My baking background really comes out in this recipe. Instead of serving chilled shrimp on shredded lettuce (or in a ring) as in a traditional shrimp cocktail, I use them to top crème brûlée–style custards made with goat cheese, horseradish and dill. This appetizer looks stunning when brought to the table.

HORSERADISH SHRIMP COCKTAIL ON GOAT CHEESE CRÈMES

MAKES SIX 5 OZ (150 G) SERVINGS • SERVES 6 •
PREP: 35 MINUTES, PLUS CHILLING • COOK: 30 MINUTES

MAKE AHEAD
You can refrigerate the prepared ramekins without the shrimp topper, covered, for up to 8 hours.

GOAT CHEESE CRÈMES
1 cup (250 mL) whipping cream
½ cup (125 mL) 2% milk
5 oz (150 g) fresh goat cheese
1 large egg
1 large egg yolk
2 Tbsp (30 mL) Prepared Horseradish (page 154)
2 Tbsp (30 mL) chopped fresh dill
1 Tbsp (15 mL) fresh lemon juice
½ tsp fine sea salt

SHRIMP
1 lemon, cut in half
1 onion, peeled and sliced
1 (14 oz/400 g) bag frozen 16/20 shrimp or 21/30 shrimp, in their shells, thawed
2 Tbsp (30 mL) mayonnaise
1 Tbsp (15 mL) Prepared Horseradish (page 154)
1 Tbsp (15 mL) chopped fresh dill
1 Tbsp (15 mL) fresh lemon juice
1 Tbsp (15 mL) capers
¾ cup (175 mL) finely shredded radicchio

1. Preheat the oven to 300°F (150°C). Place six 5 oz (150 g) ramekins or ovenproof glass jars in a roasting pan.

2. For the crèmes, place the cream and milk in a medium saucepan over medium heat and bring it to just below a simmer. Set aside.

3. Place the goat cheese in a mixing bowl, beat it to smooth it out a little and then beat in the egg and egg yolk, switching to a whisk to make sure the mixture is smooth. Whisk in the horseradish, dill, lemon juice and salt. Slowly whisk in the hot cream.

4. Use a ladle to divide the cream mixture evenly among the ramekins (they will be about half-full). Pour boiling water into the roasting pan until it reaches the level of the custards.

5. Bake, uncovered, for 25 to 30 minutes, until the custards jiggle only slightly in the centre. Let the brûlées cool in the pan on a wire rack for 5 minutes, then carefully transfer the ramekins from the pan to the rack to cool completely. Chill, uncovered, for at least 2 hours.

6. For the shrimp, place 8 cups (2 L) of water, the lemon and onion in a large saucepan and bring to a boil over high heat. Add the shrimp and reduce the heat to medium, so it is at a gentle simmer. Cook the shrimp for 3 to 4 minutes, until fully pink. Drain the shrimp, and discard the lemon and onion. Run the shrimp under cold water for 1 minute and then peel them. Set aside.

7. Prepare a dressing by mixing the mayonnaise, horseradish, dill, lemon juice and capers together in a medium bowl. Add the shrimp and toss well to coat. Cover and chill until ready to serve.

8. To serve, place each ramekin on a small serving plate. Arrange a few shrimp on top of each crème and top with the shredded radicchio.

> I love making bread in the winter, mainly because I'm spending more time indoors and love the aroma of it baking! I'm particularly fond of this recipe because it uses a German bread-baking trick of adding day-old bread that has been soaked in hot water. This adds moisture, body and a well-developed flavour to the newly made loaf.

PUMPKIN SEED MULTIGRAIN BREAD

MAKES TWO 9 × 5-INCH (2 L) PULLMAN LOAVES · SERVES 12 TO 16 ·
PREP: 30 MINUTES, PLUS RISING · COOK: 1 HOUR, PLUS COOLING

MAKE AHEAD

Freshly baked bread is tops, of course, but you can store this bread, well wrapped, on the counter (do not refrigerate) for a few days. It even makes great toast for a few days after that. Or freeze it, well wrapped, for up to 3 months. Thaw at room temperature before slicing to serve.

STARTER

2 ½ cups (300 g) dark or medium rye flour, plus extra for sprinkling

1 ¼ cups (310 mL) lukewarm water

1 tsp instant dry yeast

1 tsp black pepper

1 tsp honey

SOAKER

3 cups (140 g) torn-up pieces of day-old bread, including crusts (white, whole wheat or rye bread)

Boiling water, to cover

DOUGH

4 cups (600 g) bread flour

2 ½ cups (375 g) whole wheat flour

1 pkg (2 ¼ tsp/8 g) instant dry yeast

½ cup (125 mL) coffee or strongly brewed tea, at room temperature

2 Tbsp (32 g) fancy molasses

1 Tbsp (15 g) fine sea salt

1 cup (170 g) cooked wheat, spelt or rye kernels ("berries")

2 cups (240 g) roasted, unsalted pumpkin seeds

¼ cup (40 g) flax seeds

1 egg whisked with 2 Tbsp (30 mL) water, for egg wash

Sunflower, pumpkin and flax seeds, for sprinkling

1. For the starter, place the rye flour, water, yeast, pepper and honey in a medium bowl and stir by hand to make a thick paste. Sprinkle a little rye flour on top (this prevents a crust from forming), wrap the bowl in plastic wrap and set on the counter for at least 12 hours but no more than 24 hours.

2. For the soaker, place the torn-up bread pieces in a bowl and cover with the boiling water. Let sit until cooled to room temperature. Squeeze the excess water from the bread into a bowl. Set aside the bread and reserve ½ cup (125 mL) of the soaker liquid for the final dough.

3. For the final dough, place the bread flour, whole wheat flour and yeast in the bowl of a stand mixer fitted with the hook attachment and give it a quick stir. Add all of the starter, the reserved soaker liquid, the squeezed-out bread, the coffee (or tea), molasses and salt and mix on low speed for 5 minutes, until evenly combined.

Recipe continues ▶

HELPFUL HINT

The bread you use for the soaker will influence the flavour of the baked bread. A dark rye will add deep flavour (and colour), while a fluffier Italian loaf will result in a lighter, milder-tasting loaf. Pumpernickel adds a nice hint of sweetness.

4. Add the cooked grain kernels, and the pumpkin and flax seeds and continue to mix on low speed for another 10 minutes (the dough will be sticky, but this length of time develops the elasticity of the dough). Cover the bowl with plastic wrap without it touching the dough and let the dough rise at room temperature for just 30 minutes (it will only rise a little).

5. Grease two 9 × 5-inch (2 L) loaf pans. Turn the dough out onto a generously floured work surface, dust the dough with flour and divide it in half. Flatten each piece with your hands and then roll them up into a loaf shape. Place each loaf in a loaf pan and cover with a tea towel. Let rise at room temperature for 1 hour until almost doubled in size.

6. Preheat the oven to 350°F (180°C). Brush each loaf with egg wash and sprinkle with seeds. Use a serrated knife to score a line down the length of the loaf. Bake the loaves for 1 hour, until the tops are a deep brown. Immediately turn them out of their pans to cool on a wire rack for at least 1 hour. Serve warm (they will still be quite warm, even after an hour) or at room temperature.

ADD SPARKLE

To make this bread more Christmas-y, I add 1 tsp each of cinnamon and anise seed and ½ tsp of ground cloves to the recipe when I add the pumpkin seeds. This gives the bread an aroma and taste that remind me of Pfeffernüsse cookies, and makes it a lovely addition to a cheese board or charcuterie plate.

> The sauce for this Belgian version of a beef stew uses dark beer to add depth of flavour and prunes to add a subtle sweetness. The prunes break down as the stew cooks, so it's hard to tell they are there.

BELGIAN BEEF CARBONNADE

SERVES 6 • PREP: 20 MINUTES • COOK: 105 MINUTES

MAKE AHEAD

A stew like this improves as it sits. You can refrigerate the cooled beef carbonnade in an airtight container for up to 2 days, or freeze it for up to 3 months. It's a perfect dish to have on reserve for a busy January weeknight!

3 Tbsp (45 mL) vegetable oil, divided
2 lb (900 g) diced stewing beef, cut into 1-inch/2.5 cm cubes
¼ cup (35 g) all-purpose flour
Salt and black pepper
1 medium onion, peeled and diced
1 celery stalk, diced
1 medium carrot, peeled and diced
½ lb (225 g) cremini mushrooms, quartered
2 tsp chopped fresh thyme
1 cup (170 g) pitted prunes, cut in half
2 cups (500 mL) low-sodium beef stock
1 cup (250 mL) dark beer, such as a stout or porter
1 Tbsp (15 mL) packed light brown sugar
1 Tbsp (15 mL) red wine vinegar

1. Preheat the oven to 325°F (160°C).

2. Place 1 ½ Tbsp (22 mL) of the oil in a heavy-bottomed ovenproof medium Dutch oven over medium-high heat. In a bowl, toss the stewing beef with the flour and season lightly with salt and pepper. Shake off and reserve any excess flour, add half the meat to the pan and brown for 2 to 3 minutes, until dark brown, and then transfer to a plate. Repeat with the remaining oil and beef. Set aside.

3. Reduce the heat to medium and place the onions, celery, carrots, mushrooms and thyme in the saucepan. Sauté the vegetables for about 5 minutes, until the onions are translucent. The moisture from the vegetables will loosen any flour stuck on the bottom of the pan. Add the reserved flour and stir for another minute.

4. Stir in the prunes and then the stock and beer and bring to a simmer. Once the liquid is simmering, reduce the heat to reach a gentle simmer. Cover the pan and cook in the oven for 90 minutes, or until the meat is tender but not falling apart. (Alternatively, simmer the stew gently over low heat on the stove for 90 minutes.)

5. Immediately before serving, stir in the sugar and vinegar and season to taste.

HELPFUL HINTS

I like to dice my own beef for stew. A whole cut is often cheaper, and I can choose how lean the meat is (I prefer a boneless blade roast over an inside or outside round, which is too lean) and what size to dice it. As with any stew, cut the beef and the vegetables to about the same size.

BEYOND THE HOLIDAYS

If you are not making the beef carbonnade as part of a whole holiday menu, serve it with crusty bread or Buttery Soft Dinner Rolls (page 99), Mashed Potatoes with Green Onions (page 100), Ultimate Roasted Potatoes (page 101) or even Potato Gnocchi with Herb Butter and Parmesan (page 115).

Belgian Beef Carbonnade (page 75); Winter Salad with Roasted Pear, Feta and Hazelnut Dressing (page 77)

WINTER SALAD WITH ROASTED PEAR, FETA AND HAZELNUT DRESSING

(V)

(GF)

SERVES 6 • PREP: 20 MINUTES • COOK: 30 MINUTES

MAKE AHEAD
You can refrigerate the roasted pears in an airtight container for up to 5 days. Reheat them gently in a baking dish, uncovered, in a 325°F (160°C) oven for about 15 minutes before serving.

ROASTED PEARS
4 medium-ripe pears (Bartlett, Bosc or Forelle)
1 shallot, peeled and thinly sliced
1 Tbsp (15 mL) pure maple syrup or 1 Tbsp (18 g) honey
1 Tbsp (15 mL) fresh lemon juice
5 to 6 sprigs fresh thyme
Salt and black pepper

SALAD
1 recipe Hazelnut Dressing (page 149)
12 cups (3 L) mixed salad greens, such as curly endive, Belgian endive, radicchio, frisée, oak leaf (feuille de chêne), arugula and/or spinach
Drizzle of extra virgin olive oil
Salt and black pepper
3 oz (90 g) crumbled feta cheese
¼ cup (32 g) chopped toasted hazelnuts

1. Preheat the oven to 375°F (190°C).

2. For the roasted pears, cut each pear into 8 wedges and carve out and discard the cores. Toss the pears with the shallot, maple syrup (or honey), lemon juice, thyme, salt and pepper. Arrange in a ceramic or glass baking dish in a single layer and roast, uncovered, for 20 to 30 minutes, stirring once or twice, until the pears are fork-tender. Set aside.

3. For the salad, drop a generous spoonful of the hazelnut dressing onto the centre of 6 salad plates and spread it out a little. Arrange the greens on top, drizzle with a little olive oil and sprinkle lightly with salt and pepper. Arrange the warm pear wedges on the greens, and sprinkle with feta and chopped hazelnuts.

HELPFUL HINT
Spreading a layer of the dressing onto your salad plate is a restaurant trick. While the dressing peeks out appealingly from *underneath* the lettuce, it won't wilt the greens, which means you can assemble the salad and let it sit at the table throughout the meal.

Part of our annual holiday schedule is a November visit to Jasper Park Lodge, Alberta, in the heart of the Rocky Mountains, for a special Christmas-themed event. Guests attend cooking classes and decorating seminars, and every evening ends with dancing. During the quiet moments, I love to sit by the giant stone fireplace with a fancy coffee . . . and this recipe is a tribute to the whole experience.

"THE JASPER" FANCY COFFEE

SERVES 4 • PREP: 10 MINUTES

MAKE AHEAD
You can whip the cream for this coffee 1 to 2 hours ahead of your guests arriving and chill it in a covered bowl. If you want to whip it up to 1 day ahead, add 1 tsp (5 mL) of instant skim milk powder as you whip it and then chill it. The milk powder stabilizes the cream so it holds its volume longer.

½ cup (100 g) decorator's or coarse white sugar
Pinch of ground cinnamon, plus extra for garnish
1 egg white, lightly whisked
¾ oz (22 mL) Homemade Irish Cream Liqueur (page 80)
½ oz (15 mL) orange liqueur
½ oz (15 mL) Irish whiskey or brandy
6 oz (175 mL) hot coffee
½ cup (125 mL) whipping cream, whipped and lightly sweetened
4 thin strips of orange zest or Candied Orange Peel (page 318)

1. Have ready four 8 oz (250 mL) coffee glasses. Stir the sugar and cinnamon together and place it in a saucer. Dip the rim of each coffee glass into the egg white and then into the cinnamon sugar.

2. Pour the Irish cream, orange liqueur and whiskey (or brandy) into each coffee glass and top with hot coffee.

3. Scoop the whipped cream into a piping bag fitted with a large star tip. Pipe a dollop of cream on top of each coffee and top with a strip of orange zest, twisted (or a strip of candied orange peel). Garnish with a pinch of cinnamon and serve immediately.

HOMEMADE IRISH CREAM LIQUEUR

MAKES 3 ½ CUPS (825 ML) · PREP: 5 MINUTES ·
COOK: 3 MINUTES, PLUS CHILLING

1. Have ready enough mason jars with sealable lids, or smaller bottles
   with caps or stoppers, to hold 3 ½ cups (825 mL) of liquid.

2. Heat the cream in a small saucepan over medium heat with the cinnamon stick, until it is just below a simmer. Add the chocolate and
   whisk until it has fully melted into the cream. Whisk in the instant
   coffee and vanilla.

3. Remove the pan from the heat and let the cream mixture cool for
   about 15 minutes (this allows the cinnamon to infuse a little more).
   Whisk in the condensed milk and whiskey.

4. Pour the Irish cream into the jars or bottles and chill until needed.
   Serve over ice. If gifting, include a label specifying to keep the
   liqueur refrigerated.

MAKE AHEAD
You can refrigerate this liqueur in an
airtight container for up to 1 month.

1 cup (250 mL) half-and-half cream
1 cinnamon stick
1 oz (30 g) dark couverture/baking
  chocolate, chopped
1 tsp instant coffee powder
1 tsp pure vanilla extract
1 can (10 oz/300 mL) sweetened
  condensed milk
1 cup (250 mL) Irish whiskey

HELPFUL HINT
While Irish whiskey is the standard alcohol of choice for this recipe, I've often used the leftover brandy
from the bottle I buy for my fruitcakes. Other more distinctive-tasting spirits, such as Scotch whisky
(with its smoky/peat notes) or rum, might not work as well.

THE MAIN EVENT

YOU GET THE CALL . . . this year it's YOUR turn to host the big family dinner. No pressure, just make the best meal your family has ever had! I still remember the very first big family holiday dinner I hosted. It was my first Thanksgiving out of university, years before I studied to become a chef, and I was proud to have an apartment with a decent kitchen (even then, it was a priority for me!). I can't recall the turkey and stuffing, although I'm sure there were phone calls home to Mom to guide me through it, but I do remember being immensely proud of the pumpkin pie—my first ever attempt. It was only as I was bringing it to the table that I realized I had completely forgotten to add any sugar to the filling! I made a 180 back to the kitchen, poked holes into the filling with a skewer and poured maple syrup overtop, hoping it would seep in. It didn't.

On that note, I now share with you the wisdom accumulated over the years that have followed that very first festive meal. I've included three menus, one of them a vegetarian option, that will help you tailor the dinner to Thanksgiving or Christmas. I offer traditional preparations and some more unconventional ones, or combine a couple if you have both vegetarians and meat eaters in your group. This is your year!

Get Set for the Main Event

No holiday meals have more tradition and greater expectations associated with them than the Thanksgiving and Christmas dinners. If you are the cook in charge of one or both of these meals, here are two turkey menus with all the trimmings—one classic, the other less so—and tips on how to make the whole experience stress-free. Regardless of the menu you choose, feel free to add or change different items to suit the preferences and traditions of your own family, or select dishes from the other menus in this book.

PLAN YOUR SERVING STYLE. Family-style or buffet? Serving your meal family-style means setting a table with plates, cutlery and glasses and bringing the food to the table on platters and in bowls so that guests can help themselves as the dishes are passed around. If your group is more than 12, I recommend having two bowls or platters of each item, so that everyone can get a full plate faster. We often opt for a buffet instead. We set a long table with dinner plates and all of the delicious items we've prepared, and then ask guests to help themselves. They can easily pop up from the dining table to have seconds, and as the host, I can easily see when I need to top up platters, re-warm gravy or consolidate dishes to make cleaning up simpler.

CHOOSE YOUR SEATING STYLE. If everyone knows each other, or if your tradition includes designated seats for everyone in the family, your guests can seat themselves. Otherwise, you might choose to plan the seating beforehand and put out name cards to help guests find their seat.

STOCK UP ON DRINKS. You know your crowd, so plan wine, beer, cocktails and non-alcoholic options to suit your group and your dishes. Whether you are setting up a beverage station for people to serve themselves, or designating one or two people to manage the drinks, fill a large cooler with ice to store white wines, water (still and sparkling) and a selection of other non-alcoholic drinks. Set out the appropriate glasses nearby. You can even plug in a portable burner or slow cooker to hold a saucepan of mulled cider or hot chocolate.

SET THE PACE. Depending on the time of day and the guests you've invited, your gathering might be a long, relaxed affair with everyone lingering over dessert or it could be a faster-paced event. As the host, you set the tone and the pace. If you're in the kitchen, you could designate someone to get the door, take coats or serve drinks. Or perhaps you prefer to put on some music, introduce guests to each other and stay with them until everyone arrives before you head back to the kitchen. Once everyone is at the table, take a breath, enjoy the moment and the conversation (and the delicious feast) and don't rush. The minute you leave the table to clear plates or tidy up, people will follow, so gauge whether it's time for people to jump to help with the dishes or whether you'd rather linger over those last few bites.

CONSIDER YOUR CROWD. If you have kids in your group, or if you're serving a crowd and prefer to have your guests mingle while you bring together the meal on your own in the kitchen, put out a cheese board and a few snacks—even just rolls or other child-friendly foods, to keep everyone happy before the main event. Most parents arrive with activities to keep their kids occupied, but set aside some space the young ones can call their own (but near enough to the adults for supervision).

ORCHESTRATE DESSERT. You may have your own holiday dessert traditions, but at our house, we take a little break between the main meal and dessert to get up from the table, clean up a touch and stretch and move around! To bring everyone back together—and because I always offer a variety of cookies, cakes, squares and puddings—I like to set up a dessert buffet and be at hand to chat with my guests and help serve them desserts. Whether everyone heads back to the dining table with their desserts, or mills about the kitchen or living room more informally, is up to you.

Menu

A Traditional Thanksgiving

CHEESE BOARD, page 35

WINTER CRUDITÉS WITH DIPS, page 48

SPINACH, MUSHROOM AND PARMESAN SQUARES, page 55

~

WHOLE ROASTED TURKEY WITH CARAMELIZED ONION AND APPLE STUFFING,
CRANBERRY SAUCE AND GRAVY, page 93

BUTTERY SOFT DINNER ROLLS, page 99

MASHED POTATOES WITH GREEN ONIONS, page 100

and/or ULTIMATE ROASTED POTATOES, page 101

ROASTED CARROTS AND PARSNIPS, page 106

BRUSSELS SPROUTS WITH LEMON AND ASIAGO, page 107

~

Choose 1 or more from:

MICHAEL'S FAVOURITE DATE SQUARES, page 229

CARAMEL APPLE BARS, page 234

CINDERELLA PUMPKIN PIE, page 256

APPLE MINCEMEAT MINI PIES, page 254

PECAN BUTTER TART CHEESECAKE, page 268

A Christmas Feast

CRÈME BRÛLÉE EGGNOG, page 108

CHEESE BOARD, page 35, WITH CLASSIC OAT CRACKERS, page 41

JALAPEÑO CORNBREAD MADELEINES, page 47

WINTER CRUDITÉS WITH DIPS, page 48

MINI TOURTIÈRES, page 53

MARINATED BONELESS TURKEY BREAST ROAST WITH PANCETTA GRAVY, page 90

CRANBERRY SAUCE, page 147

BUTTERY SOFT DINNER ROLLS, page 99

POTATOES AU GRATIN, page 103

and/or SPICED SWEET POTATO WEDGES, page 104

ROASTED CARROTS AND PARSNIPS, page 106

BRUSSELS SPROUTS WITH LEMON AND ASIAGO, page 107 *OR*

SPINACH FLORENTINE WITH 'NDUJA, page 123

Choose 1 or more from:

CINDERELLA PUMPKIN PIE, page 256

LEMON MERINGUE BÛCHE DE NOËL, page 271

LIME CHIFFON CAKE WITH RASPBERRY SWISS MERINGUE BUTTERCREAM, page 275

FLOURLESS CHOCOLATE MONT BLANC TORTE, page 277

GINGERBREAD WHITE CHOCOLATE MOUSSE CAKE, page 286

A DICKENS OF A PLUM PUDDING, page 295

ASSORTED COOKIES, pages 193 to 221, IF YOU HAVE ANY ROOM LEFT

> This hearty soup has an elegant side because of the delicate flavours
> of the leeks and the celeriac (celery root). Once cooked, celeriac is smooth
> and seems creamy even before you add the cream. This soup is a wintertime
> staple in our house. When spring finally rolls around I serve it chilled
> like a traditional vichyssoise.

GF

LEEK, POTATO AND CELERIAC SOUP

SERVES 6 TO 8 • PREP: 15 MINUTES • COOK: 25 MINUTES

1. Melt the butter in a stockpot over medium heat. Add the leeks and sauté for about 5 minutes, until tender but not brown. Add the potatoes, celeriac, thyme, bay leaf and nutmeg and stir. Pour in the stock, season lightly with salt and pepper, and bring to a simmer.

2. Cover and reduce the heat so the soup simmers gently. Cook until the potatoes are tender, about 20 minutes.

3. Remove and discard the bay leaf. Purée the soup until smooth in a blender or with an immersion blender. Return the soup to the stockpot over medium heat, stir in the cream and season to taste.

4. Serve the soup in bowls or soup cups, garnished with fresh chives and crumbled blue cheese.

MAKE AHEAD
You can refrigerate this soup in an airtight container for up to 3 days, or freeze it for up to 3 months. Reheat it directly from the freezer in a saucepan over low heat, or thaw it overnight in the fridge and warm over medium-low heat.

2 Tbsp (30 g) butter
2 cups (175 g) sliced leek, white and
  light green parts only (about 1 large)
¾ lb (340 g) peeled and diced russet
  or Yukon Gold potatoes (about
  2 medium)
2 cups (250 g) peeled and diced
  celeriac (about 1 small)
2 tsp chopped fresh thyme
1 bay leaf
Pinch of ground nutmeg
4 cups (1 L) chicken stock or vegetable
  stock (gluten-free, if required)
Salt and black pepper
½ cup (125 mL) whipping cream
Chopped fresh chives and crumbled
  blue cheese, for garnish

HELPFUL HINTS
Using a high-powered blender gives this soup a very velvety texture. If you are using an immersion blender or a food processor, strain the soup through a fine-mesh sieve after blending for the same silky consistency.

ADD SPARKLE
For a formal dinner party, ladle out and garnish this soup in the kitchen rather than serving it more casually at the table. For a festive touch, replace the blue cheese garnish with cooked lobster, crab, shrimp, scallops or even smoked salmon or trout.

This marinated turkey recipe, which I call my turketta, strays from the traditional whole turkey (page 93). It's a nice option if you have a small kitchen or if your family insists on turkey for Thanksgiving *and* Christmas, but you'd rather not serve the same menu twice. Porchetta is a boneless herb-rubbed pork loin that is roasted until the skin crisps up. Here I use similar flavours but with turkey. For a fully gluten-free option, substitute Caramelized Onion Cream (page 120) for the gravy.

without the gravy

MARINATED BONELESS TURKEY BREAST ROAST WITH PANCETTA GRAVY

SERVES 6 TO 8 (WITH ENOUGH FOR LEFTOVERS) •
PREP: 20 MINUTES, PLUS MARINATING • COOK: 105 MINUTES

1. It's best to prepare the marinade right before using it. Purée the oil, onion, garlic, lemon zest, sage, thyme, salt, chili flakes and pepper in a food processor or blender until evenly combined.

2. Remove and discard any bones from the turkey breasts. Place the turkey, skin side down, in a casserole dish or other pan. Set aside ¼ cup (60 mL) of the marinade for the sauce and pour the rest over the turkey. Cover the dish with plastic wrap and let the turkey marinate in the fridge for at least 3 hours, or up to a maximum of 24 hours.

3. Preheat the oven to 400°F (200°C). Using butcher's twine, tie the turkey breasts together, skin sides facing out, leaving as much of the marinade between them as possible. Pat the outside of the breasts with paper towels and transfer to a roasting pan. Rub the turkey skin with butter and season lightly with salt and pepper.

4. Roast the turkey, uncovered, for 20 minutes. Reduce the oven temperature to 350°F (180°C) and roast for 60 to 70 minutes more, basting the turkey with the juices often, until the centre of each breast registers 170°F (77°C) on a meat thermometer. Transfer the turkey to a cutting board, cover with aluminum foil and let it rest while you prepare the gravy.

5. For the gravy, use the roasting pan if it has toasted bits that aren't burnt, otherwise heat a clean medium saucepan over medium heat. Add the pancetta and cook until crisp, stirring occasionally, about 5 minutes. Spoon the cooked pancetta onto a plate and drain the fat into a measuring cup.

Recipe continues ▶

MAKE AHEAD

You should start marinating the turkey at least 3 hours (up to a maximum of 24 hours) before it is to go in the oven. Any cooked leftovers (hello, turkey sandwich!) will keep, well wrapped, for up to 4 days in the fridge and up to 3 months in the freezer. Thaw in the fridge before using.

TURKEY

¼ cup (60 mL) extra virgin olive oil
1 medium onion, peeled and chopped
3 cloves garlic, chopped
Finely grated zest of 1 lemon
8 large fresh sage leaves
2 Tbsp (30 mL) fresh thyme leaves
2 tsp salt, plus extra for the turkey
1 tsp chili flakes
½ tsp black pepper, plus extra for the turkey
2 turkey breasts, each about 2 ¼ lb/1 kg
3 Tbsp (45 g) butter

GRAVY

1 cup (125 g) uncooked diced pancetta
3 Tbsp (45 g) combined pancetta fat and butter
¼ cup (35 g) all-purpose flour
2 cups (500 mL) low-sodium or no-salt-added chicken or turkey stock

Ultimate Roasted Potatoes (page 101); Cranberry Sauce (page 147); Marinated Boneless Turkey Breast Roast (page 90);

6. Measure 3 Tbsp (45 mL) of the fat back into the pan, supplementing with butter if needed. Add the flour, and stir with a wooden spoon over medium heat until the roux becomes the colour of peanut butter, about 7 minutes.

7. Add the reserved ¼ cup (60 mL) of marinade, stirring well, and then whisk in 1 cup (250 mL) of the stock, waiting until it begins to bubble before whisking in the remaining 1 cup (250 mL). Bring the gravy to a simmer, add the cooked pancetta and season to taste with salt and pepper.

8. To serve, untie the turkey, cut into ½-inch (1 cm) slices and serve with the gravy.

HELPFUL HINT

Traditional porchetta seasoning also includes rosemary and fennel, but I find these flavours can be overwhelming and not always family-friendly, which is why I don't use them in this turketta.

> If your Thanksgiving or Christmas dinner tradition involves the classics, here is a traditional stuffed holiday turkey for you. Pick your preferred potatoes (mashed, roasted, au gratin or sweet potato), ready the cranberry sauce, root vegetables and Brussels sprouts and you're set.

WHOLE ROASTED TURKEY WITH CARAMELIZED ONION AND APPLE STUFFING, CRANBERRY SAUCE AND GRAVY

SERVES 12 • PREP: 30 MINUTES • COOK: 3 HOURS AND 20 MINUTES

MAKE AHEAD

Leftover turkey can be wrapped well and refrigerated for up to 3 days, or diced or left in larger pieces and frozen in airtight containers for up to 3 months. Thaw it overnight in the fridge before using.

½ cup (115 g) unsalted butter, at room temperature
1 Tbsp (15 mL) finely chopped fresh thyme
Salt and black pepper
1 leek, white and light green parts only, washed and sliced
16 lb (6.75 kg) fresh whole turkey

STUFFING

1 recipe Caramelized Onion and Apple Dressing (page 153), made without the egg, uncooked

GRAVY

2 oz (60 mL) dry white vermouth
⅓ cup (50 g) all-purpose flour
3 cups (750 mL) chicken or turkey stock (including strained pan juices)

1 recipe Cranberry Sauce (page 147), for serving

1. Preheat the oven to 325°F (160°C).

2. Stir the butter with the thyme and a generous pinch of salt and pepper. Set aside. Arrange the sliced leeks in the centre of a large roasting pan and place the turkey on top. Spoon the dressing into the cavity of the turkey. Pat the skin dry with a paper towel and rub the thyme butter over the entire surface of the bird, finishing with a sprinkle of salt and pepper.

3. Cook the turkey, uncovered and basting it every 20 minutes or so (more often as the turkey gets closer to being done), for 2 ½ to 3 hours. Use a meat thermometer to check whether it is done: the recommended temperatures are 170°F (77°C) in the breast, 180°F (82°C) in the thigh and 165°F (74°C) in the centre of the stuffing.

4. Transfer the turkey to a cutting board or platter to rest uncovered for 20 minutes while you prepare the gravy and bring your other dishes to the table.

5. To make the gravy, strain the drippings from the roasting pan through a fine-mesh sieve into a bowl. Separate the fat from the pan juices using a gravy-separating pitcher or by skimming off the fat that floats to the top with a baster or a spoon. Reserve both the fat and the pan juices (add the pan juices to your stock measurement).

6. Discard the leeks if they are scorched; if they are not, reserve them to add back to the gravy at the end, if you wish.

Recipe continues ▶

7. Place the roasting pan on the stove over medium heat and add the vermouth, using a wooden spoon to loosen the caramelized bits at the bottom of the pan. Add ¼ cup (60 mL) of the pan drippings and the flour, continuing to stir over medium heat until a nutty aroma develops, about 4 minutes (for a darker gravy, let the flour turn light brown, an extra 2 minutes).

8. Switch to a whisk and slowly pour in 1 cup (250 mL) of the stock while whisking continuously. As soon as the gravy thickens, whisk in another 1 cup (250 mL). Once the gravy thickens again and begins to bubble, whisk in the remaining 1 cup (250 mL) of stock in a slow steady stream and let it reach a full simmer before adding the reserved leeks (if using) and seasoning to taste.

9. To serve, carve the turkey into slices, and serve with the stuffing, gravy and cranberry sauce.

HELPFUL HINTS

If you have the choice, carve the turkey in the kitchen rather than at the table. This way you can carve the whole breasts off the bone and slice them nicely on a cutting board, and then take off the thighs and legs, pull away the meat and arrange it on a large platter. This platter can be covered and kept warm in a 300°F (150°C) oven while you organize everything else.

I do find it true that, generally, whole turkey takes 20 minutes per pound (450 g) to cook at 325°F (160°C), but it takes longer once you add the stuffing (and depends on how tightly it is packed into the turkey), so always use a thermometer to be sure.

For a gluten-free alternative to the gravy, see the note on my Spinach Florentine recipe, page 123.

Having so many side dishes on hand at Thanksgiving or Christmas can present vegetarian guests with plenty of choices, but this meatless version of tourtière provides an option for a grand main dish. The Mushroom and Brie Wellington with Caramelized Onion Cream (page 120) is also a lovely option if you want a vegetarian main dish that can be brought to the table and "carved."

can be vegan

VEGETARIAN TOURTIÈRE

MAKES ONE 9-INCH (23 CM) PIE • SERVES 8 • PREP: 30 MINUTES • COOK: 95 MINUTES

1. Place the TVP in a bowl, stir in 1 cup (250 mL) of lukewarm water and set aside.

2. Place the oil in a large sauté pan and warm over medium heat. Add the onions, celery and carrots, sautéing until the onions are translucent, about 5 minutes. Add the garlic and sauté for 1 minute more. Stir in the diced potatoes, thyme, sage, salt, pepper, allspice and nutmeg, and then pour in the stock and cider. Bring to a simmer and cook, covered, for 15 minutes.

3. Add the TVP and continue to simmer, now uncovered, until all of the liquid has been absorbed, about 20 minutes. Cool to room temperature and then chill until ready to assemble.

4. Preheat the oven to 400°F (200°C). Have ready an ungreased 9-inch (23 cm) pie plate and a baking tray lined with parchment paper.

5. On a lightly floured surface, roll out the first disc of dough to a circle just under ¼ inch (0.5 cm) thick and line the pie plate. Spoon the chilled filling into the pie shell, pressing down to fill in any gaps.

6. Roll out the second disc of dough to the same thickness as the first and cut a few vents for steam to escape. Place this top crust over the filling, trimming and pinching the edges to seal them.

7. Place the dish on the baking tray and bake for 15 minutes, then reduce the oven temperature to 375°F (190°C) and bake for another 45 minutes, until the crust is golden brown.

8. Let the tourtière cool for 20 minutes before slicing.

MAKE AHEAD

You can refrigerate the cooked filling in an airtight container, or the baked tourtière, well wrapped, for up to 1 day. Reheat the pie in a 325°F (160°C) oven for about 30 minutes. To freeze, assemble the tourtière in the pie shell then wrap and freeze for up to 3 months. Thaw in the fridge overnight before baking.

1 ½ cups (375 mL) textured vegetable protein (TVP)

1 Tbsp (15 mL) extra virgin olive oil

1 ½ large onions, finely diced

1 celery, finely diced

1 medium carrot, finely diced

2 cloves garlic, minced

½ lb (225 g) potatoes, peeled and diced into ½-inch (1 cm) dice (about 1 medium potato)

1 Tbsp (15 mL) chopped fresh thyme

1 Tbsp (15 mL) chopped fresh sage

1 tsp salt

1 tsp black pepper

¾ tsp ground allspice

½ tsp ground nutmeg

1 ½ cups (375 mL) vegetable stock

1 cup (250 mL) apple cider

1 recipe double-crust pie dough (or vegan option) (page 315), shaped into 2 discs and chilled

Step 2

Step 4

Step 5

Soft, squishy dinner rolls are a staple for many households over the holiday season. They nestle in between the turkey and gravy on your Thanksgiving plate, they are the base for a midnight sandwich and they can be baked small for sliders (Mini Chicken Schnitzel Sliders, page 61) if you're hosting a crowd.

BUTTERY SOFT DINNER ROLLS

MAKES 24 DINNER ROLLS, 48 MINI ROLLS FOR SLIDERS •
PREP: 25 MINUTES, PLUS RISING • COOK: 25 MINUTES

MAKE AHEAD

The rolls are best served warm on the day they are baked, but you can store them, well wrapped, at room temperature for 2 to 3 days. Reheat them in a 300°F (150°C) oven for 5 minutes. You can also freeze baked rolls, well wrapped or in an airtight container, for up to 2 months. Thaw at room temperature before serving.

4 ½ cups (675 g) all-purpose flour
2 Tbsp (25 g) granulated sugar
1 pkg (2 ¼ tsp/8 g) instant dry yeast
1 ½ tsp fine sea salt
1 cup (250 mL) 2% milk, warmed to
    115°F (46°C)
⅓ cup (80 mL) warm water
    (115°F/46°C)
1 large egg, at room temperature
¼ cup (60 g) unsalted butter, at room
    temperature, plus extra for the pan
2 tsp fresh lemon juice
1 egg whisked with 2 Tbsp (30 mL)
    water, for egg wash

1. Combine all of the ingredients except the egg wash in a large mixing bowl or in the bowl of a stand mixer fitted with the hook attachment. Mix the dough by hand or at low speed until it comes together.

2. If mixing by hand, turn the dough out onto a work surface once the dough becomes too difficult to mix with a spoon and knead until smooth, about 5 minutes. If using a mixer, knead the dough on low for 3 minutes more once it has come together.

3. Place the dough in an ungreased bowl, cover with plastic wrap and let rise at room temperature until doubled in size, about 45 minutes.

4. Rub the bottom and sides of a 9 × 13-inch (22.5 × 32.5 cm) baking pan with an even layer of soft butter. Turn the dough out onto a lightly floured work surface and divide into 24 equal pieces.

5. Shape the dough into balls and arrange them in the prepared pan. Cover with a tea towel and let rise at room temperature for 30 minutes.

6. Preheat the oven to 350°F (180°C). Unwrap the rolls, brush with the egg wash and bake for about 25 minutes, until golden brown on top. Let them cool in the pan on a rack for 20 minutes, then serve warm, or transfer them to a wire rack to cool completely.

HELPFUL HINT

For full-sized round buns, divide the dough into 18 pieces, shape each into a ball and arrange on 2 parchment-lined baking trays, leaving plenty of space between them. Right before baking, flatten the buns gently with the palm of your hand (just a quick tap down) and then brush with egg wash and bake for 20 to 25 minutes.

ADD SPARKLE

When I'm using these rolls for sliders or burgers, I sprinkle them with sesame and poppy seeds after brushing with the egg wash.

> If there is gravy on the table, then mashed potatoes are in order. I love making that divot in the top of my scoop so a little pool of gravy can sit right inside.

 GF

 V

MASHED POTATOES WITH GREEN ONIONS

SERVES 6 TO 8 GENEROUSLY · PREP: 15 MINUTES · COOK: 20 MINUTES

1. Place the diced potatoes in a large saucepan of generously salted cold water and bring to a boil, uncovered, over high heat. Reduce the heat to medium-high and simmer until the potatoes are fork-tender, about 20 minutes. Drain the potatoes in a colander.

2. Add the butter to the saucepan in which you boiled the potatoes (the heat of the pan will melt it) but do not return to the stovetop. Press the potatoes through a ricer directly into the pot. Return the saucepan to low heat and stir in the sour cream and milk until smooth. Stir in the green onions and season to taste with salt and pepper. Serve immediately.

Photo on page 105

MAKE AHEAD

Mashed potatoes can be tricky to make in advance, but here's a tip from my restaurant days. Peel and dice the potatoes the evening before and chill, covered, in a bowl of water with a pinch of salt. Up to 1 hour before serving time, drain and boil the potatoes in fresh water and prepare as before. Transfer the mashed potatoes to a metal bowl, cover tightly with plastic and place over a saucepan filled with 2 inches (5 cm) of water over medium-low heat. The steam from the water below will keep the potatoes hot. Stir the potatoes well, transfer to a serving dish and bring to the table.

4.4 lb (2 kg) Yukon Gold potatoes,
    peeled and evenly diced (about
    10 medium)
Salt
6 Tbsp (90 g) butter
1 cup (250 mL) full-fat sour cream
1 cup (250 mL) 2% milk
1 bunch green onions, thinly sliced
Black pepper

HELPFUL HINTS

This recipe makes a generous 6 to 8 portions intentionally because you can never tell how big a scoop your guests will take and you NEVER want to run out of mashed potatoes.

I swear by a potato ricer for the fluffiest mashed potatoes, but mashing by pushing through a food mill or by hand is the next-best option. Using a mixer or beaters risks overworking the potatoes, which makes them gluey.

A good roasted potato should be crispy and golden on the outside and fluffy on the inside. This requires a two-step cooking method: first, parboiling the potatoes and then, slow-roasting them while the turkey or tourtière is in the oven.

ULTIMATE ROASTED POTATOES

without pan drippings

SERVES 6 TO 8 • PREP: 15 MINUTES • COOK: 75 MINUTES

MAKE AHEAD

It's best not to parboil potatoes too far in advance of roasting them because, not being fully cooked, the centres may turn black. Peel and quarter the potatoes the evening before and chill, covered, in a bowl of water with a pinch of salt. Drain them and parboil in fresh salted water as in method.

4.4 lb (2 kg) russet potatoes, peeled and cut into quarters (or eighths, if very large) (about 4 large)
½ cup (115 g) butter (and/or drippings from the turkey)
2 Tbsp (30 mL) olive or vegetable oil
Salt and black pepper
2 tsp finely chopped fresh thyme
¼ cup (60 mL) chopped Italian parsley

1. Preheat the oven to 325°F (160°F) (if the turkey isn't already in there).

2. Place the potatoes in a large saucepan and cover with cold salted water. Bring to a simmer over medium-high heat and cook until a knife can pierce through a potato but with resistance, about 12 minutes.

3. Drain the potatoes well and spread them out to dry on a baking tray for 10 minutes.

4. Place a large, heavy-bottomed metal roasting pan on the stove and melt the butter with the oil over medium-high heat. Add the potatoes, season them lightly with salt and pepper, add the thyme and toss them well to coat in the butter. Move the potatoes around so they are flat side down in the pan. Once they just begin to show signs of browning, 3 to 5 minutes, transfer the uncovered pan to the oven.

5. Roast the potatoes for about 1 hour, turning them carefully and regularly so that they brown on all sides (if you have a turkey in the oven, you can spoon a little of the drippings from the turkey pan over the potatoes as you stir). Sprinkle on the parsley right before serving.

Photo on page 91

101
—
THE MAIN
EVENT

> A creamy, cheesy scalloped-potato-style dish is always a crowd-pleaser.
> If you want to take this dish to the next level, crumble in cooked bacon
> (for non-vegetarians) and sliced green onions as you assemble the gratin . . .
> *et voilà*, Baked Potato Gratin!

POTATOES AU GRATIN

SERVES 8 TO 12 · PREP: 20 MINUTES · COOK: 80 MINUTES

MAKE AHEAD

You can assemble and bake this dish (without browning the top) and store it, covered with plastic or parchment (not foil), in the fridge for up to 1 day. To re-warm, place the gratin in the oven, covered, for 40 minutes at 300°F (150°C) and then uncovered for 10 minutes at 400°F (200°C).

6 Tbsp (90 g) butter, plus extra for the pan

6 Tbsp (50 g) all-purpose flour

4 cups (1 L) 2% milk

1 Tbsp (15 mL) Dijon mustard

1 clove garlic, minced

3 cups (330 g) coarsely grated Gruyère cheese

1 cup (90 g) coarsely grated old Cheddar cheese

2 Tbsp (30 mL) dry white vermouth

Salt and black pepper

3 lb (1.5 kg) Yukon Gold potatoes, peeled and thinly sliced (about 7 medium)

1. Preheat the oven to 350°F (180°F). Grease a 9 x 13-inch (3 L) or other similarly sized ceramic casserole or baking dish with butter.

2. Melt the butter in a medium saucepan over medium heat and then stir in the flour with a wooden spoon. Continue to cook, stirring continuously, for about 4 minutes, until the mixture smells slightly nutty but has not changed colour. Add the milk in 3 parts, beating well with a whisk and letting the mixture thicken between each addition. Whisk in the Dijon and garlic.

3. Reduce the heat to medium-low and add the cheeses in 3 parts, whisking until the cheese has melted between additions. Whisk in the vermouth and season to taste with salt and pepper. Keep this sauce warm over low heat.

4. Cover the bottom of the casserole dish with a layer of sliced potatoes, overlapping them a little. Ladle about 1 cup (250 mL) of the cheese sauce overtop (it doesn't have to cover the potatoes completely). Repeat with the remaining potatoes and sauce for about 6 layers, finishing with a layer of sauce. Place a piece of parchment over the dish (it can touch the sauce) and then cover loosely with aluminum foil.

5. Bake the gratin for about 1 hour, until the potatoes yield easily when a knife is inserted. Remove the foil and parchment and increase the oven temperature to 400°F (200°C).

6. Cook the gratin until the top is brown and bubbling, about 10 minutes. Let cool for 15 minutes before serving.

HELPFUL HINT

If your turkey is in the oven at 325°F (160°C), put the potatoes in for an extra 15 minutes at this temperature and do the 400°F (200°C) gratinée step once the turkey is out of the oven and resting.

These sweet potatoes provide a lovely complexity to a holiday plate because they are baked with ras el hanout, a Moroccan spice blend of cumin, coriander, cinnamon, paprika, cardamom, ginger, turmeric and a hint of chili. I love the sweet taste of the potato against the earthiness of the spices, and they smell fantastic when baking. Serve either hot or at room temperature.

SPICED SWEET POTATO WEDGES

SERVES 8 • PREP: 5 MINUTES • COOK: 40 MINUTES

1. Preheat the oven to 375°F (190°C). Have ready a 9 x 13-inch (3 L) baking dish or line a baking tray with parchment paper.

2. Toss the sweet potato wedges with the oil to fully coat them. Stir in the ras el hanout and season with salt and pepper and toss again. Spread the wedges in a single layer in the casserole dish or on the baking tray.

3. Roast the potatoes, stirring occasionally, until fork-tender, 35 to 40 minutes. Sprinkle with lime juice right before serving.

MAKE AHEAD

These are so quick to prepare that I don't stress about preparing any part of the recipe ahead of time. You can refrigerate leftovers, well wrapped, for up to 3 days. To reheat, place the potatoes in a single layer in a casserole dish or on a baking tray and roast for 12 to 15 minutes at 350°F (180°C). They will be a little more wrinkled than the first time around, but still delicious.

3 lb (1.5 kg) sweet potatoes, peeled and cut into wedges (about 4 medium)
¼ cup (60 mL) extra virgin olive oil
1 ½ Tbsp (22 mL) ras el hanout
Salt and black pepper
Juice of 1 lime

Clockwise from top left: Spiced Sweet Potato Wedges (page 104); Mashed Potatoes with Green Onions (page 100); Roasted Carrots and Parsnips (page 106); Brussels Sprouts with Lemon and Asiago (page 107)

Roasted root vegetables, including these carrots and parsnips, don't need to be complicated to be delicious. Adding Chinese five-spice powder—a blend of cinnamon, cloves, fennel, star anise and Sichuan peppercorns—lends complexity to this dish, but you can leave it out if you prefer.

GF

Ve

ROASTED CARROTS AND PARSNIPS

SERVES 6 TO 8 • PREP: 10 MINUTES • COOK: 45 MINUTES

1. Preheat the oven to 350°F (180°C). Have ready a 9 x 13-inch (3 L) baking or casserole dish.

2. Toss the carrots and parsnips with the oil, Chinese five-spice powder and salt and pepper. Spread the vegetables in the baking dish and cover with the lid, parchment or aluminum foil.

3. Roast the vegetables for 20 minutes, and then uncover and roast for another 20 to 25 minutes, stirring occasionally, until fork-tender. Serve immediately.

Photo on page 105

MAKE AHEAD
You can peel and cut the carrots and parsnips up to 1 day ahead, toss them with the oil, spice, and salt and pepper and then refrigerate them in an airtight container until you're ready to roast them.

1 lb (450 g) peeled and diced carrots
   (2 to 3 large)
1 lb (450 g) peeled and diced parsnips
   (3 to 4 large)
3 Tbsp (45 mL) extra virgin olive oil
1 ½ tsp Chinese five-spice powder
Salt and black pepper

HELPFUL HINT

Carrots and parsnips can be a challenge to cut because they are thick at 1 end and thin at the other, which means the pieces might roast unevenly. I use a rolling cut. Place your whole, peeled carrot on the cutting board and cut chunks at an angle across the diameter, rotating the carrot as you cut, so that no 2 pieces are the same shape but are all about the same size. This style sits nicely in the roasting pan and on your dinner plate.

Brussels sprouts are the ideal winter vegetable. Their flavour sweetens up after the first hard frost, and they store well over the winter, to be enjoyed all season long. Add a little cheese and lemon, and ta-da . . . you have a hit on your hands.

BRUSSELS SPROUTS WITH LEMON AND ASIAGO

GF

V

SERVES 6 TO 8 · PREP: 15 MINUTES · COOK: 12 MINUTES

MAKE AHEAD

Blanch your Brussels sprouts 1 day ahead (step 1) and refrigerate them in an airtight container until it is time to pop them in the sauté pan and finish off the dish.

2 ¼ lb (1 kg) fresh Brussels sprouts
2 Tbsp (30 mL) extra virgin olive oil
Salt and black pepper
Juice of 1 lemon
¾ cup (75 g) finely grated Asiago cheese
Walnut or extra virgin olive oil, for drizzling
3 Tbsp (45 mL) chopped fresh chives
¼ cup (60 mL) Toasted Buckwheat Kasha (page 158) or lightly toasted walnut pieces

1. Trim the bottoms of the Brussels sprouts and cut them in half. Bring a saucepan of water to a full boil over high heat and blanch the Brussels sprouts for 2 minutes. Drain them in a colander and immediately run them under cold water to stop the cooking. Let them drain well.

2. Heat a sauté pan over high heat and add the 2 Tbsp (30 mL) of olive oil. Add the sprouts and sauté for about 7 minutes, letting them brown a bit as you warm them through and season it with salt and pepper. Add the lemon juice to the pan, toss well and then transfer the sprouts to a serving platter.

3. Top the sprouts with the cheese and drizzle with some walnut (or olive) oil, nudging them around a little to allow the cheese to melt in. Sprinkle with the chives and toasted buckwheat kasha (or walnuts). Serve immediately.

Photo on page 105

Homemade eggnog is a real treat. Essentially it is a custard sauce spiked with your choice of rum, brandy or whiskey. When you make eggnog from scratch, you'll realize it has an angelic airiness that is nothing like the store-bought version. I like to rim my glasses with crushed caramelized sugar because the combination of that and the rich eggnog reminds me of decadent crème brûlée desserts.

CRÈME BRÛLÉE EGGNOG

SERVES 6 TO 8 • PREP: 20 MINUTES • COOK: 8 MINUTES

1. Line a small baking tray with parchment paper and set aside.

2. Place 1/3 cup (70 g) of the granulated sugar, the water and lemon juice in a small saucepan and stir to mix. Bring to a full boil over high heat, without stirring, and boil until the sugar turns a light amber, about 90 seconds. Remove from the heat.

3. Immediately pour the sugar onto the prepared tray, swirling the tray to get the sugar into as thin a layer as possible before it sets. Let the sugar mixture cool in the pan on a wire rack until set, about 30 minutes.

4. Break the sugar into pieces. Crush them in a resealable bag with a rolling pin, or pulse them in a food processor, until coarsely ground.

5. In a small saucepan over medium heat, bring the milk and the nutmeg to just below a simmer. Whisk the egg yolks and the remaining sugar together in a small bowl.

6. Add a ladleful of the hot milk to the egg mixture and whisk well. Whisking continuously, slowly add up to half of the hot milk to temper the egg mixture. Add the tempered egg mixture to the saucepan of milk and reduce the heat to medium-low. Stir with a wooden spoon until the custard is well combined and coats the back of the spoon, about 3 minutes.

7. Strain the custard through a fine-mesh sieve into a clean bowl and let it cool to room temperature. Cover and chill completely.

MAKE AHEAD
You can refrigerate the eggnog base in an airtight container for up to 3 days.

⅔ cup (140 g) granulated sugar, divided
1 Tbsp (15 mL) water
1 tsp fresh lemon juice
3 cups (750 mL) 2% milk
¼ tsp finely grated nutmeg
6 large egg yolks (reserve 1 egg white for rimming the glass)
6 to 8 oz (175 to 250 mL) rum, brandy, whiskey or a combination
1 cup (250 mL) whipping cream

ADD SPARKLE
To make a very fluffy, light eggnog, whip 2 egg whites (reserved from separating the yolks) with 3 Tbsp (36 g) of granulated sugar until it holds a soft peak when the beaters are lifted. Whisk in this meringue by hand after you've whisked in the whipped cream. Heavenly!

8. When ready to serve, whisk the rum (or brandy or whiskey) into the chilled eggnog custard. Whip the cream with electric beaters, or use a stand mixer fitted with the whip attachment, at high speed until it holds a soft peak when the beaters are lifted. Whisk the whipped cream by hand into the eggnog.

9. To serve, lightly whisk the reserved egg white with a fork and place it in a small dish. Place the crushed caramelized sugar in a small saucer, reserving some for garnish. Dip the rim of each glass into the egg white and then into the caramelized sugar. Carefully ladle the chilled eggnog into each glass (without disturbing the sparkling rim) and top with a sprinkle of the reserved caramelized sugar.

AN ELEGANT EVENING

FOR NEW YEAR'S EVE, Michael and I like to host a few friends and prepare an elegant plated dinner. While Christmas dinner, open houses and other holiday gatherings are more family-style, with platters being passed around or guests helping themselves from a buffet table, we take the time at New Year's to plate each course and serve it.

We start the evening, regardless of the weather, with Champagne and oysters outside on the porch and then we move inside for the evening. You'll notice that the dinner is not a long, drawn-out eight-course affair. We are rarely able to stay awake until midnight, and these days our friends with teenagers need to get home to keep their house parties in check!

CHAMPAGNE SPARKLER   112

~

OYSTERS WITH MIGNONETTE   113

POTATO GNOCCHI WITH HERB BUTTER
AND PARMESAN   115

~

WHOLE ROASTED BEEF TENDERLOIN
WITH HORSERADISH HOLLANDAISE   117

MUSHROOM AND BRIE WELLINGTON
WITH CARAMELIZED ONION CREAM   120

SPINACH FLORENTINE WITH 'NDUJA   123

~

served with one of

CITRUS MASCARPONE AND
PISTACHIO TART   262

FLOURLESS CHOCOLATE
MONT BLANC TORTE   277

HONEY BUTTERMILK PANNA COTTA
VERRINES WITH PASSIONFRUIT   304

CRANBERRY ORANGE STEAMED
PUDDINGS   312

A PETITS FOURS PLATE
OF MACARONS   219;
BRAZILIAN BRIGADEIROS   244;
and/or HAZELNUT ORANGE
PANFORTE   248

Opposite: Champagne Sparkler (page 112); Oysters with Mignonette (page 113)

Since I rarely make it to midnight these days (it's the early morning baker in me), enjoying my Champagne at the start of the evening is better than trying to wait until the clock strikes twelve. This cocktail is aromatic with just a hint of herbs and sweetness. It's nice as a sipper on its own or paired with fresh oysters. Thanks to the bubbles, the blackberries bounce around inside the glass—how festive!

CHAMPAGNE SPARKLER

SERVES 6 • PREP: 10 MINUTES • COOK: 5 MINUTES

1. Place the sugar, water and 12 sprigs of thyme in a small saucepan over medium heat and bring to a simmer. Let the syrup simmer for 5 minutes (there is no need to stir), and then remove from the heat and let cool to room temperature (leave the thyme in). Strain the infused syrup through a fine-mesh sieve into a mason jar, cover and chill until ready to use.

2. To mix the cocktails, measure 1 Tbsp (15 mL) of thyme syrup into each Champagne flute and add ½ oz (15 mL) of elderflower liqueur. Drop 3 blackberries into each glass and slowly pour in the Champagne (or Cava) until it almost fills the glass. Drop a thyme sprig into each flute and serve immediately.

MAKE AHEAD

The thyme syrup keeps for up to 3 months in the fridge, although you definitely want to assemble these cocktails immediately before serving.

½ cup (100 g) granulated sugar
½ cup (125 mL) water
12 sprigs fresh thyme, plus 6 for garnish
3 oz (90 mL) St. Germain elderflower liqueur
18 fresh blackberries
1 bottle (750 mL) chilled Champagne or Cava

HELPFUL HINT

If you are using Champagne for this cocktail, don't spend big money on a high-end or vintage bottle. Other options include a Crémant de Bourgogne or other sparkling wine from a different region in France. If you'd rather use Italian Prosecco in place of Champagne, make sure it is extra dry—Prosecco is often sweeter than its sparkling friends.

OYSTERS WITH MIGNONETTE

GF

SERVES 6 • PREP: 20 MINUTES

MAKE AHEAD

Oysters will keep in the fridge for up to 1 week. Do not soak or store them in tap water. Instead, place them in a bowl or, if you've bought a lot (a case is typically 100 oysters), empty a crisper drawer and store them in there. Keep them refrigerated but not covered. If the shell is tightly closed, then the oyster is fresh. If it has opened, and doesn't close when you tap it on the counter, then discard it.

MIGNONETTE

2 small shallots, finely minced
⅓ cup (80 mL) white wine vinegar
⅓ cup (80 mL) red wine vinegar
Pinch of salt

OYSTERS

36 fresh oysters
2 lemons, cut into wedges

1. For the mignonette, stir the shallots, vinegars and salt together in a small bowl. Chill until ready to serve.

2. For the oysters, arrange a bed of crushed ice on a platter large enough to hold all of the oysters. Scrub the oysters with a brush under cool running water to remove any loose bits of shell or sediment.

3. Place a tea towel on a cutting board and hold the oyster in place with another tea towel. To shuck the oyster, insert the oyster knife just off-centre from the hinge (the pointed end that holds the shell closed). Shimmy your knife in between the top and bottom shells and once about ½ inch (1 cm) of it is inside the shell, twist the knife so that the top shell releases. Carefully run the knife along the inside of the top shell to loosen the shell from the oyster and discard shell.

4. Try to keep the bottom shell level so you don't lose the liquor (the oyster juices). Run the knife underneath the oyster meat to release it from the bottom shell. It will catch at 1 point in particular, called the adductor, but just keep your knife close to the base of the shell as you push through it. Place the oyster in its bottom shell on the bed of ice. Continue shucking the remaining oysters.

5. To serve, arrange the lemon wedges and mignonette in small dishes on the side, so guests can help themselves to oysters and dress their own.

HELPFUL HINTS

I prefer to order my oysters from a proper fish shop rather than simply buying them from the counter at a grocery store. I like to have a conversation with the person I'm buying my oysters from, so I know the shellfish are at their freshest and I can learn when and where they were harvested. If you are picking up your oysters on the day you want to shuck them, ask your fishmonger for a bag of crushed ice and see if they have extra seaweed. This way you can set your oysters on their shells on the ice and arrange the seaweed around them.

ADD SPARKLE

Truffles take these gnocchi to a whole new level of elegance. Omit the chives and tarragon from the herb butter and add a touch of truffle oil or truffle paste. Or, if you were lucky enough to receive a fresh white truffle for Christmas, thinly slice it over the gnocchi right before serving.

POTATO GNOCCHI WITH HERB BUTTER AND PARMESAN

MAKES 6 AS AN APPETIZER, 4 AS A MAIN COURSE • PREP: 25 MINUTES • COOK: 1 HOUR

MAKE AHEAD

You can prepare the gnocchi up to 1 day ahead. Refrigerate the uncooked pieces in a single layer on the baking tray uncovered. To freeze them, place the gnocchi on their tray in the freezer for a few hours, and then package them in airtight containers. They can be boiled from frozen, but cook them for 5 to 6 minutes.

GNOCCHI
2 ¼ lb (1 kg) russet potatoes, skins on (about 2 to 3 medium)
2 cups (300 g) all-purpose flour
1 large egg
1 tsp fine sea salt
Black pepper

HERB BUTTER AND CHEESE
3 Tbsp (45 g) butter
2 Tbsp (30 mL) chopped fresh Italian parsley
2 Tbsp (30 mL) chopped fresh chives
1 Tbsp (15 mL) chopped fresh tarragon
Salt and black pepper
Parmesan cheese, for grating

1. For the gnocchi, simmer the potatoes in a large saucepan of salted water over high heat until the flesh is tender and the skins crack, about 50 minutes. Drain the potatoes and let cool in the saucepan for 15 minutes.

2. Peel the potatoes while they are still warm, discarding the skins. Push the warm potatoes through a ricer or a food mill, or use a handheld potato masher. Stir in the flour, egg, salt and a pinch of pepper until the mixture comes together. The dough should not stick to your hands—if it feels tacky, stir in a little more flour.

3. Line a baking tray with parchment paper. Turn the dough out onto a large cutting board and divide it into 8 pieces. Roll out each piece of dough into a long rope about 1 inch (2.5 cm) wide.

Recipe continues ▶

115
—
AN ELEGANT
EVENING

4. Cut each rope into about 1-inch (2.5 cm) pieces and arrange them in a single layer on the baking tray. Chill, uncovered, until ready to cook.

5. Bring a large saucepan of salted water to a boil over high heat. Add the gnocchi, dropping them in quickly but carefully, a few at a time, so they hit the water individually (this way they won't stick together). Let the water return to a boil and cook the gnocchi for 3 to 4 minutes, until they float to the top of the water. Drain the gnocchi.

6. For the herb butter, return the saucepan to a low heat (no need to wash it) and melt the butter. Add the still-warm gnocchi, followed by the parsley, chives and tarragon. Season lightly with salt and pepper, stirring gently to coat the gnocchi.

7. Spoon the gnocchi to individual plates or pasta bowls. Finish with a generous grating of Parmesan cheese and serve immediately.

Step 3

Step 4

I like to roast beef tenderloin whole for a fancy dinner because, once carved, the pink interior of the beef is revealed. The slices can be arranged on a platter, but for New Year's Eve, I plate individual dishes and then serve my guests. This menu doesn't have its own potato dish to serve with the main course, because I start with the Potato Gnocchi. If you'd like to include a potato, try the Ultimate Roasted Potatoes (page 101) or Spiced Sweet Potato Wedges (page 104).

WHOLE ROASTED BEEF TENDERLOIN WITH HORSERADISH HOLLANDAISE

GF

SERVES 8 · PREP: 30 MINUTES · COOK: 80 MINUTES, PLUS RESTING

MAKE AHEAD
You can trim and tie the roast up to 1 day ahead and refrigerate it, well wrapped. Pull it from the fridge 20 to 30 minutes before you plan to put it in the oven to warm up a little bit. If making everything at once, prepare the Horseradish Hollandaise while the beef is resting.

BEEF
1 whole beef tenderloin (5 ½ to 6 ⅔ lb/2.5 to 3 kg)
½ cup (125 mL) Dijon mustard (gluten-free, if required)
2 Tbsp (30 mL) chopped fresh thyme
Coarse sea salt and black pepper

HORSERADISH HOLLANDAISE
1 cup (225 g) unsalted butter
3 large egg yolks
3 Tbsp (45 mL) dry white wine
3 Tbsp (45 mL) fresh lemon juice
3 Tbsp (45 mL) Prepared Horseradish (page 154)
Salt and black pepper

1. Preheat the oven to 400°F (200°F). Have ready a roasting pan fitted with a wire roasting rack.

2. For the beef, trim the head (the wide portion) and the tail (the skinny portion) from the tenderloin. Next, trim away the chain—the piece of meat that runs along the length of the tenderloin. (Use these pieces in Beef Rendang, page 136, or Beef Wonton Soup, page 129.) Using a sharp knife, remove and discard the silver skin (the white connective tissue) from the beef. Once trimmed, it should weigh 2.9 to 3.3 lb (1.3 to 1.5 kg).

3. Using butcher's twine, tie the roast so that it holds its shape. Tie the twine tightly around the width of the roast at 2-inch (5 cm) intervals and then run it all the way around the length of the roast, looping it through the width ties and knotting where the ends meet. It does not have to look particularly neat, since it will be trimmed away before carving the roast.

4. Mix together the mustard and thyme and add salt and pepper. Rub this mixture over the tenderloin, coating the meat completely, and then place the roast in the roasting pan.

5. Roast the tenderloin, uncovered, for 10 minutes and then reduce the oven temperature to 300°F (150°C). Continue roasting the meat for about 1 hour more, until the internal temperature registers 120 to 125°F (49 to 52°C) on a meat thermometer.

6. Remove the pan from the oven and let the tenderloin rest on a cutting board, loosely covered with a piece of aluminum foil, for 15 minutes, until the internal temperature rises to 130°F (54°C), medium-rare, on a meat thermometer.

Recipe continues ▶

7. Meanwhile, make the hollandaise. Melt the butter in a saucepan over medium heat and set aside (but keep it warm and melted).

8. Place the egg yolks, white wine, lemon juice and horseradish in a metal bowl set over a saucepan of gently simmering water. Whisk vigorously until the mixture more than doubles in volume and holds a ribbon when the whisk is lifted, about 4 minutes.

9. Remove the bowl from the heat and secure the bowl in place with a tea towel (or have someone hold it). Whisking constantly, slowly drizzle in the warm, melted butter in a thin stream. Make sure the butter is fully worked in before adding more. Continue whisking until all the butter, except the milk solids at the bottom of the pan, has been added. Season to taste with salt and pepper.

10. To serve, cut away and discard the butcher's twine. Slice the roast across the grain, serving two ¾-inch (1.8 cm) slices or one 1 ½-inch (3.5 cm) slice per person. Arrange the beef on individual plates (along with potatoes, if serving, and vegetables) and spoon a little of the sauce around the beef. Serve immediately.

HELPFUL HINTS

Tenderloin is very lean, so serve it to a crowd that prefers meat done rare to medium-rare. Medium and beyond tenderloin can seem dry and tough. Resting the roast for 15 minutes lets the juices settle in the meat, so the juices won't run onto your cutting board when you slice it.

I like to make hollandaise sauce lemony and light, not heavy and buttery. This version has a modest horseradish warmth. If you like more kick, you can whisk in more horseradish after you've added the butter. Keep this recipe on hand for eggs Benedict! You can also substitute it with the Caramelized Onion Cream, page 120, if you prefer.

This dish is worthy of presenting at the table to be carved, at holiday time or any special occasion. A filling of thyme-scented mushrooms and melted Brie are revealed when the golden puff pastry is sliced. Serving it with the Caramelized Onion Cream makes it worthy of a main course, although it can also be served as a side dish with scrambled eggs at a decadent holiday brunch.

MUSHROOM AND BRIE WELLINGTON WITH CARAMELIZED ONION CREAM

SERVES 6 · PREP: 30 MINUTES · COOK: 1 HOUR

1. For the Wellington, heat a large sauté pan over medium-high heat and add the oil (or butter), shallots (or onions) and mushrooms. Sauté the mushrooms until they are fully cooked and any liquid has evaporated, about 10 minutes.

2. Stir in the garlic and thyme and season lightly with salt and pepper, cooking the mixture for 1 minute more. Add the brandy and remove the mushrooms from the heat to cool to room temperature. Then stir in the breadcrumbs and the pieces of Brie.

3. Preheat the oven to 400°F (200°C) and line a baking tray with parchment paper.

4. Place the puff pastry sheets on top of each other on a work surface. Use a sharp knife to trim off 2 strips, each 1 ½ inches (3.5 cm) wide, from opposite sides (creating a rectangle shape) of each piece of pastry and set aside. (You will have 4 strips in total.)

5. Place 1 sheet of pastry onto the prepared baking tray. Brush the edges with the egg wash and use the reserved strips to create a frame on the pastry base, trimming them as needed so that they fit snugly and then brushing them with the egg wash. Spoon the cooled mushroom filling into the centre of the pastry frame then spread it out so that it covers the entire pastry base (but not the strips creating the frame) and press it in firmly.

6. Place the second sheet of pastry overtop, stretching it if needed, to have it reach the edges of the base pastry. Brush the top of the Wellington with the egg wash. Using kitchen scissors, snip little air vents into the top of the Wellington.

Recipe continues ▶

120
—
SET FOR
THE
HOLIDAYS

MAKE AHEAD

You can assemble the Wellington up to 1 day ahead and refrigerate it unbaked and well wrapped. It is best freshly baked, although reheated leftovers are still quite scrumptious. You can refrigerate the onion cream in an airtight container for up to 3 days, or freeze it for up to 3 months. Thaw overnight in the fridge and then gently reheat over medium heat, stirring occasionally until it begins to bubble, about 6 minutes.

WELLINGTON

1 Tbsp (15 mL) extra virgin olive oil or butter

2 shallots, sliced, or 1 small onion, diced

1 ¼ lb (565 g) cremini mushrooms, sliced

2 cloves garlic, minced

2 tsp chopped fresh thyme

Salt and black pepper

1 oz (30 mL) brandy

½ cup (65 g) dry breadcrumbs

4 oz (120 g) Brie cheese, cut into pieces

2 sheets (1 lb/450 g) butter puff pastry, thawed

1 egg mixed with 2 Tbsp (30 mL) water, for egg wash

CARAMELIZED ONION CREAM

1 recipe Caramelized Onions (page 152)

1 oz (30 mL) brandy

1 cup (250 mL) whipping cream

Salt and black pepper

7. Bake for 10 minutes and then reduce the oven to 375°F (190°C) and cook for another 35 to 40 minutes, until the pastry is a rich golden brown. Allow the Wellington to cool for 10 minutes.

8. For the onion cream, place the caramelized onions in a medium saucepan over medium heat to warm them. Stir in the brandy and the cream, and bring the mixture to a simmer. Season to taste with salt and pepper.

9. Slice the Wellington into individual portions and serve with the warm caramelized onion cream on the side.

Step 5

ADD SPARKLE

Sprinkle a little truffle oil into the cooled mushroom mixture before assembling the Wellington. When baked, the truffle oil will release its aroma and the Wellington will smell even better when carved and plated.

> This side dish reminds me of an old-school steakhouse, where you order your steak à la carte and your side dishes separately. I love creamed spinach, and this version uses a spicy Calabrian-style spreadable sausage to add great flavour and a nice kick of chili heat.

SPINACH FLORENTINE WITH 'NDUJA

GF

SERVES 6 • PREP: 15 MINUTES • COOK: 10 MINUTES

MAKE AHEAD

You can refrigerate this dish in an air-tight container for up to 1 day. Reheat it over medium-low heat before serving, stirring often until warmed through.

2 oz (60 g) 'nduja spicy sausage, diced (gluten-free)

1 cup (250 mL) 2% milk

1 Tbsp (7 g) cornstarch

1 garlic clove, minced

1 tsp Dijon mustard (gluten-free, if required)

Pinch of ground nutmeg

1 cup (110 g) coarsely grated Swiss cheese

¼ cup (25 g) grated Parmesan cheese

1 pkg (10 oz/300 g) frozen chopped spinach, thawed

Salt and black pepper

1. Heat a medium saucepan or sauté pan over medium heat and add the sausage, stirring until it is fully cooked, about 5 minutes. Transfer the sausage meat to a plate and set aside, but leave any residual oil in the pan.

2. Whisk the milk, cornstarch, garlic, mustard and nutmeg together in a small bowl and add to the saucepan. Whisk over medium heat until the milk begins to bubble, about 4 minutes. Reduce the heat to medium-low and whisk in the cheeses in 3 parts, whisking until the cheese has melted between each addition.

3. Squeeze out any excess water from the thawed spinach. Stir the spinach into the cheese sauce, stirring well to break down any clumps. Stir the reserved sausage meat back into the pot, season to taste with salt and pepper and serve warm.

123
—
AN ELEGANT
EVENING

HELPFUL HINTS

If cooking for gluten-intolerant guests, double check with your butcher that the 'ndjua you buy is gluten-free. If 'nduja isn't available, substitute double the amount of spicy Italian sausage and prepare it just like the 'nduja.

This creamy spinach dish works well under a bed of fluffy Potato Gnocchi with Herb Butter and Parmesan (page 115). I've also doubled the sauce base before (all the ingredients except the spinach) to make a creamy spinach sauce to serve with roasted chicken or as a gluten-free alternative to gravy with the Whole Roasted Turkey (page 93).

WHEN IT'S ALL OVER
(LEFTOVERS AND LIGHTER MEALS)

ONE OF THE PERKS of hosting "the main event" is that you own the leftovers! While you can dole out some to relatives, make sure you save some for yourself. After you've had that essential ham, turkey or beef sandwich, portion out and freeze diced ham, roast beef or shredded turkey to make these hearty winter dishes all through the cold-weather months, well beyond the holiday season.

If you are hitting the reset button to start the new year by eating simpler foods and more vegetables, or taking a break to recalibrate yourself mid-holiday, here are some flavourful one-pot meals that are a snap to make. Some are vegan, some are low in fat, and all of them make use of vegetables that are readily available in the winter without breaking the bank.

> A snowy Sunday is the perfect time to get a pot of this soup simmering. If
> the gang has been outside shovelling or skating, a hot bowl of hearty soup
> will make for a warm welcome back indoors.

HAM AND SPLIT PEA SOUP

SERVES 8 TO 10 · PREP: 15 MINUTES · COOK: 2 ½ HOURS

1. Add the oil to a stockpot over medium heat, followed by the onions, celery and carrots. Sauté the vegetables for about 5 minutes, until translucent. Stir in the garlic, thyme and bay leaves and sauté for 1 minute more. Add the peas and stock (or water) and then the ham bone.

2. Simmer, loosely covered and stirring occasionally, for about 2 ½ hours, until the split peas break down and thicken the soup.

3. Remove and discard the ham bone and bay leaves and stir in the diced ham. Season to taste with salt and pepper and stir in the parsley before serving.

MAKE AHEAD

This soup actually tastes even better the day after it's made. You can refrigerate it in an airtight container for up to 5 days. While the soup will thicken up a great deal once chilled, it will thin out as it warms. Reheat in a saucepan over medium heat for about 10 minutes, until simmering.

2 Tbsp (30 mL) extra virgin olive oil
1 medium onion, diced
2 stalks celery, diced
3 medium carrots, peeled and diced
4 cloves garlic, minced
1 Tbsp (15 mL) chopped fresh thyme
2 bay leaves
2 cups (450 g) yellow split peas
8 cups (2 L) chicken stock or water
1 ham bone, from roasted ham or ham
   hock, meat trimmed away
2 cups (325 g) diced cooked ham
Salt and black pepper
¼ cup (60 mL) chopped Italian parsley

HELPFUL HINT

A slice of fresh or toasted Pumpkin Seed Multigrain Bread (page 73) is perfect with this soup. To make a complete meal, I serve it with spinach greens topped with sliced red onion, sliced apple and Hazelnut Dressing (page 149).

Here is a recipe with all the key elements that cabbage rolls offer but without the work of filling and rolling the cabbage leaves. While the rolls are traditionally made with ground beef or pork, leftover turkey works just as well in this thick soup. It's a lovely alternative to the more usual turkey rice soup.

TURKEY CABBAGE ROLL SOUP

SERVES 8 · PREP: 15 MINUTES · COOK: 45 MINUTES

1. Cook the bacon in a large, heavy-bottomed stockpot over medium heat until crisp, about 8 minutes. Transfer the bacon to a plate, and drain off and discard all but 2 Tbsp (30 mL) of the remaining fat.

2. Add the onions, celery and carrots to the stockpot and sauté over medium heat until the onions are almost translucent, about 5 minutes. Add the garlic and cook for 1 minute more.

3. Stir in the cabbage and add the tomatoes, stock (or water), vinegar, rice, horseradish, paprika, celery salt and bay leaves and stir. Cover the pot, bring it to a full simmer and then reduce the heat to a gentle simmer and cook for 20 minutes.

4. Add the cooked turkey and continue to simmer, covered, until the rice is fully cooked, about 20 minutes more. Season to taste with salt and pepper.

5. Remove and discard the bay leaves and stir in the cooked bacon. Serve warm, garnished with a dollop of sour cream.

MAKE AHEAD

The flavour of this soup improves as it sits, so I prefer to serve it 2 or 3 days after I make it. Keep in mind that the rice and cabbage keep absorbing liquid as the stew sits, so you may have to add a little water with each reheating. You can refrigerate it in an airtight container for up to 3 days, or freeze it for up to 3 months. Thaw overnight in the fridge and warm over medium heat for about 10 minutes, until simmering.

3 strips bacon, diced
1 medium onion, diced
1 stalk celery, diced
1 medium carrot, peeled and coarsely grated
1 clove garlic, minced
6 cups (1.5 L) diced green or Savoy cabbage
2 (each 28 oz/796 mL) cans diced tomatoes
2 cups (500 mL) chicken stock (gluten-free, if required) or water

¼ cup (60 mL) cider vinegar
½ cup (93 g) long-grain brown rice (such as basmati)
2 Tbsp (30 mL) Prepared Horseradish (page 154)
1 Tbsp (10 g) sweet paprika
2 tsp celery salt
2 bay leaves
3 cups (375 g) diced cooked turkey meat
Salt and black pepper
Sour cream, for garnish

HELPFUL HINTS

I like to use brown rice for this soup, since it tends to hold its shape better than white rice, especially when frozen.

To make a soup and salad supper out of this recipe, I serve a side salad of winter greens (a mix of romaine, radicchio, endive) and sliced cucumber with Buttermilk Ranch Dressing and Dip (page 148) and a sprinkling of sunflower seeds or Toasted Buckwheat Kasha (page 158) on top.

Wontons are a fantastic way to make a full meal out of a small amount of leftover beef. Folding up the wontons is fun and quick—unless you are looking to be a master folder in a famous dumpling house in Hong Kong. This soup is family-friendly: it is mildly flavoured, and slurping and splashing as you eat is fully expected.

BEEF WONTON SOUP

SERVES 4 · MAKES 3 TO 4 DOZEN WONTONS · PREP: 20 MINUTES · COOK: 10 MINUTES

1 cup (140 g) finely diced cooked beef

1 cup (60 g) finely diced king oyster mushrooms

¾ cup (175 mL) green onions, thinly sliced, divided

1 clove garlic, minced

2 tsp finely grated fresh ginger

4 Tbsp (60 mL) soy sauce, divided

3 tsp toasted sesame oil, divided

1 large egg

1 Tbsp (7 g) cornstarch

48 wonton wrappers

6 cups (1.5 L) unsalted or low-sodium beef stock

8 baby bok choy, cut in half

1. Toss the beef with the mushrooms, ½ cup (125 mL) of the green onions, the garlic, ginger, 1 Tbsp (15 mL) of the soy sauce and 1 tsp of the sesame oil in a bowl.

2. In a separate bowl, whisk the egg and cornstarch together and then stir them into the beef.

3. Line a baking tray with parchment paper. Separate the wonton wrappers and have a dish of cool water on hand.

4. To fill the wontons, hold a wonton wrapper in your hand and rub water around the edges.

5. Spoon about 1 tsp (5 mL) of the beef filling into the centre of the wrapper and bring the edges together in a half-moon shape (if the wonton wrappers are square, bring the edges together to form a triangle).

6. Pinch the edges to secure them and place the wonton on the prepared baking tray. Fill and fold the remaining wrappers, placing them in a single layer on the baking tray. Cover loosely with a tea towel and chill until ready to cook. (You may not use all of the wonton wrappers.)

Recipe continues ▶

HELPFUL HINTS

To keep your soup hot for longer, run your soup bowls under hot water right before you fill them.

To make a full meal of this soup, I add a simple side salad of snap peas, bean sprouts and sliced mushrooms tossed with French Vinaigrette (page 147) to which I add a touch of grated fresh ginger and sesame oil.

7. Bring the beef stock to a simmer in a medium saucepan over medium-high heat. Add the remaining 3 Tbsp (45 mL) of soy sauce and 2 tsp of sesame oil.

8. Bring a large saucepan of unsalted water to a full boil over high heat. Drop half of the wontons into the water and boil until they float, about 4 minutes. Use a slotted spoon or a spider to transfer the wontons to large soup bowls. Repeat with the remaining wontons.

9. Drop the bok choy into the boiling water and blanch for 2 minutes, to soften the leaves. Arrange 4 cooked bok choy halves in each bowl. Ladle the beef broth overtop and sprinkle each bowl with the remaining ¼ cup (60 mL) of sliced green onions. Serve immediately.

Step 5 Step 6

HELPFUL HINT

I serve this comfort food supper with Brussels Sprouts with
Lemon and Asiago (page 107) and a dollop of Roasted Applesauce (page 152) or even
a little Horseradish Cream (page 154) or Dijon mustard.

A croque monsieur is a French version of a grilled ham and cheese sandwich—the difference is that after being toasted, the sandwich is topped with a béchamel sauce, sprinkled with cheese and broiled. This bread pudding, made of assembled ham and cheese sandwiches, has the same finishing feature.

CROQUE MONSIEUR BAKE

SERVES 8 TO 10 • PREP: 20 MINUTES • COOK: 1 HOUR

MAKE AHEAD

You can assemble the bread pudding, without the béchamel, the day before you wish to bake it. Refrigerate it, covered, overnight. Refrigerate the béchamel sauce in an airtight container for up to 3 days. Reheat over medium heat, stirring often, for about 8 minutes to soften it before using.

BREAD PUDDING

¼ cup (60 g) butter
1 clove garlic, minced
12 thick slices day-old French bread
2 ½ cups (275 g) coarsely grated
    Gruyère cheese
1 ½ cups (240 g) diced cooked ham
¼ cup (60 mL) grainy mustard
4 large eggs
3 ½ cups (825 mL) 2% milk
1 tsp salt
½ tsp black pepper

BÉCHAMEL

2 Tbsp (30 g) butter
2 Tbsp (17 g) all-purpose flour
1 cup (250 mL) 2% milk
½ tsp fine sea salt
¼ tsp black pepper
¼ tsp ground nutmeg
1 cup (110 g) coarsely grated Gruyère
    or Swiss cheese

1. Preheat the oven to 350°F (180°C).

2. For the bread pudding, melt the butter with the garlic and brush it over the bottom and sides of a 12-cup (3 L) casserole dish. Brush any remaining garlic butter onto the slices of bread.

3. Toss the cheese, ham and mustard together. Arrange 6 of the bread slices on a work surface and spoon the ham mixture over them. Cover with the remaining bread slices, making sandwiches. Depending on the size of your dish (and the bread), you may want to cut the sandwiches in half. Arrange them in the casserole dish.

4. Whisk the eggs and then whisk in the milk, salt and pepper until evenly combined. Pour over the sandwiches and press them down with a spatula to encourage the bread to soak up the liquid. Bake, uncovered, for 45 minutes.

5. Meanwhile, for the béchamel, melt the butter over medium heat in a medium saucepan and stir in the flour with a wooden spoon. Continue to cook, stirring continuously, for about 3 minutes until the mixture smells slightly nutty but has not changed colour.

6. Add a third of the milk and whisk until smooth (it will thicken up quickly). Whisk in the remaining milk and add the salt, pepper and nutmeg. Whisk until the sauce thickens and begins to bubble, about 1 minute. Remove from the heat until ready to use.

7. After the croque monsieur has baked for 45 minutes, increase the oven temperature to 400°F (200°C).

8. Spoon the béchamel sauce evenly over the sandwiches. Sprinkle the top with the grated cheese and bake for 15 minutes, until the cheese has browned and the pudding is bubbling and puffy at the edges.

9. Let the bread pudding cool on a wire rack for 15 minutes. Spoon onto plates and serve warm.

> Cauliflower is an ideal curry vegetable because it absorbs colour and flavour so easily. This South Asian curry is simple and quick to make, and I take the time to create my own masala for a more intense flavour.

CHICKPEA AND CAULIFLOWER CURRY

SERVES 4 • PREP: 15 MINUTES • COOK: 25 MINUTES

MAKE AHEAD

I love this curry reheated for lunch the next day. Leftovers can be refrigerated in an airtight glass or metal container (avoid plastic because the turmeric can stain it) then reheated over medium heat until simmering, about 10 minutes.

RAITA

2 cups (500 mL) coarsely grated English cucumber (unpeeled)
Pinches of salt and granulated sugar
1 ½ cups (375 mL) plain yogurt (3% fat or higher)
¼ cup (60 mL) chopped fresh mint
¼ tsp ground coriander
Juice of 1 lime

CURRY

2 Tbsp (30 mL) vegetable oil
1 medium onion, diced
2 tsp ground cumin
2 tsp ground coriander
2 tsp ground turmeric
2 tsp garam masala
1 to 3 small red chilies (your choice), sliced (optional)
3 cloves garlic, minced

1 ½-inch (3.5 cm) piece of fresh ginger, finely grated
2 cups (500 mL) crushed tomatoes
2 cups (500 mL) vegetable stock
8 cups (600 g) fresh cauliflower florets (about 1 small head)
1 can (19 oz/540 mL) chickpeas, drained and rinsed
1 cup (250 mL) frozen peas
½ cup (125 mL) plain yogurt (3% fat or higher)
Salt and black pepper
4 cups (1 L) cooked basmati rice or quinoa, for serving
½ cup (125 mL) fresh cilantro leaves
Fresh lime juice

1. For the raita, toss the grated cucumber with a pinch of salt and sugar and let sit in a bowl at room temperature for about 30 minutes. Squeeze the cucumber to press out excess liquid and stir the cucumber into the yogurt. Stir in the mint, coriander and lime juice and chill, covered, until ready to serve.

2. For the curry, heat the oil in a large sauté pan over medium-high heat. Add the onions, cumin, coriander, turmeric, garam masala and chilies (if using) and sauté for 2 to 3 minutes, until the onions are sizzling. Add the garlic and ginger and sauté for 1 minute more.

3. Pour in the tomatoes and stock and bring to a full simmer, stirring often. Add the cauliflower and reduce the heat to a gentle simmer. Cook, uncovered and stirring often, until the cauliflower is tender, about 20 minutes.

4. Add the chickpeas and frozen peas to warm them through, stir in the yogurt and season to taste with salt and pepper.

5. Divide the rice (or quinoa) between bowls, spoon the curry on top and sprinkle with cilantro leaves and lime juice. Serve immediately with a dollop of raita.

HELPFUL HINTS

For a richer variation, replace the yogurt in the curry with 3 Tbsp (45 g) of butter or ¼ cup (60 mL) of whipping (35%) cream. Store-bought garam masala usually contains ground cumin and coriander as well as hints of sweeter spices such as cinnamon and cardamom. If necessary, you could use 1 ½ Tbsp (14 g) of garam masala in place of the cumin, coriander, turmeric and the smaller measure of garam masala in this recipe.

> Rendang is a Malaysian style of curry that is immensely fragrant (and can be very spicy). I came to appreciate how delicious it is when visiting Malaysia. Unlike a saucy South Asian or Thai curry, this braised dish becomes drier as it cooks, intensifying the flavours.

BEEF RENDANG

SERVES 4 · PREP: 15 MINUTES · COOK: 1 HOUR

1. Cut the dried tops off the lemongrass. Peel away and discard the outer layer if it is dry. Finely chop the lemongrass and place it in the bowl of a food processor with the onions, garlic, chilies, ginger and oil. Purée until this chili paste is as smooth as possible.

2. Heat a large sauté pan over medium-high heat and add the chili paste, stirring constantly until it just begins to stick, about 4 minutes. Stir in the star anise, cardamom, cinnamon and tamarind paste and stir for 1 minute more (the tamarind paste will eventually dissolve into the liquid).

3. Add the coconut milk and water, stirring to melt the chili paste into the liquids. Once simmering, reduce the heat to medium-low and add the beef.

4. Simmer, uncovered, for about 1 hour, stirring often, especially during the last 20 minutes of cooking. (The sauce will reduce significantly and stick to the beef, and the rendang will deepen to a dark red-brown in the last 10 minutes.)

5. Remove and discard the star anise, cardamom pods and cinnamon stick. Season to taste with salt.

6. Serve the rendang with the rice. Sprinkle chopped cilantro over each serving.

MAKE AHEAD
Refrigerate the rendang in an airtight container for 3 days, or freeze for up to 3 months. Thaw overnight in the fridge and warm over medium heat until simmering, about 15 minutes.

2 stems lemongrass
1 medium onion, peeled and chopped
3 cloves garlic, peeled
3 to 4 fresh red Thai chilies
1 ½-inch piece (3.5 cm) fresh ginger, peeled and sliced
3 Tbsp (45 mL) vegetable oil
3 whole star anise
3 whole green cardamom pods
1 cinnamon stick
1 Tbsp (25 g) tamarind paste
1 can (13 ½ oz/400 mL) coconut milk
1 cup (250 mL) water
1 ½ lb (675 g) diced cooked beef (see note)
Salt
4 cups (1 L) cooked long-grain rice, such as basmati or jasmine
½ cup (125 mL) chopped fresh cilantro

HELPFUL HINTS

Traditionally, beef rendang is made with raw stewing beef, and of course you can use that here. Replace the cooked beef with the same weight of raw boneless beef blade, cut into cubes, and cook for 90 minutes instead of 1 hour.

Malaysian cuisine is known for its sweat-inducing heat (I love it!) and this recipe makes a fiery stew, especially if you use the small red Thai chilies. Make a milder version by using fewer chilies, removing the seeds from the Thai chilies, or replacing the chilies with a single red bell pepper for no heat at all.

For a full meal, serve the rendang over rice with crunchy Quick Cabbage Slaw (page 65), which helps cut the heat, just as raita does with a South Asian curry.

> This vibrant curry is packed with fresh vegetables and served over a bed of rice noodles. If you don't have any leftover turkey, diced cooked chicken works just as well.

THAI TURKEY COCONUT CURRY

SERVES 6 • PREP: 15 MINUTES • COOK: 10 MINUTES

1. Place the stock, coconut milk, garlic, ginger, lemongrass, lime zest and five-spice powder in a stockpot over medium heat and bring to a simmer. Add the beans, snap peas, mushrooms and bell pepper to the stockpot, return to a simmer and cook for about 2 minutes, just until the beans are tender. Stir in the turkey and season to taste with salt and pepper.

2. To serve, rinse the cooked rice noodles in a colander under hot water and divide them between 6 bowls. Ladle the soup into the bowls and top with the bean sprouts, basil, cilantro and peanuts. Season to taste with lime juice and hot sauce. Serve immediately.

MAKE AHEAD

Unlike most wintry soups, this one is best eaten right after it's made, to retain the fresh flavours and colours.

3 cups (750 mL) chicken or vegetable stock (gluten-free, if required)
1 can (13 ½ oz/400 mL) coconut milk
2 cloves garlic, minced
1 Tbsp (6 g) finely grated fresh ginger
1 piece fresh lemongrass, bruised with the back of a knife
Finely grated zest of 1 lime
2 tsp Chinese five-spice powder
1 ½ cups (150 g) green beans, cut in half
1 ½ cups (150 g) snap peas, trimmed
1 ½ cups (100 g) quartered button mushrooms
1 red bell pepper, seeded and diced
2 cups (250 g) diced cooked turkey meat
Salt and black pepper
1 pkg (8 oz/225 g) rice stick noodles, cooked and drained
2 cups (150 g) fresh bean sprouts
½ cup (125 mL) fresh basil leaves
¼ cup (60 mL) fresh cilantro leaves
¼ cup (37 g) chopped peanuts
Fresh lime juice and hot sauce, to taste

HELPFUL HINT

This soup is super quick to make and hearty enough to serve as a main course. I like that a flavourful dish like this can be made from scratch without relying on bottled sauces containing unnecessary fat, sugar and salt.

This wintry bowl of colourful goodness is proof that meals made with vegetables can be hearty and fulfilling without adding excessive legumes or grains. The sparkle of olives and lemon brings to mind the light flavours of the Mediterranean—and warm sunny days on a terrace or at the beach.

Ve

ROASTED SQUASH AND TOMATO BOWL WITH WHITE BEANS, SPINACH AND OLIVES

SERVES 4 (ON ITS OWN) OR 6 (OVER COOKED QUINOA OR RICE) •
PREP: 15 MINUTES • COOK: 30 MINUTES

1. Preheat the oven to 350°F (180°C).

2. Heat the oil in a large ovenproof sauté pan over medium heat and add the caramelized onions, stirring to warm them through.

3. Stir in the squash and tomatoes, tossing to coat with the onions. Add the garlic, oregano and chili flakes, and season lightly with salt and pepper.

4. Roast the vegetables in the oven, uncovered and stirring once or twice, for about 30 minutes, until the squash is fork-tender.

5. Return the pan to the stovetop over medium heat. Add the white beans and spinach and stir gently until the spinach has wilted (it will look like a lot of spinach leaves at first, but they reduce considerably as they wilt), about 3 minutes.

6. Stir in the olives and lemon juice and season to taste.

7. Serve immediately in individual bowls over cooked quinoa or brown rice (if using).

MAKE AHEAD

This quick meal also works well as a make-ahead dish for busy weeknights or for packed lunches. You can refrigerate this in an airtight container for 3 days and warm it over medium heat until simmering, about 10 minutes. I don't recommend freezing this dish because the tomatoes will go very soft and fall apart once thawed.

3 Tbsp (45 mL) extra virgin olive oil
1 cup (250 mL) Caramelized Onions (page 152)
2 cups (400 g) diced butternut squash
2 cups (300 g) grape or cherry tomatoes
2 cloves garlic, minced
1 Tbsp (15 mL) chopped fresh oregano (or 1 ½ tsp dried)
Pinch of dried chili flakes
Salt and black pepper
1 (19 oz/540 mL) can white kidney beans, drained and rinsed
6 cups (1.5 L) fresh spinach leaves
½ cup (65 g) pitted green olives
Juice of 1 lemon
4 cups (1 L) cooked quinoa or brown rice (optional)

MISO SOBA NOODLE BOWL

SERVES 4 · PREP: 15 MINUTES · COOK: 15 MINUTES

MAKE AHEAD

This dish is best enjoyed right after it's prepared. The noodles take such a short time to cook that I like to have my vegetables chopped before I cook the eggs and noodles, so I'm not caught off guard.

4 whole eggs (in the shell)
1 pkg (12.8 oz/363 g) buckwheat soba noodles
8 cups (2 L) mushroom or vegetable stock
2 medium carrots, peeled and thinly sliced
2 Tbsp (30 mL) dark (red) miso
3 to 4 dashes soy sauce
Dash of toasted sesame oil
1 pkg (420 g) firm tofu, diced
6 cups (1.5 L) spinach leaves
5 oz (150 g) enoki mushrooms, bottoms trimmed
2 green onions, thinly sliced
4 tsp finely grated fresh ginger

1. Fill a saucepan with hot water and gently add the eggs. Bring the water to a full boil over high heat, uncovered, and then add the soba noodles and continue to boil for 2 minutes. Drain the noodles and eggs into a colander and rinse with cold water to stop the cooking. Remove the eggs and set aside.

2. Place the stock and carrots in a saucepan over medium heat and bring to a simmer. Cook for 3 to 4 minutes, until the carrots are tender but not overly soft.

3. Place the miso paste in a small bowl and whisk a little warm stock into it. Return this mixture to the saucepan (this prevents lumps). Add the soy sauce and sesame oil to taste and keep the stock warm over medium-low heat.

4. Warm 4 large soup or pasta bowls. Peel the eggs. Rinse the soba noodles in the colander under hot water to warm them and loosen them.

5. Divide the noodles between the bowls and arrange the tofu, spinach leaves and mushrooms on top. Ladle the hot broth into each bowl and top with an egg (cut in half, if you wish), green onions and fresh ginger. Serve immediately.

HELPFUL HINTS

The goal when boiling the eggs for this recipe is to have a semi-soft yolk. The size of the saucepan you use and the power of your stove will affect how quickly the water boils. A smaller saucepan and a quick-to-heat burner will cook your eggs in less time than a larger saucepan on a slower burner. After you've made this recipe once, adjust the cooking time as needed.

I like that I can find all of the ingredients for this recipe at my regular grocery store. If you visit an Asian grocery store, pick up a little bottle of togarashi, a blend of sesame seeds, chili flakes and orange peel (and a few spices) that's traditionally used in udon noodle soup for a bit of heat.

I seem to eat a lot of noodle dishes in the winter, likely because I can load them up with vegetables. Glass noodles, also known as cellophane noodles or Chinese vermicelli, are widely available and easy to work with and, because they are made from starch and water, they are gluten-free.

SICHUAN SPICY GREENS AND GLASS NOODLE BOWL

SERVES 6 · PREP: 15 MINUTES · COOK: 10 MINUTES

1. Have all of your ingredients ready to use. Place the glass noodles in a bowl and cover with warm tap water. Let sit for 15 minutes, then drain and set aside.

2. Trim the bok choy and gai lan. Bring a large saucepan of salted water to a boil over high heat, add the bok choy and gai lan and blanch for 1 minute. Drain them into a colander and then rinse under cold running water to cool. Set aside.

3. Heat a wok or non-stick saucepan over medium heat and add 2 Tbsp (30 mL) of the vegetable oil, the chilies, shallots, garlic and ginger and stir to coat, letting the shallots and garlic brown a little, about 1 minute.

4. Add the coriander, cinnamon and cardamom and stir for a few seconds. Add the drained noodles and cabbage and increase the heat to medium-high, stirring constantly until the cabbage and noodles soften up. Add the vinegar and sesame oil and season to taste with salt or soy sauce. Divide the noodles between 6 bowls (you can heat the bowls first by running them under hot water if you wish).

5. Return the wok or saucepan to the stove over medium heat. Add the remaining 1 Tbsp (15 mL) of vegetable oil and the bok choy and gai lan. Toss to warm through, about 2 minutes, and arrange the vegetables over the noodles.

6. Garnish each serving with avocado, green onions and sesame seeds and serve immediately.

MAKE AHEAD

This is even quicker if you blanch your bok choy and gai lan 1 day ahead. Drain the vegetables well, cool completely and refrigerate in an airtight container.

1 pkg (14 oz/400 g) glass noodles (mung bean or sweet potato vermicelli)

1 ½ lb (675 g) baby bok choy or Shanghai bok choy (about 6)

1 lb (450 g) gai lan (about 12 stalks)

3 Tbsp (45 mL) vegetable oil, divided

5 to 6 whole Thai red chilies, sliced, or 6 to 8 Sichuan peppercorns

2 shallots, thinly sliced

2 cloves fresh garlic, sliced

1 ½-inch (3.5 cm) piece of thinly sliced ginger, cut into julienne strips

1 tsp ground coriander

¼ tsp ground cinnamon

¼ tsp ground cardamom

2 cups (500 mL) finely shredded cabbage (Napa or Savoy)

3 Tbsp (45 mL) black vinegar

Dash of toasted sesame oil

Salt or soy sauce (gluten-free, if required)

2 avocados, peeled and quartered, for garnish

3 green onions, thinly sliced, for garnish

Sesame seeds, for garnish

SAVOURY SUPPORTING ACTS

FRENCH VINAIGRETTE

MAKES ABOUT 1 CUP (250 ML) • PREP: 5 MINUTES

MAKE AHEAD

You can refrigerate the French vinaigrette in a 1-cup (250 mL) mason jar for up to 1 week. The oil will set up in the fridge, so let the vinaigrette sit at room temperature for about 20 minutes before serving.

¼ cup (60 mL) red wine vinegar

3 Tbsp (45 g) minced shallot, about 1 large

2 tsp Dijon mustard (gluten-free, if required)

2 tsp honey

½ cup (125 mL) extra virgin olive oil

¼ cup (60 mL) water

Salt and black pepper

1. Whisk the red wine vinegar, shallot, mustard and honey together. Slowly drizzle in the olive oil while whisking, followed by the water. Season to taste with salt and pepper and then chill until ready to use.

HELPFUL HINTS

For a faster and easier prep, I simply shake all of the ingredients thoroughly in a sealed mason jar and then pop it in the fridge. I add water to my classic vinaigrette so that it's thinner than a regular vinaigrette and won't weigh down my greens. The water also lowers the fat ratio slightly without compromising the flavour.

CRANBERRY SAUCE

MAKES ABOUT 4 CUPS (1 L) • PREP: 5 MINUTES • COOK: 25 MINUTES

MAKE AHEAD

You can refrigerate the cranberry sauce in an airtight container for up to 2 weeks, or freeze it for up to 3 months.

4 cups (440 g) fresh or frozen cranberries

1 cup (250 mL) water

Pinch of ground cloves

¾ cup (150 g) granulated sugar

¼ cup (60 mL) pure maple syrup

1 oz (30 ml) orange liqueur

1. Place the cranberries, water and cloves in a saucepan over medium heat and bring to a simmer. Reduce the heat to medium-low for a gentle simmer, and cook, uncovered, for 10 minutes (or 15 minutes if starting with frozen cranberries), stirring occasionally, until most of the cranberries pop.

2. Add the sugar and maple syrup and cook for another 10 minutes, until the cranberries have broken down and are shiny and translucent. Add the orange liqueur and cook for just 1 minute before removing from the heat to cool. Chill for at least 2 hours before serving.

Buttermilk is the key to the ranch flavour in this dressing and dip. Its consistency makes it perfect as a dressing for a green salad or as a dip for vegetables (Winter Crudités, page 48).

BUTTERMILK RANCH DRESSING AND DIP

MAKES ABOUT 1 CUP (250 ML) • PREP: 3 MINUTES

1. Whisk all of the ingredients together with salt and pepper to taste (ranch dressing typically uses a fair bit of black pepper). Transfer to an airtight container and chill until ready to use.

HELPFUL HINT

For a thicker ranch dressing that you can use as a dip for potato chips, increase the mayonnaise to ⅓ cup (80 mL) and add 2 Tbsp (30 mL) of instant skim milk powder. The proteins in the milk powder will thicken the dip without changing the flavour.

MAKE AHEAD

You can refrigerate this in an airtight container until the expiry date of the buttermilk or sour cream you made it with, whichever is first.

½ cup (125 mL) buttermilk
½ cup (125 mL) sour cream or plain Greek yogurt (0% fat is fine)
3 Tbsp (45 mL) mayonnaise
2 green onions, finely chopped
1 clove garlic, minced
Salt and black pepper

Once you've made this easy blue cheese dressing and dip, you'll never buy store-bought again. Use it to dress a salad, or to dunk chicken wings in as I do on a sports-watching Sunday. The hint of garlic is Michael's little addition, and it really makes the dip!

MICHAEL'S BLUE CHEESE DRESSING AND DIP

MAKES ABOUT 1 ¾ CUPS (425 ML) • PREP: 5 MINUTES

1. Stir together the sour cream, mayonnaise, mustard and garlic until combined. Stir in the blue cheese, but leave most of the crumbles intact. Season to taste with salt and pepper. Chill, covered, until ready to serve.

MAKE AHEAD

You can refrigerate this in an airtight container until the expiry date on the sour cream you made it with.

½ cup (125 mL) full-fat sour cream
½ cup (125 mL) mayonnaise (gluten-free, if required)
1 tsp Dijon mustard (gluten-free, if required)

1 clove garlic, minced
6 oz (180 g) crumbled blue cheese
Salt and black pepper

This virtuous dressing and dip is a personal favourite, and I keep it on hand year-round to use as a salad dressing or dip for vegetables. It is lighter and smoother than guacamole with bright, fresh herbs.

AVOCADO YOGURT DRESSING AND DIP

GF

V

MAKES ABOUT 1 ½ CUPS (375 ML) • PREP: 5 MINUTES

MAKE AHEAD
You can refrigerate this in an airtight container for up to 4 days.

1 ripe avocado
¾ cup (175 mL) Greek yogurt (0% fat is fine)
2 green onions, sliced
½ cup (125 mL) fresh basil leaves, mint leaves, cilantro leaves, dill fronds, or any combination
6 Tbsp (90 mL) rice vinegar
Salt and black pepper

1. Cut the avocado in half and spoon the flesh into a blender or food processor. Add the yogurt, green onions, herbs and rice vinegar and purée until smooth. Season to taste, transfer to an airtight container and chill until ready to use.

HELPFUL HINT
Use this dip in place of mayonnaise on sandwiches.

Puréeing toasted hazelnuts right into this dressing makes it thick and almost creamy. I like to use this style of dressing on hardier winter greens like radicchio and frisée—delicate greens, such as Boston lettuce, will collapse under its weight. You could even toss it over warm cooked pasta like a pesto with a little diced cooked chicken or turkey and a handful of chopped basil.

HAZELNUT DRESSING

GF

Ve

MAKES ABOUT 1 CUP (250 ML) • PREP: 5 MINUTES

MAKE AHEAD
You can refrigerate this in an airtight container for up to 2 weeks.

½ cup (65 g) toasted hazelnuts, peeled
3 Tbsp (45 mL) fresh lemon juice
1 Tbsp (15 mL) pure maple syrup
1 tsp Dijon mustard (gluten-free, if required)

6 Tbsp (90 mL) hazelnut oil or mild extra virgin olive oil, plus extra for serving
2 Tbsp (30 mL) water
Salt and black pepper

1. Place the hazelnuts, lemon juice, maple syrup and mustard in the bowl of a food processor and pulse until evenly combined and quite smooth (it will be a thick paste).

2. With the food processor running, slowly drizzle in the oil followed by the water. Season to taste with salt and pepper. Cover and chill until ready to serve.

Buttermilk Ranch Dressing (page 148); Avocado Yogurt Dressing (page 149); Raspberry Olive Tapenade (page 151); Michael's Blue Cheese Dressing (page 148)

Raspberries may seem like an odd addition to a salty olive sauce,
but the fruit lightens up the olives and adds a festive touch. This tapenade
makes a lovely addition to a Winter Crudités platter (page 48) or an
antipasto or cheese platter (page 35).

RASPBERRY OLIVE TAPENADE

MAKES ABOUT 1 ½ CUPS (375 ML) • PREP: 5 MINUTES

MAKE AHEAD
You can refrigerate this in an airtight
container for up to 1 week.

1 ½ cups (195 g) pitted kalamata olives
½ cup (25 g) sliced sundried
    tomatoes
½ cup (85 g) fresh raspberries (or
    frozen, thawed)
1 clove garlic, minced
6 leaves fresh basil
1 tsp finely grated lemon zest
Juice of 1 lemon
3 Tbsp (45 mL) extra virgin olive oil
Black pepper

1. Place all of the ingredients in the bowl of a food processor and pulse
   until finely chopped (you don't want a paste). Transfer to an airtight
   container, season to taste with pepper and chill until ready to serve.
   If gifting, spoon the tapenade into little jars and partner with a piece
   of cheese or a cheese board for the perfect host gift.

HELPFUL HINT
This tapenade has many uses:
• Spoon it over a small uncut wheel of Brie and bake for 10 to 15 minutes at 375°F (190°C) for a gooey delicious treat.
• Toss it into a pan of cooked linguini with a few shrimp for a quick and tasty supper.
• Spoon it over cooked or smoked salmon for an easy sauce.
• Use it to dress watermelon cubes hollowed slightly with a melon baller, and then top with a cube of feta. Spear
  these canapés with a frilly toothpick!

ADD SPARKLE
Make your own palmiers by spreading the tapenade evenly over a sheet of puff pastry. Roll up the pastry from
opposite ends so they meet in the middle and then slice into ½-inch (1 cm) pieces. Arrange them on a baking tray
lined with parchment paper, leaving an inch (2.5 cm) between them, and bake in a 400°F (200°C) oven for about
15 minutes, turning them over halfway through cooking. Serve warm or at room temperature.

Roasting the apples for this classic accompaniment to ham concentrates their flavour
and produces a texture that is thicker than that of store-bought applesauce.
Any variety of apple—or a blend of apples—works here.

ROASTED APPLESAUCE

MAKES ABOUT 2 ½ CUPS (625 ML) • PREP: 10 MINUTES • COOK: 40 MINUTES

1. Preheat the oven to 375°F (190°C).

2. Toss the sliced apples with the lemon juice, honey, melted butter and
   salt to coat well. Spread in a large ungreased casserole or other
   ceramic baking dish (the apples can overlap) and roast, uncovered
   and stirring occasionally, until the apples are fork-tender, about
   40 minutes. Allow the apples to cool to room temperature.

3. Purée the cooled apples in a food processor or blender. If the applesauce is too thick (this will depend on the apple variety), add ¼ to
   ½ cup (60 to 125 mL) of water as you blend. Chill the applesauce
   until ready to serve.

MAKE AHEAD
You can refrigerate the applesauce in
an airtight container for up to 3 weeks,
or freeze it for up to 3 months. Thaw
overnight in the fridge.

2 lb (900 g) apples, peeled and sliced
2 Tbsp (30 mL) lemon juice
2 Tbsp (37 g) honey
2 Tbsp (30 g) butter, melted
Pinch of salt

These onions are the ultimate flavour-builder for cold-weather dishes, so an essential during
the holiday season. Use them to add oomph to soup or a sandwich of leftover turkey or beef.

CARAMELIZED ONIONS

MAKES ABOUT 2 CUPS (500 ML) • PREP: 10 MINUTES • COOK: 40 MINUTES

1. Heat a stainless steel, cast iron or enamel coated sauté pan over
   medium heat and add the butter (or oil). (Don't use a non-stick pan;
   you want the onions to stick a little.) Add the onions, thyme and a little
   salt and pepper and stir to coat the onions. Cook, stirring often with a
   wooden spoon, until the onions begin to caramelize, about 15 minutes.
   About halfway through cooking, when brown bits start sticking to the
   bottom of the pan, add a splash of the Sherry (or wine) and use the
   wooden spoon to loosen all those flavourful bits. Continue to cook the
   onions, adding splashes of Sherry (or wine) to lift the browned bits,
   until they are a rich brown, an additional 20 to 25 minutes.

2. Remove the pan from the heat and let the onions cool. Chill until
   needed.

MAKE AHEAD
You can refrigerate these in an airtight
container for up to 2 weeks, or freeze
them for up to 2 months. Thaw overnight in the fridge before using.

3 Tbsp (45 mL) butter or extra virgin
   olive oil
3 medium onions, sliced
2 tsp chopped fresh thyme
Salt and black pepper
¼ cup (60 mL) dry Sherry or dry
   white wine

> What's the difference between stuffing and dressing? Dressing involves the same ingredients and preparation as stuffing, but it is cooked *outside* the bird whereas stuffing is cooked in it. This dressing is vegetarian, but as a stuffing it wouldn't be.

CARAMELIZED ONION AND APPLE DRESSING

V

if cooked
on its own

SERVES 6 TO 8 • PREP: 10 MINUTES • COOK: 1 HOUR

MAKE AHEAD

You can prepare the dressing 1 day ahead and refrigerate it, well wrapped, overnight. Cook it straight from the fridge, but add an extra 10 to 15 minutes to the cooking time.

2 Tbsp (30 g) butter, plus extra for greasing the pan
6 cups (1.5 L) diced day-old crusty bread (crusts left on), cut into 1-inch (2.5 cm) cubes
1 ½ cups (375 mL) chicken or vegetable stock
1 large egg
2 Tbsp (30 mL) chopped fresh sage
¾ tsp fine sea salt
1 cup (250 mL) Caramelized Onions (page 152)
½ cup (35 g) diced dried apples

1. Preheat the oven to 350°F (180°C). Lightly grease a 12-cup (3 L) baking dish with butter.

2. Place the diced bread in a large bowl. Whisk the stock, egg, sage and salt together and pour over the bread. Add the caramelized onions and apples and toss well, giving the bread a few minutes to soak up the liquid.

3. Transfer the dressing to the prepared pan and dot the top with butter. Lightly cover the dish with aluminum foil and bake, covered, for 20 minutes. Remove the foil and continue to bake for another 30 to 40 minutes, until the top is a rich golden brown.

4. Let the dressing cool for 10 minutes before serving.

ADD SPARKLE

I'm a bit of a purist when it comes to dressings and stuffings. I see them as a way to elevate the flavour of a roast, so I don't add too many extras like nuts or sausage (just that little bit of apple for subtle sweetness). That said, a classic holiday side dish such as this is very personal. If you need to put in raisins or leave out the apples to keep Aunt Penny happy, then do it.

> Making prepared horseradish is easier than you might think, especially when you realize that you control the heat. Just a warning: if you like it hot, you may want to get a pair of goggles ready!

Ve

PREPARED HORSERADISH

MAKES 2 CUPS (500 ML) • PREP: 15 MINUTES

1. Have ready a clean 2-cup (500 mL) canning jar or other glass jar with a sealable lid.

2. Use a food processor fitted with a shredding blade to grate the horseradish (you can grate by hand using a box grater, but it is tiring work and your eyes may get irritated). Stir in the water. The longer you let the horseradish sit with the water, the hotter it will get. For mild horseradish, stir in the vinegar right after adding the water; for extra-hot horseradish, let it sit for 5 minutes before adding the vinegar. Season to taste with salt.

3. Spoon the horseradish into the jar, seal tightly and chill until ready to use.

MAKE AHEAD

Look for fresh horseradish in grocery stores from October onward, and get an early start on the holidays. You can refrigerate homemade prepared horseradish in an airtight container for up to 6 months.

2 cups (350 g) peeled and diced fresh horseradish
⅓ cup (80 mL) distilled water
½ cup (125 mL) white vinegar
Pickling salt

> Horseradish cream makes an original gift. While it needs to be refrigerated, it's one of those "extras" that any host would be happy to receive as a gift. In addition to being delicious served with ham (or on the requisite ham sandwich the next day), it is delectable alongside roast beef or smoked salmon.

V

HORSERADISH CREAM

MAKES ABOUT 1½ CUP • PREP TIME: 5 MINUTES

1. Stir together the crème fraîche (or sour cream), horseradish and mustard until well mixed. Spoon into a serving bowl.

MAKE AHEAD

The horseradish cream will keep in a jar or an airtight container in the fridge for up to 1 month.

1 cup (250 mL) crème fraîche or full-fat sour cream
½ cup (125 mL) Prepared Horseradish (above) or store-bought
1 tsp Dijon mustard

Pickled Hot and Sweet Peppers (page 157); Fermented Cucumber Pickles (page 156); Horseradish Cream (page 154); Prepared Horseradish (page 154)

> Pickles are a great addition to a cheese board or for any event that calls
> for finger foods, and making them doesn't have to be a full-day process of
> putting up enough to get you through the winter—we're not pioneers!
> I prefer fermented pickles (think deli pickles) to vinegar pickles, and this
> small-batch half-sour version only takes a few days to ferment.

FERMENTED CUCUMBER PICKLES

MAKES 8 CUPS (2 L) OF PICKLES · PREP: 10 MINUTES, PLUS FERMENTING

GF

Ve

1. Wash and air-dry an 8-cup (2 L) glass jar (or 2 smaller ones). Wash the cucumbers and cut them into thick slices or sticks. Arrange the cucumbers in the jar, along with the garlic, dill and peppercorns.

2. Bring the water to a full boil and stir in the salt. Pour over the cucumbers to cover completely. Weigh down the cucumbers with a ceramic or glass saucer or a small dish (do not use metal) and cover the jar with a piece of cheesecloth or a clean tea towel. Do not secure the jar with a lid.

3. Let the jar sit on the counter for 24 hours (optimally at about 70 to 75°F/21 to 24°C), stirring once during that time.

4. After the first day, remove the cover and weight. If blue or green spots (mold) have developed, discard the pickles (the temperature was likely too warm). If a film has developed on the brine, simply remove it with a spoon. (It is safe to eat.)

5. Taste a pickle to see if you like the level of sour. If it is not yet sour enough, cover the jar again, return it to the counter, stir once in 24 hours and taste again the following day. The longer they sit, the more they will sour. Repeat for up to 3 days (the pickles won't sour further after 3 days).

6. Once the pickles have soured to your liking, transfer them to a clean jar, seal with a secure lid and refrigerate. If gifting, make sure to include a tag on the jar that says to refrigerate them.

MAKE AHEAD
You can store these pickles in an air-tight container in the fridge for up to 3 months.

2 English cucumbers
2 whole garlic cloves, peeled
½ bunch fresh dill
6 whole black peppercorns
4 cups (1 L) distilled water
1 ½ Tbsp (22 g) pickling salt

HELPFUL HINTS
Use distilled water, which has no trace elements in it, to make the brine (trace metals in tap water can discolour foods, such as turning garlic cloves blue). It is also crucial to use pickling salt. The added iodine in table salt can discolour foods too.

These peppers can be stored in your pantry or given away to stock the pantries of friends and family. I love getting a jar of pickled hot peppers—I use them all winter long to spice up stews and sauces, and I use the hot pickle juice to add spice to salsa or guacamole.

PICKLED HOT AND SWEET PEPPERS

GF

Ve

MAKES 12 CUPS (3 L) • PREP: 30 MINUTES, PLUS RESTING TIME •
COOK: 20 MINUTES

MAKE AHEAD
You can make these pickles at any time of the year. The canning process ensures the pickled peppers will keep for over a year in a cool, dark place. Once you open the jar, they will keep, refrigerated, for up to 6 months.

6 cups (1.5 L) mixed whole chili
   peppers (sweet and/or hot)
8 cups (2 L) distilled water
½ cup (125 g) pickling salt
8 cups (2 L) white vinegar
½ cup (100 g) granulated sugar
3 whole garlic cloves, peeled

1. Have ready three 4-cup (1 L) canning jars or other glass jars with sealable lids. Wash the whole chili peppers and drain well. If adding a few sweet peppers to the mix (see the note below), cut them into large pieces that fit into your jars and discard their seeds.

2. Place all of the peppers in a large bowl. Bring 7 cups (1.75 L) of the water and the salt to a boil and pour over the peppers. Let sit on the counter for 4 hours, then drain and rinse (this step will help to keep the peppers crisp).

3. Fill a large stockpot with water and bring to a boil over high heat. Place the vinegar, sugar and garlic cloves in a second stockpot and bring to a full boil over medium-high heat.

4. Use rubber tongs (or jar tongs) to immerse the glass jars in the boiling water for a few seconds and then drain on a tea towel. Pack the peppers into the jars and ladle the hot vinegar overtop, adding enough to reach to ¼ inch (0.5 cm) from the top of each jar. Add 1 garlic clove to each jar.

5. Place rubber-ringed lids in a heatproof bowl, cover with a little cool water and then pour a ladleful of boiling water over (the rubber needs to be softened but not boiled). Set the lids on each jar and secure in place with the second, threaded ring, twisting only until "finger tight" (do not overtighten).

6. Use the rubber tongs to carefully drop the jars into the boiling water, ensuring the jars are submerged. Boil for 10 minutes, transfer to the towel to drain and then set aside to cool completely. Label each jar with the name of the pickles and the date. If gifting, a simple ribbon securing a slotted spoon to the jar adds the necessary festive touch.

HELPFUL HINT
The ratio of sweet to hot peppers is really up to you. I like to mix up the colours and varieties, but even a jar of jalapeño pepper rings is a "warmly" welcomed gift in mid-winter.

> Buckwheat groats are oddly shaped hulled seeds from the buckwheat plant.
> When the groats are toasted, they are called kasha. Fully cooked, they make
> a thick porridge, but here I simply soak them and then toast them with a hint
> of honey. They crisp up to the texture of toasted nuts.

TOASTED BUCKWHEAT KASHA

MAKES ABOUT 1 ½ CUPS (375 ML) · PREP: 5 MINUTES PLUS RESTING TIME ·
COOK: 25 MINUTES

1. Rinse the kasha in a fine-mesh sieve under cool running water until the water rinses clear. Place it in a heatproof bowl and pour the boiling water overtop. Immediately cover the bowl with plastic wrap and let sit until the water has been absorbed, about 20 minutes.

2. Rinse the kasha again in a fine-mesh sieve under cool running water, set the sieve over a bowl and let the kasha sit to dry, fluffing it occasionally with a fork, about 20 minutes.

3. Preheat the oven to 350°F (180°C) and line a baking tray with parchment paper.

4. Toss the dry kasha with the maple syrup and spread it in an even layer on the baking tray. Bake for about 25 minutes, stirring occasionally, until it is a rich golden brown.

5. Remove from the oven and let cool on the tray. Crumble the grains and transfer them to an airtight container until ready to use.

MAKE AHEAD
Toasted kasha will keep in an airtight container at room temperature for up to 1 month.

½ cup (80 g) buckwheat kasha
⅓ cup (80 mL) boiling water
2 Tbsp (30 mL) pure maple syrup

HELPFUL HINT
Sprinkle toasted kasha over a salad to add a little crunch or over a soup as a garnish instead of nuts.

Baking
for the Holidays

(AND ALMOST EVERY DAY)

Holiday Baking Essentials

Baking at holiday time means so much more than treating ourselves to a fancier dessert or an extra cookie (or three). The holidays are about sharing, and so is baking: there is a sense of giving something of ourselves when we bake for others. We are devoting time to preparing ingredients, measuring, mixing, baking, waiting, cooling, chilling and packaging . . . all in anticipation of the eventual eating and appreciating.

And I love it! I am thrilled to see family members baking together, making a party out of preparing recipes that have been passed down through generations, and also creating new traditions. In this baking section, I've included some of my own family favourites as well as some new treats that now regularly appear on my holiday table. As in part one of this book, I have included instructions about prepping ahead of time, how to store your goodies and how long they will keep.

The holidays always seem to catch us by surprise, but with some guidance and planning, you can achieve all your baking goals for the holiday season. Remember that many of these recipes also make great desserts at any time of year. A good Lemon Twinkle Cookie is a lovely treat with fresh strawberries in June, while the Lime Chiffon Cake with Raspberry Swiss Meringue Buttercream would make an ideal birthday cake. So, holiday or not, let your baking spirit shine through. Here are some basic tips about the tools you'll need and the ingredients you'll want to have on hand to get you in the baking spirit.

TOOLS

While you can never have too many festively-shaped cookie cutters, there are other baking tools that will make your baking sessions more productive. Here is my list of essential tools, in order of importance.

MEASURING TOOLS—Good-quality measuring cups and spoons AND a scale are critical to recipe success. You'll notice that all of the dry ingredients in the recipes in this book are listed by volume (cups and teaspoons) and by weight (grams). If you are new to weighing ingredients, I recommend giving it a try. Weighing leaves little room for error, and items like flour, chocolate, honey and butter are more precisely (and much more tidily) measured by weight.

OVEN THERMOMETER—This tool may seem an odd choice for the second-most important one on the list, but I'd be lost without it. Ovens vary greatly in how quickly they heat up, how they hold the heat and how their temperature oscillates throughout baking. Just because you set your oven to 350°F (180°C) and it beeps to tell you it's heated, it doesn't mean it is. This affordable tool sits inside your oven and tells you the precise temperature (and how much it drops when you open your oven door). You can even move the thermometer around the oven to check if you have any "hot spots," so you can rotate your baking trays for even results. If you find your oven is more than 25°F (10 to 15°C) off, call in a repairperson to calibrate it.

BAKING PANS—A springform pan is my go-to for any round cake or cheesecake that I wish to extract easily, and a good mix of other shapes and sizes of baking trays and pans will come in handy. Basic metal pans are best (as opposed to glass, ceramic or silicone). I find that light and dark metal work equally well. The butter and sugar in a recipe affect how an item bakes more than the shade of the metal pan.

PARCHMENT PAPER—This grease- and moisture-resistant paper keeps items from sticking to your pan and makes clean-up a snap. If you're baking cookies, the paper can be re-used. I typically lightly grease my cake pans with butter before lining them with paper so that the paper sticks to the pan, giving the cake a clean, defined shape (no puckering or rough edges).

ELECTRIC BEATERS OR STAND MIXER—If you are doing some serious baking, you will need powerful support to bring volume to your whipping cream and egg whites, or to take some of the effort out of making cookie doughs. Handheld electric beaters can take on most mixing and whipping tasks, but for things like bread doughs and larger batches of cake and cookie batters, the powerful motor of a stand mixer will do a better job.

SILICONE SPATULAS—These sturdy tools are ideal for mixing cookie doughs and simple batters, and their flexible heads are heatproof and flexible, so every drop can be scraped from your bowl or pan.

ICE CREAM SCOOPS—I use my ice cream scoops for far more than scooping ice cream. They are great for portioning muffin batter, cookie dough and truffles/candies because each scoop makes an even and tidy serving. I suggest three sizes: a mini scoop for mini muffins and confections, a medium scoop for cookies and a regular-sized scoop for larger items, such as full-sized muffins and large desserts—and for ice cream.

OFFSET SPATULAS—These metal spreaders with a "step" near the handle become an extension of your hand when spreading frosting onto cakes, lifting tart slices from the pan and transferring warm cookies to a cooling rack. They typically come in small and large sizes—choose small, large or both.

PIPING BAGS AND TIPS—Now that disposable piping bags are readily available, I use them more often than the old-fashioned fabric ones. Having an assortment of tip shapes and sizes gives you creative control over piping spritz cookies, adding décor to cakes and, of course, decorating cut-out cookies.

METAL COOLING RACK—Although a cork or tile trivet keeps your counters safe, it can keep the heat trapped in the pan and prevent your baked goods from cooling quickly enough. The result? A soft or overbaked exterior. Choose a wire rack instead, so air can circulate under and around the tray or baked goods.

CANDY THERMOMETER—If making candies and other confections is a part of your holiday baking plans, a candy thermometer is essential. It will ensure that your sugar cooks to the right temperature so it sets to the correct consistency and help you temper your chocolate so it sets up at room temperature.

INGREDIENTS

During the holiday baking season, we lean toward certain ingredients: dried fruits and nuts figure prominently, and I know that I use more butter pre-holiday than at any other time of the year. Here are some tips for buying, using, storing and enjoying these ingredients.

BUTTER—When it comes to baking, I always use unsalted butter because it is fresher and sweeter tasting, and I am in control of the salt. In regular cooking, unless specified, salted or unsalted is fine.

When butter is specified to be at room temperature, 65 to 68°F (18 to 20°C) is the ideal range. I pull my butter from the fridge, cut it into pieces and let it sit for 1 hour. Try to avoid softening the butter in the microwave—its temperature will be uneven.

CHOCOLATE—Couverture chocolate is also known as baking chocolate, and it comes in squares, blocks or chips called callets. This chocolate is designed to be melted and worked smoothly into cake batters—Flourless Chocolate Mont Blanc Torte, page 277, for example—or other doughs and fillings. Dark, milk and white are the three basic types of couverture chocolate. Each type melts and sets up differently and has its own sweetness and intensity, so they are not interchangeable in recipes. Dark chocolate comes in two intensities: semisweet (milder) or bittersweet (stronger). You may notice that some couverture chocolate labels show a percentage on them—this refers to the cocoa content. The higher the percentage, the more bitter the chocolate. Semisweet chocolate can range between 51% to 65% cocoa solids, and bittersweet ranges between 66% to 74%. If a recipe benefits from using one over the other, I specify either semisweet or bittersweet. If not, I call for dark chocolate and you can choose whichever one you prefer.

Chocolate chips, on the other hand, are designed to hold their shape when baked, so white, milk and dark chocolate chips can be interchanged in my recipes.

When I make chocolate candies, I use a process called tempering, which can only be done with couverture/baking chocolate. Tempering involves heating and cooling chocolate to specific temperatures so the cocoa butter crystals within the chocolate bond together just so; properly done, this is what makes chocolate set up at room temperature with a satin finish, gives it a snap when you bite in and prevents any streaking as the chocolate sits. The temperatures vary between dark chocolate and milk and white chocolates. See Chocolate Barks (page 240) for the precise method and temperatures.

If any of your chocolate develops a dusty coating, called "bloom," it means that the chocolate has undergone a temperature change at some point and that some of the cocoa butter in the chocolate has risen to the surface. The chocolate is still perfectly fine to use, bloom and all. Store chocolate in a cool, dark place but do not refrigerate it.

CITRUS—I love citrus during the winter. In the countries where they're grown, these fruits are most often in season around holiday time, which means an abundance of choice. Get creative: a blood orange, tangerine, Minneola tangelo, clementine or mandarin orange zest and juice can be substituted for a navel orange 1:1 in most cases. When I call for orange, lemon or lime juice in a recipe, I always use freshly squeezed, and when I zest I finely grate it. Both the zest and the juice can be frozen, separately. I loosely pack zest into a small airtight container, so I can spoon out what I need easily and return the container to the freezer. Both will keep for up to 3 months, and the juice can be thawed in the fridge or on the counter.

DRIED FRUITS—I stock up on all my dried fruits as I head into the holiday baking season. Raisins, cranberries and dates are the most common, but I also use currants, cherries, figs and blueberries. Store dried fruits at room temperature in an airtight container. Don't worry if a white dust develops on their edges, particularly on dates and figs; their sugars are simply rising to the surface and the fruits are still fine to eat. I find that dried fruits stored in an airtight container will keep for more than six months, so I don't bother freezing them.

MILK AND OTHER DAIRY—When baking with milk, I typically use 2%, although you can use 1% without compromising the recipe. I don't recommend baking with skim milk because its lack of milk fat makes it like baking with water. The same is true for fat-free yogurts and sour creams. Starches and gelatins are used to thicken these fat-free products, and these additives change texture when stirred or heated, so your baked goods could end up dry or crumbly. Use full-fat sour cream and yogurt in baking, unless otherwise specified.

Whipping cream is typically 35% fat, and a minimum of 30% fat is needed for the whipped cream to be able to hold air (which is why you cannot substitute with half-and-half). Half-and-half cream is 10% fat.

Buttermilk is low in fat (around 1%), has a thick consistency and a real tang to it. Originally the by-product of the butter-making process (hence the name), it is now manufactured independently. I prefer using real buttermilk for my recipes, but if you are in a pinch you can make 1 cup (250 mL) of "buttermilk" by measuring 1 Tbsp (15 mL) of white vinegar or lemon juice into a liquid measuring cup and topping it with 1% or 2% milk to reach the 1-cup (250 mL) line.

If you are looking for dairy alternatives, almond milk is my preferred option for baking, as its texture and fat content mimic dairy milk best. Coconut milk (in Tetra-Paks, not cans) is second best. Rice milk is like skim milk; it is simply too thin and watery to work well in baking.

NUTS—Many traditional holiday baked goods contain nuts and dried fruits, and with good reason. Not that long ago, drying these ingredients to preserve them over the winter took a great deal of work, making them especially prized. To use large quantities of nuts and dried fruits all at once was a sign of celebration and even prosperity.

I stock up on shelled nuts over the holidays because stores sell through their stock regularly, which means the nuts are nice and fresh. Store most nuts in an airtight container in a cool, dark place for up to three months. Firmer nuts, like hazelnuts and almonds, will keep longer than tender, oily nuts, such as walnuts and pecans. If I know I won't use leftover nuts within a few months of my holiday baking frenzy, I freeze them in their airtight containers and they will last for up to another six months.

Toasting nuts heightens their flavour, adds crunch and also freshens them up. When I am gearing up for the holidays, I'll often toast large quantities of nuts to save myself that step when I'm mixing up a cookie dough or fruitcake batter. To toast nuts, spread them in a single layer on a parchment-lined baking tray and bake in a 350°F (180°C) oven, stirring once or twice. Walnuts and pecans will take 10 to 12 minutes, almonds and hazelnuts 15 to 18 minutes. Cool the nuts on the tray to room temperature and then pack them away in an airtight container.

Note that hazelnuts need to be peeled after toasting because their papery skins taste bitter if left on. I pop the toasted, cooled hazelnuts into a dry colander in the sink.

Do not wet them; instead, use a dry towel to rub them vigorously in the colander. The skins will break down, fall off and drop through the holes of the colander, making the peeled hazelnuts easier to pick out and then store. Discard the skins.

SALT—I prefer to use fine sea salt in baking (unless I am sprinkling flaked sea salt on top of something like chocolate bark). Fine salt dissolves into batter or dough easily, whether it is sea salt or regular fine salt (which you can use if you prefer). Salt in baking is there for the same reason as it is cooking: to heighten flavour. You can cut out or reduce the salt in any of my baking recipes without compromising how the recipe will turn out (except in recipes with yeast where salt slows the fermentation, allowing for better flavour to develop), but you may have to adjust to a taste change, as you would if you reduced the salt in savoury cooking.

SPICES—Spices are another key holiday baking ingredient. Store them in an airtight container in a cool, dark place for up to 1 year. After that, they will still be edible but their flavour may have faded. Do not refrigerate your spices—they will lose their flavour faster and can pick up "fridge taste." Cinnamon is a holiday classic, with the supporting spices of ginger, nutmeg, cloves and allspice often blended with it to give desserts a truly festive aroma and flavour. Cardamom is an Olson family staple

at Christmastime, used in Icelandic recipes like the Vínarterta Linzer Cookies (page 216). I normally use pre-ground spices for baking because that fine a grind is hard to achieve at home with a coffee grinder.

VANILLA AND OTHER FLAVOURINGS—I'm such a vanilla fan that I will not skimp when it comes to this flavouring. I call for whole vanilla bean in recipes when using heat because taking the time to extract the flavour from the bean makes for a more aromatic and intensely vanilla-flavoured dessert. I use vanilla bean paste, which already has the flavours extracted from the seeds, when I want the flecks of vanilla seeds in the paste to add flair to my baked goodies. When the seeds won't be seen, or if you can't find vanilla bean paste, vanilla extract in the same measure works fine. Be sure to buy pure vanilla extract, as it makes such a difference to the quality of your baked goods. If you are using vanilla bean paste or extract in place of a whole vanilla bean, 1 Tbsp (15 mL) equals the flavour from one bean.

Some flavourings, such as peppermint and almond extracts, can also be purchased in natural or artificial form, and I stick to natural there as well. Others, such as rum and coconut, are only available as artificial extracts. I *do* use rum extract when I want to add an eggnog flavour to a recipe without actually adding rum itself. Most natural extracts are sold in a dark glass bottle, and can be stored for a year or more in a cool, dark place.

SEASONAL PASTRIES AND SWEET BREADS

HOLIDAY BAKING IS more than just cute cookies and grand desserts. Breads, muffins, coffee cakes and other treats wiggle themselves into the holiday season (and, well, any time of the year) quite easily. It's my habit to tackle this style of baking in the morning, not just because many of these items are "breakfast-y," but because taking that little bit of time to bake first thing is satisfying and fills the house with the aroma of baked goods, which sets a good tone for the rest of the day.

Opposite: Kouign Amann (page 184)

> "Healthy" muffins are sometimes misidentified as being heavy, dense or bland, but those words won't pop into your mind when you bite into one of these moist, tender and tasty gems. They're naturally sweet with the banana and tart with the cranberries, and they smell like banana bread when they bake—which is a real treat around the holidays or afterward.

BANANA CRANBERRY VIRTUOUS MUFFINS

MAKES 12 MUFFINS • PREP: 10 MINUTES • COOK: 25 MINUTES

1. Preheat the oven to 350°F (180°C) and grease a 12-cup muffin pan or line the cups with foil liners.

2. Place the mashed bananas in a large mixing bowl and whisk in the yogurt, sugar, oil, egg, egg white and vanilla. Add the flour, oats, baking powder and cinnamon and stir until combined. Stir in the cranberries.

3. Scoop the batter into the muffin cups and sprinkle the tops with a few oats.

4. Bake for about 25 minutes, until a skewer inserted in the centre of a muffin comes out clean. Cool in the pan on a wire rack.

MAKE AHEAD

You can store baked muffins in an air-tight container at room temperature for 3 days. Or freeze them, well wrapped, in a resealable bag or an airtight container for up to 3 months. Thaw them at room temperature until soft.

1 ½ cups (225 g) mashed ripe bananas (about 3 large)
⅔ cup (160 mL) plain Greek yogurt (non-fat is OK)
⅓ cup (70 g) coconut palm sugar
¼ cup (60 mL) vegetable oil
1 large egg
1 large egg white
2 tsp pure vanilla extract
1 ½ cups (225 g) whole wheat flour
½ cup (50 g) regular rolled oats (not instant), plus extra for sprinkling
2 tsp baking powder
½ tsp ground cinnamon
1 cup (110 g) fresh or frozen, thawed, cranberries

ADD SPARKLE
Turn these into more decadent muffins by stirring in ½ cup (85 g) of chocolate chips and ½ cup (50 g) of walnut or pecan pieces. Santa might even prefer these to the usual cookies with his midnight glass of milk!

This moist lemon cake is lighter than a pound cake, and with its buttery crumble topping, it has a dressy feel that suits the holidays. I love a slice with a cup of tea when I'm seeking a quiet moment in the busy-ness of the season.

LEMON CRUMBLE LOAF CAKE

MAKES ONE 9 × 5-INCH (2 L) LOAF   •   SERVES 16   •   PREP: 20 MINUTES   •
COOK: 70 MINUTES

1. Preheat the oven to 325°F (160°C). Grease a 9 × 5-inch (2 L) loaf pan and line the bottom and sides with parchment paper.

2. For the crumble, stir the flour, sugar, lemon zest, baking powder and salt together. Add the melted butter and stir with a fork until the mixture is rough and crumbly (it will be soft). Set aside.

3. For the cake, sift the flour, sugar, baking powder and salt into a large mixing bowl if using electric beaters, or into the bowl of a stand mixer fitted with the paddle attachment. Add the butter and lemon zest and beat on low speed until large pieces of butter are no longer visible.

4. In a bowl, whisk the sour cream, eggs, egg yolk and vanilla together. Add all at once to the flour mixture and beat on low speed until the batter is moistened. Increase the speed to medium, mixing until the batter is smooth, about 30 seconds (the batter will be thick). Stir in the raspberries, blueberries or chopped cranberries (if left whole, the cranberries float to the top of the cake!) (if using). Scrape the batter into the prepared pan, level the top and sprinkle with the crumble.

5. Bake for 60 to 70 minutes, until a skewer inserted in the centre comes out clean. Cool the loaf cake in the pan on a rack for 20 minutes, then turn out and let cool completely on a wire rack.

MAKE AHEAD
You can store the loaf, well wrapped or in an airtight container, for up to 4 days at room temperature, or freeze it for up to 3 months. Thaw at room temperature before serving.

CRUMBLE
¾ cup (110 g) all-purpose flour
⅓ cup (70 g) granulated sugar
1 Tbsp (15 mL) finely grated lemon zest
¼ tsp baking powder
Pinch of fine sea salt
¼ cup (60 g) unsalted butter, melted

CAKE
2 cups (300 g) all-purpose flour
¾ cup (150 g) granulated sugar
2 tsp baking powder
½ tsp fine sea salt
½ cup (115 g) unsalted butter, at room temperature and cut into pieces
1 Tbsp (15 mL) finely grated lemon zest
⅔ cup (160 mL) sour cream
2 large eggs
1 large egg yolk
2 tsp pure vanilla extract
1 cup (250 mL) fresh raspberries, blueberries or chopped cranberries (optional)

ADD SPARKLE
This loaf can also be served as a plated dessert. To finish a holiday meal, serve slices of it with a spoonful of Festive Red Berry Compote (page 320) or the Lemon Curd from the Lemon Meringue Bûche de Noël (page 271) on the side.

A buckle is a fruit-laden coffee cake, with a fruit layer sandwiched between cake layers, nestled under a crumble to protect the fruit from drying out. It is pretty enough to double as a casual dessert.

RED BERRY BREAKFAST BUCKLE

MAKES ONE 9-INCH (23 CM) BUCKLE • SERVES 12 TO 16 • PREP: 35 MINUTES • COOK: 50 MINUTES

1. Preheat the oven to 350°F (180°C). Grease and line the bottom and sides of a 9-inch (23 cm) springform pan with parchment paper.

2. Sift the flour, sugar, baking powder and salt into a large mixing bowl if using electric beaters, or into the bowl of a stand mixer fitted with the paddle attachment. Add the butter and mix on medium-low speed until no large pieces of it are visible.

3. In a separate bowl, whisk the buttermilk, egg and vanilla together. Add all at once to the flour mixture and mix on medium-low speed until the batter is smooth, about 1 minute (it will be dense).

4. Dollop two-thirds of the batter into the prepared pan. Lightly dust your fingertips with flour and press the batter into an even layer to cover the bottom of the pan. Spoon the cooled fruit compote over the batter, and then spoon small dollops of the remaining batter overtop (the fruit will not be completely covered).

5. Sprinkle the crumble topping over the buckle and bake for about 50 minutes, until a skewer inserted in the centre comes out clean of crumbs.

6. Cool the buckle in its pan on a wire rack. Release the sides of the springform pan and slide the cake off the base onto a platter, peeling away and discarding the parchment. Dust with icing sugar before serving.

MAKE AHEAD

You can store the baked cake, well wrapped, at room temperature or in an airtight container in the fridge for up to 4 days. Or freeze it, well wrapped, for up to 3 months. Thaw at room temperature for about 2 hours before serving. The crumble topping may have lost its crunch, but it will taste just as delicious as when freshly baked.

2 cups (300 g) all-purpose flour
¾ cup (150 g) granulated sugar
2 tsp baking powder
¼ tsp fine sea salt
6 Tbsp (90 g) unsalted butter, at room temperature and cut into pieces
¾ cup (175 mL) buttermilk
1 large egg
1 ½ tsp pure vanilla extract
1 recipe Festive Red Berry Compote (page 320)
1 recipe crumble topping (from Lemon Crumble Loaf Cake, page 172), made with orange instead of lemon zest
Icing sugar, for dusting

ADD SPARKLE

Serve slices of this cake with a little dollop of sweetened whipped cream,
or a scoop of vanilla ice cream sprinkled with a pinch of cinnamon or nutmeg.

BEYOND THE HOLIDAYS

A blue fruit version of this buckle is just as tasty as the festive red one. Replace the
raspberries and cranberries with blueberries and blackberries when making the compote.

Scones are one of my favourite foods to bake all year, not just at holiday time, but the combination of blueberries and white chocolate has somehow always felt festive to me.

BLUEBERRY WHITE CHOCOLATE SCONES

MAKES TEN 3-INCH (7.5 CM) SCONES • PREP: 15 MINUTES • COOK: 16 MINUTES

1. Preheat the oven to 400°F (200°C) and line a baking tray with parchment paper.

2. Sift the flour, icing sugar, baking powder and salt into a large mixing bowl. Add the butter and, using a pastry cutter, 2 butter knives or your fingertips, work it in until large pieces are no longer visible.

3. Scoop up small handfuls of dough and flatten the butter pieces by rubbing them between your palms—do this 6 to 8 times (to build in flakiness).

4. Whisk the milk with the egg yolk (reserve the white) and vanilla bean paste and add all at once to the flour mixture. Stir just until the liquid no longer drips, but the dough has not come together fully.

5. Turn out the dough onto a clean work surface and flatten it a bit with your hands.

6. Sprinkle any dry crumbles and roughly one-third of the chocolate chips and blueberries on top.

7. Fold the dough in half and flatten again, repeating with the crumbs that fall away and half of the remaining chocolate chips and berries. Repeat again with the remaining chocolate chips and berries and then flatten the dough into a disc about 1 inch (2.5 cm) thick.

Recipe continues ▶

MAKE AHEAD

If making these ahead, here are 2 great options:

• Make the dough the day before, cut out the scones and chill overnight, well wrapped. Bake them straight from the fridge.

• Or, freeze the unbaked scones, in an airtight container, for up to 3 months. Thaw on a baking tray for 20 to 30 minutes, then bake as directed above.

2 ¼ cups (335 g) all-purpose flour
3 Tbsp (25 g) icing sugar
2 tsp baking powder
¼ tsp fine sea salt
½ cup (115 g) cold unsalted butter, cut into pieces
½ cup (125 mL) cold 2% milk
1 large egg, separated
1 tsp vanilla bean paste
½ cup (85 g) white chocolate chips
½ cup (80 g) dried blueberries
Granulated, turbinado or sanding sugar, for sprinkling

ADD SPARKLE
A little icing adds a sweet touch to these scones. Just whisk 1 cup (130 g) of icing sugar with 2 Tbsp (30 mL) of milk and drizzle with a fork over the cooled scones. Let set for 30 minutes before serving.

8. Use a 3-inch (7.5 cm) round cutter to cut out scones. Gather together the leftover scraps of dough, reshape them into a disc about 1 inch (2.5 cm) thick and repeat (you will likely only have to re-roll once).

9. Place the scones on the prepared baking tray, 2 inches (5 cm) apart. Brush the tops with the reserved egg white, lightly whisked, and sprinkle with sugar.

10. Bake for about 16 minutes, until they have browned evenly on the bottom and lightly on top. Transfer the scones to a wire rack to cool.

11. Serve the scones warm or at room temperature on the day they are baked.

Step 6

Step 7

Step 8

Step 9

> Making homemade Danishes is a labour of love and a real time commitment. While this recipe does take a little time (any yeast dough does), the lovely wreath has all the buttery softness of a traditional Danish with just a fraction of the effort required to make and assemble it.

RASPBERRY JAM DANISH WREATH

SERVES 12 • PREP: 25 MINUTES, PLUS RESTING •
COOK: 40 MINUTES, PLUS SETTING

MAKE AHEAD

You can prepare the wreath up to step 8 the day before baking and then chill in its pan until ready to bake (see note below). Alternatively, freeze in its pan for up to 3 months and thaw overnight in the fridge before letting it rise on the counter for about 2 hours before baking.

Store the baked wreath, well wrapped, for 2 to 3 days at room temperature. Do not refrigerate. You can also freeze the baked wreath, but once thawed it will likely be a little softer than when it was freshly baked.

DOUGH
3 ½ cups (525 g) all-purpose flour
¼ cup (50 g) granulated sugar
1 pkg (2 ¼ tsp/8 g) instant dry yeast
1 tsp fine sea salt
¼ cup (60 g) unsalted butter
1 cup (250 mL) 2% milk
1 large egg, at room temperature

FILLING AND ASSEMBLY
½ cup (115 g) unsalted butter, at room temperature
1 cup (250 mL) raspberry jam
1 tsp pure vanilla extract
1 tsp ground cinnamon
1 cup (170 g) frozen raspberries (still frozen)
1 cup (130 g) icing sugar, sifted
2 Tbsp (30 mL) 2% milk

1. For the dough, stir the flour, sugar, yeast and salt together in a mixing bowl, if mixing by hand, or in the bowl of a stand mixer fitted with the hook attachment. Place the butter in a small saucepan over medium heat to melt and pour the milk over it, letting it warm up to around 115°F (46°C), just above body temperature.

2. Pour the liquid over the flour mixture, add the egg and mix on low speed until the dough comes together. Increase the speed by 1 level and knead until the dough springs back when touched, about 4 minutes. (If mixing by hand, stir the dough with a wooden spoon until it becomes too difficult and then turn it out onto the counter to knead by hand for 6 minutes or until elastic, adding as little extra flour as possible as you go.)

Recipe continues ▶

❧

HELPFUL HINT
I love the smell of yeast dough and raspberries as this recipe bakes, and it seems a shame to deprive my guests of this aroma. I make and assemble the wreath the day before and chill it, loosely covered, overnight. In the morning I put it right from the fridge into a cold oven, and turn on the oven to 350°F (180°C). By the time the oven reaches full temperature, the dough has risen to its full size and I then set the oven timer for 40 minutes—so the wreath is fresh from the oven when my brunch guests arrive.

BEYOND THE HOLIDAYS
You can also use this recipe to make jam-filled sticky buns. Once you've rolled up the dough, cut it into 12 portions, arrange them in a 9 × 13-inch (22.5 × 32.5 cm) baking pan and then proof and bake as for the wreath.

3. Place the dough in an ungreased bowl, cover with plastic wrap and let rise on the counter until doubled in size, about 90 minutes.

4. For the filling, beat the butter by hand to soften it and then beat in the raspberry jam, vanilla and cinnamon.

5. Generously grease a 12-inch (30 cm) ovenproof skillet, or a 10-inch (25 cm) or 12-inch (30 cm) round baking pan. Turn the risen dough out onto a lightly floured surface and roll it into a rectangle about 20 × 10 inches (50 × 25 cm).

6. Spread the raspberry filling evenly over the dough and sprinkle the frozen raspberries on top. Starting at a long side, roll up the dough.

7. Cut the roll in half widthwise, and then cut each piece in half lengthwise so you have 4 pieces, with the jam now exposed.

8. Hold the first piece by the 2 short ends and twist them in opposite directions. Lay the twisted dough in the pan, with 1 end in the centre. Wrap the dough around the centre end in a spiral, working your way from the centre out toward the sides of the pan. Repeat with the 3 remaining pieces of dough, gradually enlarging the spiral so that it fills the pan—any spaces will fill in as the dough rises. Cover the pan with a tea towel and let the dough rise again at room temperature until almost doubled, 45 minutes.

9. Preheat the oven to 350°F (180°C). Uncover the pan and bake until the wreath is an even golden brown, about 40 minutes. Let cool completely in the pan on a wire rack before glazing.

10. Whisk the icing sugar and milk together and drizzle over the wreath. Let the glaze set for about 1 hour before serving. Serve the wreath either directly from the pan or transfer it to a cutting board and slice it into wedges to serve.

Step 6

Step 7

Step 8

A classic Italian Christmas treat, panettone is a light yeasted bread with a touch of dried fruit and a sweet cake-y character, and it looks grand on the table. If you have leftovers, use fresh panettone to make ham sandwiches or stale panettone to bake delicious Panettone Bread Puddings (page 308).

PANETTONE

MAKES ONE 9-INCH (23 CM) PANETTONE · SERVES 24 ·
PREP: 15 MINUTES, PLUS RESTING · COOK: 55 MINUTES

1. Grease a 9-inch (23 cm) springform pan and line the sides of the pan with parchment that comes up at least 7 inches (18 cm). Alternatively, you can grease a Bundt pan, angel food pan or other tall, high-sided pan of similar size.

2. Stir the raisins and candied peel in a bowl with the rum and citrus zests. Set aside.

3. Place the butter in a saucepan over medium heat to melt and then pour in the milk, heating until the milk is around 115°F (46°C), just above body temperature. Set aside.

4. Place the flour, sugar, yeast, salt and nutmeg in a large mixing bowl, if mixing by hand, or in the bowl of a stand mixer fitted with the hook attachment. Pour in the warm milk, add the egg yolks and vanilla and rum extracts and mix by hand or on low speed until everything is combined.

5. Add the macerated raisins, peel and zest (including any liquid), increase the speed 1 level and continue to mix until the dough develops elasticity, about 5 minutes (it will look stretchy and be very soft). (If mixing by hand, continue to mix until it begins to develop resistance, about 7 minutes. It will be too soft to knead on the counter.)

6. Scrape the dough into the prepared pan, dust the top lightly with flour and cover with a clean tea towel, then top with a piece of plastic wrap and set aside to rise at room temperature for 2 hours, until it more than doubles in size.

7. Preheat the oven to 350°F (180°C). Brush the top of the panettone with the egg wash and bake for 45 to 55 minutes, until the top is a deep, even brown. Release the sides of the springform pan and slide the panettone off the base, peeling and discarding the parchment, and set it on a wire rack to cool completely before slicing.

MAKE AHEAD
You can store the baked panettone, well wrapped, at room temperature for up to 2 days. Or freeze it for up to 2 months. Thaw at room temperature for at least 3 hours before serving. Do not refrigerate.

1 cup (150 g) raisins
⅔ cup (100 g) diced Candied Orange Peel (page 318) or store-bought peel
2 Tbsp (30 mL) rum
Grated zest of 1 orange
Grated zest of 1 lemon
5 Tbsp (75 g) unsalted butter
1 ½ cups (375 mL) 2% milk
4 ½ cups (675 g) all-purpose flour
6 Tbsp (75 g) granulated sugar
1 Tbsp (10 g) instant dry yeast
½ tsp fine sea salt
½ tsp ground nutmeg
4 large egg yolks
2 tsp (10 mL) pure vanilla extract
1 tsp (5 mL) rum extract
1 egg whisked with 2 Tbsp (30 mL) cold water, for egg wash

HELPFUL HINT
In the winter, the dry heat of our homes can affect how long it takes for a yeast dough to rise. Keep your rising dough away from heating vents, the top of the fridge and other traditional places you might have been told to coax rising from your dough. It'll get there without the extra heat, just give it time and keep it covered.

BEYOND THE HOLIDAYS
Instead of making a large holiday panettone, divide the recipe between 2 greased 9 x 5-inch (2 L) loaf pans and bake for 40 minutes. Cut the loaves into slices for sandwiches and toast.

I fell in love with these pastries a few years back on a visit to Montreal, a city that is pastry heaven! This layered, buttery sweet pastry was created in Brittany, a region of France famous for its butter (*kouign amann* means "cake butter" in Breton). Imagine a croissant that is a little more like puff pastry, with a caramelized sugar crust and a soft sweet interior . . . Now get ready to bake! Like many classic French pastries, kouign amann take patience and adherence to timing—they're the boss, not you, but you get to take all of the credit when friends and family rave about them.

KOUIGN AMANN

MAKES 12 PASTRIES • PREP: 30 MINUTES, PLUS RESTING AND CHILLING • COOK: 35 MINUTES

1. For the dough, combine the flour, sugar, yeast and salt in a large mixing bowl, if mixing by hand, or in a stand mixer fitted with the hook attachment. Add the water and oil and stir together on low speed until combined. Increase the speed 1 level and mix until the dough feels smooth and elastic, about 4 minutes. (If mixing by hand, stir the dough with a wooden spoon until it becomes too difficult, and then turn it out onto a work surface once combined and knead until elastic, about 6 minutes. The dough should come off the bottom and sides of the bowl but will be relatively soft.)

2. Place the dough in an ungreased bowl, cover the bowl with plastic wrap and let rise for 1 hour, until doubled in size. Punch the dough down, shape it into a 10-inch (25 cm) square (dust your hands with flour to prevent sticking), wrap in plastic and chill for at least 1 hour, or up to 8 hours.

3. For the butter, beat the butter and 2 Tbsp (25 g) of the sugar together. Line the bottom and sides of a 9 × 5-inch (2 L) loaf pan with plastic wrap and press the butter into the bottom in an even layer. Wrap well and chill for at least 1 hour.

4. If preparing the dough and butter more than 1 hour ahead, pull both out from the fridge 30 minutes before rolling. Turn the dough out onto a lightly floured surface. Place the rectangle of butter on top of the dough and fold the dough over so the sheet of butter is hidden. Press out any air pockets and pinch the dough, just a little, to enclose the butter.

5. Roll out the dough to a rectangle 12 × 18 inches (30 × 45 cm), just under ½ inch (1 cm) thick. Bring the short sides together so that they meet in the centre and then fold the dough in half like a book. Rotate the dough 90 degrees and repeat, this time folding the dough into thirds. Wrap the dough in plastic wrap and chill for 1 hour.

MAKE AHEAD

I don't recommend baking these ahead of time, since they are best enjoyed the day they are baked. They are tastiest once cool, when the caramelized sugar on the surface has had time to set and become crunchy. Timing is key when rolling, folding and letting your kouign amann rise. If you do want to make these ahead of time to freeze and bake later, make the dough, do the first 2 folds and then freeze, well wrapped, for up to 3 months. Thaw the dough overnight in the fridge before continuing with the folds that use sugar. (If you were to freeze the assembled kouign amann, the sugar would liquefy once thawed and you would end up with sticky pastries that are difficult to handle.)

DOUGH

2 ½ cups (375 g) all-purpose flour

2 Tbsp (25 g) granulated sugar

1 pkg (2 ¼ tsp/8 g) instant dry yeast

1 tsp fine sea salt

1 cup (250 mL) cool water

2 Tbsp (30 mL) vegetable oil

BUTTER AND ASSEMBLY

1 cup (225 g) unsalted butter, at room temperature

½ cup (100 g) granulated sugar, divided

Step 8

Step 9

Step 10

6. Lightly dust a work surface with ¼ cup (50 g) of the sugar and roll out the dough to a rectangle 12 × 18 inches (30 × 45 cm), just under ½ inch (1 cm) thick. Sprinkle the top of the dough with the remaining 2 Tbsp (25 g) of sugar and fold it in thirds.

7. Rotate the dough 90 degrees and repeat the rolling and folding (but not adding more sugar at this point). Wrap and chill the dough for exactly 20 minutes (any longer, the sugar will dissolve).

8. Grease a 12-cup muffin pan and set aside. Unwrap the dough and roll it (no additional flour or sugar will be needed) into a rectangle 16 × 12 inches (40 × 30 cm) and just over ¼ inch (0.5 cm) thick.

9. Trim away any rough edges and cut the dough into twelve 4-inch (10 cm) squares.

10. Bring the corners of each square into the centre, pinch them together and press down gently. Press each pastry into a muffin cup and cover the pan with a tea towel, letting the dough rise for 1 hour.

11. Preheat the oven to 350°F (180°C). Place the muffin pan on a parchment-lined baking tray and bake for 30 to 35 minutes, until the kouign amann are a rich golden brown. Carefully turn them out of the pan (they will be sticky and hot) onto a wire rack to cool completely.

Photo on page 168

HELPFUL HINTS

When you are rolling and folding the kouign amann in sugar for the final time, you need to work quickly—the more you handle the dough, the more it will warm up and then liquefy the sugar. Once you get the pastries into the pan, the pressure is off.

There are times when investing in top-quality butter really counts, and this is one of them (shortbread cookies are another). Most butter in Canada has a fat content of 80%, but premium butter has 82% (check the label). That extra 2% makes a big difference in a pastry where butter is important for flavour and texture.

HOLIDAY COOKIES

MY EARLIEST CHRISTMAS memories are of making cookies with my grandmother, and it was from her that I inherited my love of baking. These days, I am quite content to spend hours in the kitchen, whipping up batters, baking, filling and decorating away the days—especially around the holidays. But we all have busy schedules, so here's an assortment of cookie recipes, most of which can be made ahead if needed.

Opposite: Vanilla Bean Sugar Cut-Out Cookies (page 195)

Holiday Cookie Planning

I love getting ahead on my holiday cookie baking, but somehow cookies take up an awful lot of freezer space and they don't always come out of the freezer tasting as delicious as when they went in. Here are my suggestions for making the most of your time, your freezer space and your cookies.

MAKE THE DOUGH AHEAD. Most of the work (and the resulting clean-up) happens when you make the cookie dough. And unbaked dough takes up far less room in the freezer than baked cookies do. Here are some quick tips for freezing sweet and savoury cookies.

- *Drop cookie doughs* (like Snappy Gingersnaps, page 202, and Coconut Chocolate Oatmeal Chews, page 205): shape into balls, chill for 1 hour (so the individual cookies won't stick together) and freeze in resealable bags.
- *Rolled cookie doughs* (like Vanilla Bean Sugar Cut-Out Cookies, page 195): shape into discs, wrap well and freeze as is.
- *Sliced cookies* (like Cheddar and Chive Shortbreads, page 42): shape into a roll, wrap well and freeze as is.

LABEL EVERYTHING. Use sticky labels or masking tape and a permanent marker to label every package. Note the name of the cookies and the date you made the dough. Add any special instructions, plus the oven temperature and bake time.

ORGANIZE BY WEEK. As holiday season approaches, you tend to need more cookies. Pack a selection of cookie doughs into plastic containers, one for each week in December. Then all you have to do is pull out a container, thaw it overnight in the fridge, and slice and bake as you go. Each week, you'll fill the house with the delicious smell of baking cookies, but all the work will have happened a month ago!

FREEZE BAKED COOKIES (ONLY IF YOU MUST). As a general rule, baked cookies with less sugar, such as shortbread, freeze far better than cookies with a lot of sugar. Once thawed, the sugar in baked cookies wants to liquefy, so they may become softer or stickier than when they were first baked (popping them back in the oven isn't a predictable fix—and hence not a timesaver).

HOST A COOKIE EXCHANGE. Read all of my tips on page 191 for planning and throwing a fun cookie exchange party.

Hosting a Cookie Exchange

*I*n addition to helping you get ahead on your baking, and increasing your cookie selection, hosting a holiday cookie exchange is a great way to visit with family, friends and neighbours.

PLAN THE COOKIE MENU. When you invite your guests, ask them to bring two different cookies: a recipe that you've planned and a second that they choose, perhaps a family favourite. (If you invite more than ten people, each guest only needs to bring one type of cookie.)

BRIEF YOUR GUESTS. Ask each person to bake twelve cookies per guest plus some extras to sample on party day. Ask them to bring a label for their cookie, and to list the ingredients so other guests are aware of potential allergens and can choose cookies that meet their dietary preferences. If you know there are nut allergies in your group, you can simply avoid recipes with nuts.

PREPARE FOR THE EXCHANGE. Get baking! This is a case where my note about freezing baked cookies qualifies as an "if you must" scenario. Whether a guest or the host, you may have to bake and freeze a few cookie batches in order to have them ready for the party. Another option is to invite guests to bring a few cookie doughs along with their baking instructions, so everyone can exchange and then store the dough in the freezer and bake when ready.

PREPARE FOR THE PARTY. Guests will likely bring their own cookies in tins which can be re-used, but ask them to bring extras (or have a few on hand yourself) in cases sizes and quantities don't fit. Or you can provide festively decorated jars or baskets. (Either way, keep a few extra tins ready in case someone forgets to bring one or in case you run out of space for cookies!) Provide tongs to pick up the cookies.

PROVIDE DRINKS AND SNACKS! Before you dive into the cookie buffet, offer some treats to guests. In addition to beer and wine, you can also offer Virtuously Rich Hot Chocolate (page 15) with Snowflake Marshmallows (page 250—maybe with a splash of Homemade Irish Cream Liqueur, page 80), Crème Brûlée Eggnog (page 108), Mulled Apple Cider (page 16) or Mulled Red Wine (page 16). And don't forget about the savouries! Put out a cheese board, a crudité platter with dips (page 48) or even a few savoury squares (pages 55 to 58) to nibble on.

LET THE EXCHANGE BEGIN. Give guests time to walk around the cookie buffet table and load up their tins! Naturally, everyone should be fair and take equal amounts of each cookie, but arranging the plates and platters so they are all within easy reach will make that goal achievable. Tongs will keep the exchange food-safe and the cookies intact.

DECORATE AND PLAY. If you are making your cookie exchange a truly social affair, plan an hour of cookie decorating. Put on inspiring music, have some baked cut-out cookies and piping bags of royal icing (page 196) on hand, and let everyone get silly and decorate a few gems. You will definitely spend more time laughing than actually decorating—I speak from experience!—and isn't that the point of getting together with friends and family?

COOKIES IN A JAR

> These adorable cookie recipes are easy to assemble and make fantastic host gifts. Fill the jars with everything you need to make homemade cookies, and the recipient can bake them whenever it is convenient. I've included three recipes that vary in colour, taste and texture, so giving the full set is even more generous! You'll need a 4-cup (1 L) mason jar for each recipe.

CANDY CANE SUGAR

MAKES 2 TO 3 DOZEN COOKIES • PREP: 5 MINUTES

½ vanilla bean
1 cup (200 g) granulated sugar
pink food colouring gel (optional)
2 cups (300 g) all-purpose flour
½ tsp baking soda
½ tsp cream of tartar
¼ tsp fine sea salt
½ cup (125 mL) crushed candy canes

1. Have ready a 4-cup (1 L) mason jar with a sealable lid. With a paring knife, split the vanilla bean open and scrape out the seeds into a small bowl. Add the sugar to the seeds and rub together to infuse the flavour. Add the pink food colouring gel (if using) and mix through using a toothpick.

2. Sift the flour, baking soda, cream of tartar and salt on top of the sugar and whisk to combine. Use a canning funnel to pour half of the sugar then half of the flour into the mason jar.

3. Repeat the layers of sugar and flour, then top with crushed candy canes. Seal the jar and include a tag with the following baking instructions:

   Stir ¾ cup (175 g) of unsalted butter, melted, and 1 egg in a mixing bowl. Stir in the entire contents of the jar until blended. Drop spoon-fuls of the batter onto 2 parchment-lined baking trays, chill for 30 minutes and bake for 10 to 12 minutes at 350°F (180°C), until lightly browned at the edges. Cool on the tray and dive in!

HOLIDAY OATMEAL

MAKES 2 DOZEN COOKIES • PREP: 5 MINUTES

1. Have ready a 4-cup (1 L) mason jar with a sealable lid. Stir together the flour, both sugars, cinnamon, ginger and baking soda. Use a canning funnel to pour the mixture into the jar. Place the chocolate chips in a layer on top, followed by the cranberries and then the oats.

2. Seal the jar and include a tag with the following baking instructions:

   Pour this mix into a large bowl and stir in ½ cup (115 g) of unsalted butter, melted, and 1 egg until the mixture comes together. Drop spoonfuls of the batter onto 2 parchment-lined baking trays and bake at 375°F (190°C) for about 10 minutes until lightly browned. Enjoy warm with a glass of cold milk.

¾ cup (110 g) all-purpose flour
½ cup (100 g) granulated sugar
½ cup (100 g) packed dark brown sugar
½ tsp ground cinnamon
½ tsp ground ginger
¼ tsp baking soda
⅔ cup (115 g) chocolate chips
⅔ cup (85 g) dried cranberries
1 ¼ cups (125 g) regular rolled oats (not instant)

CHOCOLATE TOFFEE

MAKES 2 DOZEN COOKIES • PREP: 5 MINUTES

1. Have ready a 4-cup (1 L) mason jar with a sealable lid. Sift the flour, baking soda and salt together and spoon this mixture into the mason jar. Sift the cocoa powder and spoon it on top. In individual layers, add the brown sugar, then the granulated sugar, Skor bits and walnut (or pecan) pieces. Place a piece of parchment paper over the walnut pieces and spoon the chopped chocolate on top.

2. Seal the jar and include a tag with the following baking instructions:

   Melt the chocolate with 6 Tbsp (90 g) of unsalted butter and stir in the contents of the jar along with 2 eggs until combined. Drop spoonfuls of the batter onto 2 parchment-lined baking trays and bake at 350°F (180°C) for 11 to 12 minutes, until the cookies lose their shine. Cool on the trays before jumping in!

1 cup (150 g) all-purpose flour
½ tsp baking soda
¼ tsp fine sea salt
⅓ cup (40 g) cocoa powder (Dutch process or conventional)
¾ cup (150 g) packed light brown sugar
¼ cup (50 g) granulated sugar
¾ cup (120 g) Skor toffee bits
¾ cup (75 g) walnut or pecan pieces
8 oz (225 g) dark couverture/baking chocolate

This classic cut-out cookie uses the same dough as the Eggnog Buttercream Sandwich Cookies, but with vanilla bean paste in place of the eggnog flavours of rum and nutmeg. These cookies hold their shape well when baked, so are ideal for cutting out trees, stockings, wreaths and other detailed shapes.

VANILLA BEAN SUGAR CUT-OUT COOKIES

MAKES 3 TO 4 DOZEN COOKIES • PREP: 75 MINUTES (INCLUDING DECORATING), PLUS CHILLING • COOK: 14 MINUTES, PLUS SETTING AND AIR-DRYING

MAKE AHEAD

You can store these baked cookies, iced or plain, for 10 days in an airtight container at room temperature. They actually will keep for longer (about 1 month), if they are completely covered with royal icing. You can freeze undecorated baked cookies for up to 3 months. (Do not freeze decorated cookies as the icing may crack.) Thaw the cookies to room temperature before decorating.

1 cup (225 g) unsalted butter, cut into pieces and at room temperature
1 cup (130 g) icing sugar, sifted
2 large egg yolks
2 tsp vanilla bean paste
2 ½ cups (375 g) all-purpose flour
½ tsp fine sea salt
1 recipe Royal Icing (page 196)
Decorator's or sanding sugar, dragées and other edible décor, for decorating

1. Using electric beaters or a stand mixer fitted with the paddle attachment, beat the butter until smooth. Add the icing sugar. Starting on low speed, work in the sugar, and then increase the speed to medium-high and beat until fluffy, about 2 minutes.

2. Beat in the egg yolks and vanilla. Add the flour and salt and beat just until the dough comes together. Shape the dough into 2 discs, wrap in plastic and chill for at least 2 hours.

3. Preheat the oven to 325°F (160°C) and line 2 baking trays with parchment paper.

4. On a lightly floured surface, knead 1 disc of dough a little to soften it and then roll it out to just under ¼ inch (0.5 cm) thick.

5. Use a 2- or 3-inch (5 or 7.5 cm) cookie cutter to cut out cookies. Arrange on the baking trays, 1 inch (2.5 cm) apart. Repeat with the second disc of dough, re-rolling any scraps as needed.

6. Bake the cookies for 12 to 14 minutes until slightly golden at the edges. Transfer to a wire rack to cool.

7. Prepare the royal icing for flooding or piping (page 196). Decorate the cookies as you wish, sprinkling with decorator's or sanding sugar or adding dragées or other edible décor. Allow 4 to 6 hours for the icing to dry.

Photo on page 190

Here is a nice twist on the holiday classic, decorated gingerbread cookies. Speculoos are a notably buttery and nicely spiced cookie common in the Netherlands and Belgium. The subtle differences between a traditional North American–style gingerbread and this recipe are the use of honey in place of molasses and the addition of a little cardamom, ground anise and black pepper to the spice mix in place of ginger.

SPECULOOS CUT-OUT COOKIES

MAKES 4 TO 6 DOZEN COOKIES · PREP: 75 MINUTES (INCLUDING DECORATING), PLUS CHILLING · COOK: 15 MINUTES, PLUS SETTING AND AIR-DRYING

MAKE AHEAD

You can store these baked cookies, iced or plain, for 10 days in an airtight container at room temperature. They actually will keep for longer (about 1 month) if they are completely covered with royal icing. You can freeze undecorated baked cookies for up to 3 months. (Do not freeze decorated cookies as the icing may crack.) Thaw the cookies to room temperature before decorating.

SPECULOOS COOKIE DOUGH

½ cup (115 g) unsalted butter, at room temperature
½ cup (100 g) packed dark brown sugar
½ cup (150 g) honey
1 large egg, at room temperature
2 ½ cups (375 g) all-purpose flour
2 tsp ground cinnamon
½ tsp ground nutmeg
½ tsp ground cloves
½ tsp ground cardamom
½ tsp ground anise
½ tsp baking soda
½ tsp fine sea salt
¼ tsp black pepper

ROYAL ICING

4 cups (520 g) icing sugar, sifted
3 Tbsp (14 g) meringue powder
6 Tbsp (90 mL) warm water
Food colour paste (optional)
Coloured sugars and dragées, for décor

1. For the cookies, beat the butter, brown sugar and honey together using electric beaters, or in a stand mixer fitted with the paddle attachment on medium speed, or by hand, until smooth. Beat in the egg.

2. Sift the flour, cinnamon, nutmeg, cloves, cardamom, anise, baking soda, salt and pepper into a separate bowl and add all at once to the butter mixture, stirring until evenly blended (the dough will be soft). Scrape this batter onto a piece of plastic wrap, wrap and chill for at least 2 hours, until set. The dough will still feel a little soft once chilled.

3. Preheat the oven to 325°F (160°C) and line 2 baking trays with parchment paper. Roll out the dough on a lightly floured surface to just under ¼ inch (0.5 cm) thick.

4. Use cookie cutters to cut out your desired shapes and sizes and transfer these to the baking trays, 1 inch (2.5 cm) apart.

5. Bake for 12 to 15 minutes, or until lightly browned at the edges. Transfer to a wire rack to cool completely before decorating.

6. For the royal icing, place the icing sugar, meringue powder and water in the bowl of a stand mixer fitted with the paddle attachment. Beat on low speed until the icing sugar is incorporated. Increase the speed to medium and beat until the icing comes together and is fluffy, about 5 minutes. Set aside some of the royal icing in a bowl with plastic wrap placed directly on the surface of the icing, at room temperature.

7. To make a "flood" style of icing that spreads over the surface of the cookie, add just a little more water until it spreads on its own but completely covers the cookie (thicker than glaze). To get the desired consistency, you can always add more water or icing sugar, as needed. Add food colour paste in small amounts, until you reach the colour intensity you want.

8. Spoon the "flood" style icing into a piping bag fitted with a small plain tip. Pipe an outline on the cookie and then fill it in with icing, or pipe dots and use a toothpick to swirl the colours. Allow 4 to 6 hours for the icing to dry. After drying, use the reserved royal icing to pipe additional details on top of the flooded layer, then sprinkle with coloured sugars or dragées. Allow to dry for an additional 4 hours.

Photo on page 287

HELPFUL HINT

Feel free to use a mix of cookie cutter shapes and sizes and even mix the variety of cookies on the same baking tray. If there is only 1 to 2 inches (2.5 to 5 cm) difference in size between them, they will all bake in the same time.

While this classic style of French butter cookie would normally be made with salted butter, I prefer to use unsalted butter and then add the salt myself (different brands of butter can have different amounts of salt). These short-bread cookies are barely sweet—really, it's all about the butter!

BRETON SEA SALT SHORTBREADS

MAKES 2 ½ DOZEN COOKIES · PREP: 15 MINUTES · COOK: 45 MINUTES

1. Preheat the oven to 300°F (150°C) and line the cups of mini-muffin pans with paper liners (petits fours size).

2. Using electric beaters or a stand mixer fitted with the paddle attachment, beat the butter and icing sugar on medium speed until smooth and light. Beat in 2 of the egg yolks. Add the flour, cornstarch and 1 tsp salt and mix on low speed until the dough comes together.

3. Use a small ice cream scoop or 2 teaspoons to drop the dough into the lined muffin pans. Use the bottom of a glass dipped in flour to gently press the dough flat. Whisk the remaining egg yolk with 1 Tbsp (15 mL) of cold water and brush the tops of the cookies. If you wish, sprinkle the cookies with a little flaked sea salt.

4. Bake for 35 to 45 minutes, until the tops are a rich golden brown. Let cool in the pans on a wire rack.

MAKE AHEAD
You can store baked shortbread in an airtight container at room temperature for up to 3 weeks. It also freezes wonderfully well because of its low sugar content (relative to other holiday cookies). You can make the dough ahead and freeze it in a resealable bag for up to 3 months. Thaw the dough for 2 hours at room temperature before spooning it into pans and baking. Or freeze baked shortbread in an airtight container for up to 3 months and thaw at room temperature.

1 cup (225 g) unsalted butter, at room temperature
⅔ cup (90 g) icing sugar, sifted
3 large egg yolks (1 for brushing cookies)
1 ½ cups (225 g) all-purpose flour
¼ cup (30 g) cornstarch
1 tsp fine sea salt
Flaked sea salt, for sprinkling (optional)

HELPFUL HINT

Shortbread improves in texture as it sits in the pan. The longer these cookies sit, the softer and more tender they get. However, keep them away from cookies with prominent flavours (such as chocolate, spices or citrus zest) as they will absorb the odours and flavours around them.

> If you have a cookie press sitting in the back of your cupboard, now is the time to pull it out! I use a piping bag fitted with a star tip to pipe my spritz cookies into wreath shapes, but this soft batter works just as well pushed through a cookie press.

CLASSIC SPRITZ COOKIES

MAKES ABOUT 3 DOZEN COOKIES • PREP: 10 MINUTES, PLUS RESTING •
COOK: 12 MINUTES

1. Preheat the oven to 375°F (190°C) and line 2 baking trays with parchment paper.

2. Using electric beaters or a stand mixer fitted with the paddle attachment, beat the butter and sugar together on medium-high speed until fluffy and light, about 2 minutes. Add ¼ cup (35 g) of the flour and beat on medium speed. Add the egg and vanilla and beat until smooth. Add the remaining flour and the salt and beat on medium-low speed until smooth.

3. Spoon the batter into a piping bag fitted with a large star tip. Pipe circles about 1 ½ inches (3.5 cm) across onto the baking trays, 1 inch (2.5 cm) apart. If you wish, sprinkle with a little decorator's or sanding sugar or other sprinkles. Chill the trays, uncovered, for at least 10 minutes (up to 1 hour) before baking to set the cookies' shape.

4. Bake for 10 to 12 minutes, until the cookies just begin to show signs of colour at the edges. Let cool on the tray on a wire rack.

MAKE AHEAD
You can bake these cookies up to 1 week ahead and keep them in an airtight container. You can also freeze the dough, well wrapped, for up to 3 months. Thaw at room temperature until fully softened then beat by hand before piping and baking. Like shortbread, these crisp cookies freeze well after baking. Pack them in an airtight container and freeze for up to 3 months. Thaw at room temperature before serving.

1 cup (225 g) unsalted butter, very soft
½ cup (100 g) granulated sugar
2 ¼ cups (335 g) all-purpose flour, divided
1 large egg, at room temperature
2 tsp vanilla bean paste or pure vanilla extract
¼ tsp fine sea salt
Decorator's or sanding sugar or sprinkles (optional)

HELPFUL HINTS

These cookies need a little extra heat to set their detailed shape. Use an oven thermometer (page 163) to check the temperature of your oven, and expect a little browning at the edges of these cookies. Adding that little bit of flour before you beat in the egg helps to prevent the batter from curdling. Try adding a touch of flour to other cake or cookie batters if they start to curdle when you add the eggs.

For a chocolate version of this cookie, replace ½ cup (75 g) of the flour with ⅓ cup (40 g) of sifted cocoa powder.

The "snappiness" in these cookies comes from the intense ginger flavour, the added kick of black pepper and the crisp snap they make when you bite into them. If you prefer a milder cookie, reduce the ginger to taste.

SNAPPY GINGERSNAPS

MAKES 5 DOZEN GINGERSNAPS • PREP: 10 MINUTES • COOK: 25 MINUTES

1. Preheat the oven to 325°F (160°C) and line 2 baking trays with parchment paper.

2. Whisk together the melted butter, demerara (or brown) sugar, molasses, egg and egg yolk in a large mixing bowl. In a separate bowl, stir the flour, ginger, baking soda, cinnamon, salt and pepper together. Add to the butter mixture and stir until blended.

3. Use a small ice cream scoop or 2 teaspoons to shape the dough into balls. Roll each cookie in granulated sugar to coat and place on the prepared baking trays, 1 ½ inches (3.5 cm) apart.

4. Bake for 20 to 25 minutes, until the cookies brown around the edges (they will puff up while baking but then collapse as they cool, developing a lovely crackled surface). Let cool on the trays on a wire rack.

MAKE AHEAD
You can bake gingersnaps up to 1 week ahead and keep them in an airtight container at room temperature or freeze the baked cookies, well wrapped, for up to 3 months. Thaw the cookies at room temperature before serving.

¾ cup (175 g) unsalted butter, melted and cooled to room temperature
1 ¼ cups (250 g) packed demerara or dark brown sugar
¼ cup (65 g) fancy molasses
1 large egg
1 large egg yolk
2 ¼ cups (335 g) all-purpose flour
2 Tbsp (18 g) ground ginger
2 tsp baking soda
1 tsp ground cinnamon
½ tsp fine sea salt
½ tsp black pepper
Granulated sugar, for rolling

> If you can't decide between a chocolate chip cookie, an oatmeal cookie or a brownie, this is the cookie for you!

CHOCOLATE COCONUT OATMEAL CHEWS

MAKES ABOUT 3 ½ DOZEN COOKIES · PREP: 10 MINUTES · COOK: 12 MINUTES

MAKE AHEAD

You can bake these chews up to 1 week ahead and keep them in an airtight container at room temperature. Or scoop and chill the dough on baking trays, then freeze the cookies in resealable bags for up to 3 months. To bake, let the frozen cookies thaw on a baking tray for 30 minutes before putting them in the oven. You can freeze the baked cookies, but they will lose their crunchy exterior a little once thawed.

½ cup (115 g) unsalted butter, at room temperature
1 cup (200 g) packed dark brown or demerara sugar
1 large egg, at room temperature
1 tsp pure vanilla extract
½ cup (60 g) cocoa powder
⅓ cup (50 g) all-purpose flour
½ tsp ground cinnamon
½ tsp baking soda
½ tsp salt
1 ½ cups (150 g) regular rolled oats (not instant)
1 cup (175 g) chocolate chips (any type)
1 cup (100 g) flaked sweetened coconut
½ cup (70 g) dried cranberries

1. Preheat the oven to 350°F (180°C) and line 2 baking trays with parchment paper.

2. Cream the butter and brown sugar by hand until well combined (the mixture will not be creamy or fluffy). Beat in the egg then the vanilla.

3. Sift the cocoa, flour, cinnamon, baking soda and salt over the bowl and stir into the butter mixture. Stir in the oats until they are well coated with batter and then stir in the chocolate chips, coconut and cranberries.

4. Use a small ice cream scoop or 2 teaspoons to drop the batter onto the baking trays, 2 inches (5 cm) apart. Press down on them a little with the palm of your hand.

5. Bake for about 12 minutes, until they lose their shine at the edges. Let cool on the trays on wire racks.

ADD SPARKLE

Need a fun but quick hands-on dessert that all ages will love? Scoop chocolate, vanilla or candy cane ice cream between 2 of these cookies for a great ice cream sandwich. Roll the outside edges of the ice cream in crushed candy cane for extra festive flair.

These look very much like crinkle cookies, but are rolled in decorator's or sanding sugar, rather than icing sugar, before baking. They have a festive twinkle, as the light reflects the sparkling sugar. You'll definitely have a twinkle in your eye after eating one, too.

LEMON TWINKLE COOKIES

MAKES ABOUT 2 ½ DOZEN COOKIES • PREP: 15 MINUTES • COOK: 14 MINUTES

1. Preheat the oven to 325°F (160°C) and line 2 baking trays with parchment paper.

2. In a large mixing bowl, cream the butter and both sugars by hand or using electric beaters on medium. Beat in the egg yolks, vanilla and lemon zest, then the lemon juice. (If the mixture looks a little curdled, sift ½ cup/75 g of the flour into the mixture to smooth it out.) Stir in the melted white chocolate.

3. In a separate bowl, sift the flour, cornstarch, baking soda and baking powder together. Add all at once to the butter mixture and mix by hand or on low speed until combined (the dough will be soft but manageable for scooping).

4. Use a small ice cream scoop or 2 teaspoons to shape the dough into balls. Roll the balls in the sugar to coat thoroughly and arrange them on the baking trays, 2 inches (5 cm) apart. Press down gently on them with the palm of your hand.

5. Bake for 12 to 14 minutes, until a cookie can be gently lifted from the tray. Carefully smack the tray down on the counter to deflate the cookies (for the crinkle effect). Let cool on the tray for 5 minutes, then transfer to a wire rack to cool completely.

Photo on page 207

MAKE AHEAD

You can store these baked cookies for up to 5 days in an airtight container at room temperature. Or scoop the dough and freeze the cookies on a baking tray without rolling them in sugar first. Once frozen, pack them into an airtight container and store for up to 3 months. To bake, let the frozen cookies thaw on a baking tray for about 20 minutes before rolling them in sugar and putting them in the oven.

½ cup (115 g) unsalted butter, at room temperature
½ cup (100 g) granulated sugar
½ cup (65 g) icing sugar, sifted
2 large egg yolks
1 tsp pure vanilla extract
Finely grated zest of 1 lemon
3 Tbsp (45 mL) lemon juice
2 oz (60 g) white couverture/baking chocolate, melted and cooled to room temperature
1 ½ cups (225 g) all-purpose flour
2 Tbsp (15 g) cornstarch
½ tsp baking soda
½ tsp baking powder
White decorator's or sanding sugar, or granulated sugar, for rolling

Gingerbread Crinkle Cookies (page 208); Lemon Twinkle Cookies (page 206); Chocolate Crinkle Cookie (page 209)

These are soft and chewy cookies with just a hint of a crunchy shell from the icing sugar they were rolled in. They are a new holiday favourite for me.

GINGERBREAD CRINKLE COOKIES

MAKES ABOUT 4 DOZEN COOKIES • PREP: 15 MINUTES • COOK: 12 MINUTES

1. Preheat the oven to 325°F (160°C) and line 2 baking trays with parchment paper.

2. Cream the butter and brown sugar in a large mixing bowl by hand for 1 minute, until lighter in colour and smooth. Beat in the egg, then the molasses.

3. In a separate bowl, sift the flour, ginger, cinnamon, baking soda, salt, cloves and nutmeg together. Add all at once to the butter mixture, stir until evenly blended, then stir in the granulated sugar just until combined.

4. Use a small ice cream scoop or 2 teaspoons to shape the batter into balls. Roll the balls in the icing sugar to generously coat and place them on the baking trays, 2 inches (5 cm) apart. Press down on the cookies with the palm of your hand to flatten slightly.

5. Bake for 10 to 12 minutes, until they have puffed up and appear set at the edges. Carefully smack the tray down on the counter to deflate the cookies (for the crackle effect). Let cool on the tray for 5 minutes, then transfer to a wire rack to cool completely.

Photo on page 207

MAKE AHEAD
You can store these baked cookies for up to 5 days in an airtight container at room temperature. Or scoop the dough and freeze the cookies on a baking tray without rolling them in sugar first. Once frozen, pack them into an airtight container and store for up to 3 months. To bake, let the frozen cookies thaw on a baking tray for about 20 minutes before rolling them in sugar and putting them in the oven.

½ cup (115 g) unsalted butter, at room temperature
1 cup (200 g) packed light brown sugar
1 large egg, at room temperature
½ cup (130 g) fancy molasses
2 ½ cups (375 g) all-purpose flour
2 tsp ground ginger
1 ½ tsp ground cinnamon
½ tsp baking soda
¼ tsp fine sea salt
¼ tsp ground cloves
¼ tsp ground nutmeg
½ cup (100 g) granulated sugar
Icing sugar, for rolling

HELPFUL HINT
Adding the granulated sugar at the end helps the cookies become even more crinkly when they bake.

A holiday cookie tin isn't complete without a good chocolate crinkle cookie. My mom has been baking these classics for as long as I can remember.

CHOCOLATE CRINKLE COOKIES

GF

MAKES ABOUT 2 ½ DOZEN COOKIES • PREP: 15 MINUTES • COOK: 12 MINUTES

MAKE AHEAD

You can store these baked cookies in an airtight container for up to 5 days at room temperature. Or scoop the dough and freeze the cookies on a baking tray without rolling them in sugar first. Once frozen, pack them into an airtight container and store for up to 3 months. To bake, let the frozen cookies thaw on a baking tray for about 20 minutes before rolling them in sugar and putting them in the oven.

6 oz (180 g) dark couverture/baking chocolate, chopped

2 large eggs, at room temperature

½ cup (100 g) granulated sugar

1 tsp pure vanilla extract

1 tsp balsamic vinegar

2 cups (260 g) icing sugar, divided

½ cup (60 g) Dutch process cocoa powder

1 Tbsp (7 g) cornstarch

½ tsp baking powder (certified gluten-free)

½ tsp salt

½ cup (85 g) white chocolate chips

Photo on page 207

1. Preheat the oven to 350°F (180°C) and line 2 baking trays with parchment paper.

2. Melt the couverture chocolate in a metal bowl set over a saucepan filled with 1 inch (2.5 cm) of barely simmering water, stirring gently. Set aside.

3. With electric beaters or a stand mixer fitted with the whip attachment, whip the eggs with the granulated sugar, vanilla and balsamic vinegar until light and frothy, about 3 minutes (it doesn't have to hold a "ribbon"). Whisk in the melted chocolate (still warm is OK).

4. Sift in 1 cup (130 g) of the icing sugar, the cocoa powder, cornstarch, baking powder and salt and stir by hand until well combined. Stir in the white chocolate chips. The batter may seem very soft at first, but just give it a minute—it will tighten up.

5. Place some of the remaining icing sugar in a shallow dish. Use a small ice cream scoop or 2 teaspoons to drop spoonfuls of batter directly into the icing sugar, rolling to coat fully and evenly. Arrange the balls on the baking trays, 1 ½ inches (3.5 cm) apart. Gently press each cookie flat slightly with the palm of your hand to flatten slightly.

6. Bake the cookies for 10 to 12 minutes, until fully puffed up. Carefully smack the tray down on the counter to deflate the cookies (for the crackle effect). Let cool on the tray for 5 minutes, then transfer to a wire rack to cool completely.

These cookies look adorable, with a little raspberry jam peeking out of one side and apricot jam peeking out of the other. Their shape reminds me of soft, buttery kolacky, the jam- or cheese-filled Slovak pastries that my grandmother always made at Christmas.

RASPBERRY AND APRICOT JAM KOLACKY

MAKES ABOUT 3 DOZEN COOKIES • PREP: 45 MINUTES, PLUS CHILLING • COOK: 18 MINUTES

1. Using electric beaters or a stand mixer fitted with the paddle attachment, beat the butter on medium speed for 1 minute, until fluffy. Add the icing sugar and vanilla and mix, starting on low and increasing to medium, for 1 minute.

2. Sift in the flour, cornstarch and salt, add the cornmeal, and mix on medium-low speed until the dough comes together. Shape into a disc, wrap in plastic wrap and chill for at least 2 hours before rolling.

3. Preheat the oven to 325°F (160°C) and line 2 baking trays with parchment paper.

4. On a lightly floured surface, knead the dough just a little to soften it (this will prevent cracking as you roll). If you find the dough cracks as you begin to roll it, gather it up and knead again to soften it further. Roll into a circle just under ¼ inch (0.5 cm) thick. Use a 2 ½-inch (6.5 cm) fluted round cookie cutter to cut out cookies and re-roll any scraps as needed (it re-rolls nicely).

5. In the centre of each cookie, drop about ¾ tsp of raspberry jam and a spoonful of apricot, side by side. Hold 2 opposite edges of the dough in your hands and bring them together over the jam. Pinch them to seal, ensuring that some raspberry jam peeks out of 1 side and some apricot jam peeks out the other. Place the cookies on the tray, 1 ½ inches (3.5 cm) apart.

6. Brush the cookies with the egg white and then sprinkle with cinnamon sugar.

7. Bake for 15 to 18 minutes, until golden at the edges. Let cool completely on the tray on a wire rack.

MAKE AHEAD

You can store these baked cookies for 1 week in an airtight container at room temperature. As a rule, jam-filled cookies become soft and fragile if frozen and then thawed. To get ahead, make the dough and freeze it, shaped into a disc and well wrapped, for up to 3 months. To bake, thaw the dough overnight in the fridge before rolling, cutting, filling and putting the cookies in the oven.

1 cup (225 g) unsalted butter, at room temperature
½ cup (65 g) icing sugar, sifted
Scraped seeds of ½ vanilla bean or 1 ½ tsp (7 mL) vanilla bean paste
1 ¾ cups (255 g) all-purpose flour
¼ cup (30 g) cornstarch
½ tsp fine sea salt
2 Tbsp (20 g) cornmeal
½ cup (125 mL) raspberry jam
½ cup (125 mL) apricot jam
1 egg white, lightly whisked, for brushing
3 Tbsp (36 g) granulated sugar mixed with ¼ tsp ground cinnamon, for sprinkling

> The rum and nutmeg in the dough and the buttercream filling give these delicate cookies a classic eggnog flavour that's perfect for the holiday season.

EGGNOG BUTTERCREAM SANDWICH COOKIES

MAKES 2 TO 3 DOZEN SANDWICH COOKIES •
PREP: 30 MINUTES, PLUS CHILLING • COOK: 14 MINUTES, PLUS AIR-DRYING

MAKE AHEAD

You can store these baked cookies in a single layer in an airtight container for 1 week at room temperature. To make ahead, freeze the dough, shaped into a disc, well wrapped, and the buttercream, spooned into a resealable bag or container, for up to 3 months. To bake, thaw the dough overnight in the fridge before rolling, cutting, filling and baking. Thaw the buttercream at room temperature until soft, then beat it to fluff it up before piping.

EGGNOG COOKIES

1 cup (225 g) unsalted butter, cut into
    pieces and at room temperature
1 cup (130 g) icing sugar, sifted
2 large egg yolks
1 tsp pure vanilla extract
½ tsp rum extract
2 ½ cups (375 g) all-purpose flour
½ tsp fine sea salt
½ tsp ground nutmeg

BUTTERCREAM

6 Tbsp (90 g) unsalted butter, at
    room temperature
2 ¼ cups (290 g) icing sugar, sifted,
    divided
1 ½ Tbsp (10 g) custard powder
3 Tbsp (45 mL) whipping cream
1 tsp pure vanilla extract
½ tsp rum extract
½ tsp ground nutmeg
Silver dragées, for décor

1. For the cookies, using electric beaters or a stand mixer fitted with the paddle attachment, beat the butter until smooth. Add the icing sugar. Starting on low speed, work in the sugar, and then increase the speed to medium-high and beat until fluffy, about 2 minutes.

2. Beat in the egg yolks and vanilla and rum extracts. Add the flour, salt and nutmeg and beat on low speed until the dough comes together. Shape the dough into 2 discs, wrap in plastic and chill for 2 hours.

3. Preheat the oven to 325°F (160°C) and line 2 baking trays with parchment paper.

4. On a lightly floured surface, knead the first disc of dough a little to soften it and then roll it out to just under ¼ inch (0.5 cm) thick. Use a 2-inch (5 cm) cookie cutter to cut out cookies. Place on the baking trays, 1 inch (2.5 cm) apart. Repeat with the second disc of dough, re-rolling any scraps as needed.

5. Bake the cookies for 12 to 14 minutes, or until slightly golden at the edges. Transfer to a wire rack to cool.

6. For the buttercream, beat the butter with 1 cup (130 g) of the icing sugar on medium speed using electric beaters or a stand mixer fitted with the paddle attachment. Once the butter and icing sugar are well blended, add the custard powder, cream, vanilla and rum extracts and nutmeg. Beat again, starting on low and increasing the speed until all the ingredients are combined (the buttercream may not be smooth at this point).

7. Beat in the remaining 1 ¼ cups (160 g) of icing sugar on low, then increase the speed to medium-high and beat for 2 minutes, until fluffy. Spoon the buttercream into a piping bag fitted with a small star tip. Pipe a single layer of buttercream onto the bottom of a cookie and gently press a second cookie on top. Repeat with the remaining cookies.

8. Use leftover buttercream to pipe a little accent on top of each cookie, then place a silver dragée on top. Let the cookies air-dry for 1 to 2 hours.

These soft, cake-like cookies are already tasty enough to be served as a treat on their own, but the cream cheese filling makes them even better. They look stunning on a holiday dessert table.

CARROT CAKE SANDWICH COOKIES

MAKES 18 ASSEMBLED COOKIES • PREP: 25 MINUTES • COOK: 12 MINUTES

1. Preheat the oven to 350°F (180°C) and line 2 baking trays with parchment paper.

2. For the cookies, beat the butter and brown sugar together by hand until well blended and almost fluffy, about a minute. Beat in the egg, followed by the vanilla.

3. Sift in the flour, baking soda, baking powder, cinnamon, nutmeg and salt and stir until evenly combined. Stir in the carrots, followed by the oats and coconut. Stir in the currants.

4. Use a small ice cream scoop to drop levelled amounts of the batter onto the baking trays, 2 inches (5 cm) apart. It's important to drop level scoops so that the cookies bake with nice domed tops.

5. Bake the cookies for about 12 minutes, until they lift easily from the tray. Cool on the trays on wire racks.

6. For the filling, beat the cream cheese and butter by hand until smooth. Add the icing sugar and vanilla and beat again until fluffy and well blended.

7. To assemble the sandwiches, spoon the filling into a piping bag fitted with a large plain piping tip and pipe a layer of filling over the flat side of a cookie (or use a spatula to spread a generous dollop of the filling instead). Press a second cookie, flat side down, on top of the filling.

MAKE AHEAD
These cookies are soft, almost like a muffin. Unfilled, they can be stored in an airtight container at room temperature for up to 5 days, or frozen for up to 3 months. Thaw them at room temperature until soft. Once assembled, they will keep, refrigerated in an airtight container to preserve the cream cheese frosting, for up to 5 days.

COOKIES
½ cup (115 g) unsalted butter, at room temperature
½ cup (100 g) packed light brown sugar
1 large egg, at room temperature
1 tsp pure vanilla extract
1 cup (150 g) all-purpose flour
½ tsp baking soda
½ tsp baking powder
½ tsp ground cinnamon
¼ tsp ground nutmeg
¼ tsp fine sea salt
1 cup (100 g) finely grated carrots
½ cup (50 g) regular rolled oats (not instant)
½ cup (50 g) flaked sweetened coconut
½ cup (75 g) dried currants

FILLING
½ cup (125 g) cream cheese, at room temperature
¼ cup (60 g) unsalted butter, at room temperature
½ cup (65 g) icing sugar, sifted
1 tsp vanilla bean paste or pure vanilla extract

I love when different family traditions come together. When I celebrated my first Christmas with Michael, I learned about the Icelandic-Canadian tradition of vínarterta, a layered prune and cardamom shortbread torte that is cut into fruitcake-sized bites to enjoy. With my Slovak background, prune fillings in cookies were a Christmas staple. Now this linzer cookie merges our two family heritages into a delightful new holiday tradition! The original vínarterta torte benefits from freezing and then thawing, to soften up its layers, and the same goes for these cookies, making them a perfect make-ahead cookie for the holidays.

VÍNARTERTA LINZER COOKIES

MAKES ABOUT 3 DOZEN ASSEMBLED COOKIES •
PREP: 25 MINUTES, PLUS CHILLING • COOK: 11 MINUTES

1. For the cookie dough, beat the butter with the icing sugar with electric beaters or a stand mixer fitted with the paddle attachment on medium-high speed, or by hand, until fluffy. Beat in the egg yolks and vanilla and almond extracts until well combined.

2. Sift in the flour, cardamom and salt. Mix on low speed, or by hand, until evenly combined. Shape the dough into 2 discs, wrap in plastic wrap and chill until firm, at least 2 hours.

3. For the filling, place the prunes, water, sugar, butter, cardamom and cinnamon in a medium saucepan over medium heat and bring to a simmer. Simmer, uncovered, for 5 minutes and then set aside to cool to room temperature.

4. Purée the filling mixture in a blender or food processor or with an immersion blender until a thick, smooth paste. Chill until ready to use.

5. Preheat the oven to 325°F (160°C) and line 2 baking trays with parchment paper.

6. On a lightly floured surface, knead the first disc of dough slightly to soften it (this prevents the dough from cracking when rolling). Roll the dough into a circle just under ¼ inch (0.5 cm) thick.

7. Use a 2-inch (5 cm) round cookie cutter to cut out enough cookies to fill a tray, 1 inch (2.5 cm) apart. Re-roll the dough as required. Repeat with the second disc of dough.

Recipe continues ▶

MAKE AHEAD
You can store these baked and assembled cookies for up to 2 weeks in an airtight container at room temperature. Or to get ahead, make the dough, shape it into a disc, wrap and freeze it for up to 3 months. To bake, thaw the dough in the fridge overnight before rolling, cutting, filling and putting the cookies in the oven. You can even make the prune filling up to 1 month ahead and store it in a jar, refrigerated.

VÍNARTERTA COOKIES
1 cup (225 g) unsalted butter, at room temperature
2 cups (260 g) icing sugar, sifted
4 large egg yolks
1 tsp pure vanilla extract
½ tsp almond extract
3 cups (390 g) cake and pastry flour
1 ½ tsp ground cardamom
½ tsp fine sea salt

FILLING
1 ½ cups (260 g) pitted prunes
⅓ cup (80 mL) water
¼ cup (50 g) granulated sugar
1 Tbsp (15 g) unsalted butter
1 tsp ground cardamom
½ tsp ground cinnamon
Icing sugar, for assembly (optional, see Add Sparkle below)

8. Use a 1-inch (2.5 cm) or smaller cookie cutter of the same shape (or different shape) to cut out the centre of half the cookies. (Be sure you have the same number of cookies with and without the hole in the centre.)

9. Bake the cookies for 9 to 11 minutes, until they just begin to brown a little at the edges. The cookies with the holes will be done about 1 minute sooner than the others. Transfer the cookies to a wire rack to cool completely.

10. To fill the cookies, spread a spoonful of prune filling on the bottom of each whole cookie. Gently press a cookie with a hole in it on top of each one.

Step 10

ADD SPARKLE

Here are 2 options to dress up these lovely cookies:

Place the cookies with holes cut out on a parchment-lined baking tray and dust them with icing sugar before assembling (pick the cookies up from the sides when assembling, to keep the dusting intact).

Place the cookies with holes cut out on a parchment-lined baking tray. Whisk 1 cup (130 g) of sifted icing sugar with 2 Tbsp (30 mL) of water until smooth and drizzle over the cookies with a fork or in a piping bag fitted with a small tip. Let the glazed cookies air-dry for 2 hours before assembling the linzers.

> The grandest cookie of all, the French macaron is a thing of beauty. Making macarons takes patience and practice, but once you hit your stride, you'll find the repetitive action of measuring, piping and assembling very Zen-like. Here is a reliable base recipe, and some seasonal flavours and colours to suit the time of year. Get those gift boxes ready!

FESTIVE MACARONS: CANDY CANE, EGGNOG, CHOCOLATE ORANGE

GF

MAKES 2 DOZEN ASSEMBLED MACARONS • PREP: 30 MINUTES, PLUS RESTING • COOK: 15 MINUTES

MAKE AHEAD
You can refrigerate assembled macarons in an airtight container for up to 1 week. (Do not freeze them.) Let them come to room temperature before serving.

MACARON BASE
1 cup (130 g) icing sugar (replace 3 Tbsp/25 g with cocoa powder if making the Chocolate Orange macarons)

¾ cup + ⅓ cup (130 g) ground almonds

3 large egg whites, at room temperature

Flavours and colours, as noted on page 221 (optional)

2 Tbsp (30 mL) water

½ cup (100 g) granulated sugar

FILLING
3 Tbsp (45 mL) 2% milk

3 Tbsp (36 g) granulated sugar

2 large egg yolks

½ cup (115 g) unsalted butter, at room temperature

1 tsp pure vanilla extract

Flavours and colours (optional)

1. Prepare 2 baking trays: Cut 1 sheet of parchment paper for each baking tray and 1 longer sheet for a piping template. The extra length gives you a "handle" with which to pull this sheet out from beneath your top parchment after you've piped your macarons. On this template parchment, use a marker to trace circles 1 ½ inches (3.5 cm) across and at least 1 inch (2.5 cm) apart. Place this sheet on a baking tray and cover it with 1 of the smaller sheets of parchment.

2. For the macaron base, pulse the icing sugar (and cocoa powder, if using) and ground almonds in a food processor until the nuts are a fine powder. Pour into a large mixing bowl and make a well in the centre.

3. Whisk the egg whites with a fork to loosen them up, and pour half into the well in the almond mixture. Starting at the centre and working outward, use a spatula to gradually stir more and more of the dry mixture into the egg whites until fully combined (the mixture will be a thick paste). If adding colour and/or flavour (see table, page 221), add it now and stir to blend.

4. In the bowl of a stand mixer fitted with a whip attachment, whip the remaining egg whites on high speed until they hold a soft peak when the beater is lifted.

5. Place the water in a small saucepan and then add the granulated sugar (the water goes in first so that it dissolves the sugar evenly) and bring to a full boil, uncovered, over high heat. Cook without stirring until the mixture reaches 239°F (115°C) on a candy thermometer, less than 2 minutes.

Recipe continues ▶

6. With the mixer running on high speed, *carefully* pour the hot sugar mixture down the inside of the bowl and continue whipping until the whites hold a stiff peak and have cooled to body temperature, about 2 minutes.

7. Fold one-third of the whipped egg whites into the almond base. (You will be stirring more than folding, since the whites will deflate significantly.) Once they have been fully incorporated, add the remaining egg whites, folding more gently this time. Let the batter sit for 2 minutes in the bowl, without touching it.

8. Spoon the batter into a piping bag fitted with a ½-inch (1 cm) plain tip. Using the template as a guide, hold the tip of the piping bag straight down and close to the parchment and completely fill each circle just to its edge with batter. (You may have to sacrifice a few macarons as you practise piping to get the hang of it.)

9. Once you've finished piping the first tray, gently slip the template from beneath the sheet of macarons. Set the template on the second tray, cover it with the remaining sheet of parchment paper and continue piping.

10. Let the macarons set for 45 minutes to 1 hour to develop a "skin" on their surface. You should be able to touch the top of the macarons gently without your finger getting sticky, and you will notice that the surface loses its lustre slightly, going from shiny to satin.

11. Preheat the oven to 300°F (150°C). Bake the macarons for about 15 minutes, until they can be gently but easily loosened and lifted from the baking tray. Immediately after you remove the macarons from the oven, carefully lift the parchment paper from the pan and set on a wire rack to let the macarons cool completely.

12. Once cooled, gently peel the macarons from the paper. Discard the parchment paper. If you are not using the macarons immediately, store them, unfilled, in an airtight container at room temperature (do not refrigerate).

13. For the filling, place the milk, sugar and egg yolks in a small saucepan over medium heat. Gently whisk until the milk thickens and coats the back of a spoon, about 5 minutes. Remove the pan from the heat and pour the custard through a fine-mesh sieve into a bowl. Place a piece of plastic wrap directly on the surface of the custard to prevent a skin from forming and let cool completely to room temperature. (If you make the custard ahead and chill it after cooling, be sure to bring it back to room temperature before completing the buttercream.)

Step 10

Step 15

14. Once the custard has cooled, use electric beaters or a stand mixer with the whip attachment to beat the butter on high speed to soften it. Reduce the speed to medium and add the custard gradually, stopping occasionally to scrape down the sides of the bowl. If the buttercream looks curdled, simply increase the speed to high after all the custard has been added and the buttercream will smooth out (this could take 1 to 3 minutes). Once smooth, stir in the colouring and/or flavouring as desired (see table).

15. To assemble the macarons, spoon the buttercream into a small piping bag fitted with a ½-inch (1 cm) plain tip. Pipe a dot of buttercream (about 1 ½ tsp) onto the bottom of a macaron and gently press a second one onto the buttercream to make a "sandwich." To avoid crushing the delicate macarons, try to hold them by their edges rather than pressing down on their tops.

16. If gifting, pack gently but snugly in a single layer in a box or tin. Some craft stores sell boxes specifically designed to hold macarons in place.

FLAVOUR AND COLOUR ADDITIONS FOR MACARONS

	BASE FLAVOUR	BASE COLOUR	DECORATIVE TOUCH	FILLING COLOUR	FILLING FLAVOUR
CANDY CANE		Add a touch of pink food colouring paste	Sprinkle the filling of the piped macarons with finely crushed candy cane dust	Add a touch of pink food colouring gel	Stir in 2 oz (60 g) of melted and cooled white chocolate and 1 tsp of peppermint extract
EGGNOG	Stir in ¼ tsp of finely ground nutmeg	Add a touch of buttercup yellow food colouring gel	Sprinkle lightly with ground nutmeg	Add a touch of buttercup yellow food colouring gel	Stir in ¼ tsp of ground nutmeg and 1 tsp of rum extract
CHOCOLATE ORANGE	Stir in finely grated zest of ½ an orange				Stir in 1 oz (30 g) of melted and cooled bittersweet chocolate and the finely grated zest of ½ an orange

Macarons: Naughty or Nice?

When it comes to making macarons, people seem to have a love/hate relationship with these beautiful little treats. There are many great tips you can follow to help you, but also a few misleading myths. I've put all of them to the test, and here is my list of the "Nice" (truly, helpful hints) and the "Naughty" (myths).

NICE (TIPS)

STICK TO DRY DAYS. On very humid or rainy days, macarons are at risk of cracking when they bake, but there is one tip that can sometimes help: Try adding ½ tsp of meringue powder to the dry mixture if the humidity is not in sync with your baking schedule.

DRAW A TEMPLATE. I've been making macarons for years, and while I'm practised at piping, I still find using a template is the easiest way to get perfectly sized macarons every time.

USE A SCALE. Although I've also provided volume measures, using a scale aids in achieving a precise and consistent result.

KEEP "SPRINKLES" TO A MINIMUM. A little candy cane dust or ground nutmeg adds festive flair to these macarons, but don't get carried away—too much and it detracts from the beautiful shape of the macaron.

LET THE BATTER REST. This tip was an accidental discovery—I got distracted, only to discover that the time lapse made my macarons better. When I let the macaron batter sit in the bowl for 2 to 3 minutes before I put it into the piping bag, it pipes better and develops a nice satin top.

COOL THOSE MACARONS QUICKLY! Transferring the whole sheet of baked macarons from the baking tray to a wire rack lets them start cooling quickly, so you don't overbake the bottoms.

NAUGHTY (MYTHS)

AGE YOUR EGG WHITES. Some people say you should let your egg whites sit for 24 hours before using them, but I've never noticed a difference. By making a meringue that involves cooking the sugar before adding it to the egg whites, I get an even lift and a perfect "foot" (the ruffle that appears at the bottom of the macaron as it bakes) in my macarons every time.

SIFT, AND SIFT SOME MORE. Many people believe that you have to sift your almonds and icing sugar separately AND that you have to sift them together several times. However, when you grind your icing sugar and ground almonds in a food processor, as in this recipe, the mixture becomes a fine powder without a single bump or lump.

FANCY BARS AND SQUARES

I'M ALL ABOUT PRACTICALITY, and I love a good bar or square because it can easily take the place of a cookie or, when cut into a large portion, make an easy plated dessert. In this chapter I've included a mix of classics like Date Squares and Butter Tart Squares, as well as playful and inventive new options, like the Graceland Squares.

Opposite: Michael's Favourite Date Squares (page 229)

> A Canadian staple, the butter tart square has earned annual holiday cookie tin status in many households. They are easier to make than individual tarts, yet they retain the sweet maple creaminess we have come to expect from this dessert.

SIGNATURE BUTTER TART SQUARES

MAKES ONE 8-INCH (20 CM) SQUARE PAN • MAKES 25 TO 36 SQUARES • PREP: 15 MINUTES • COOK: 45 MINUTES

MAKE AHEAD

You can store the squares in an airtight container for 3 days at room temperature or for 5 days in the fridge. They can be frozen, but will soften up after thawing. If you must freeze, pack them in a single layer in an airtight container for no more than 1 month to avoid moisture building up. Thaw overnight in the fridge before serving.

BASE

1 cup (150 g) all-purpose flour
1 cup (100 g) regular rolled oats (not instant)
¼ cup (50 g) packed light brown sugar
½ cup (115 g) unsalted butter, melted

TOPPING

¾ cup (150 g) packed light brown sugar
½ cup (125 mL) pure maple syrup
2 large eggs
¼ cup (60 g) unsalted butter, melted (warm but not hot is fine)
2 tsp white or cider vinegar
1 tsp pure vanilla extract
¼ tsp fine sea salt
1 cup (150 g) raisins or pecan pieces (optional)

1. Preheat the oven to 350°F (180°C). Lightly grease and line the bottom and sides of an 8-inch (20 cm) square pan with parchment paper.

2. For the base, stir the flour, oats and brown sugar by hand in a large bowl. Add the melted butter and stir together until the mixture is rough and crumbly (like a fruit crisp topping).

3. Press into the bottom of the pan, bake for 12 minutes to set (it will not brown) and then let cool in the pan on a wire rack. Leave the oven on. While the base is cooling, prepare the topping.

4. For the topping, whisk the brown sugar, maple syrup and eggs together until combined. Whisk in the melted butter followed by the vinegar, vanilla and salt.

5. Sprinkle the raisins (or pecans) (if using) in an even layer over the bottom of the base and carefully pour the maple syrup mixture overtop (you can move the raisins or pecans around to realign them, if required).

6. Bake for 25 to 30 minutes, until the topping bubbles just around the edges and is set when the pan is gently jiggled. Let cool completely in the pan on a wire rack before cutting into squares.

❧

HELPFUL HINT

To prevent the top fluid layer from seeping around the edges and underneath the base of your tart, press the crumbly base gently up into the edges of the pan, so there is a little lip before pouring. Resist packing the base in too firmly, otherwise it can shrink away from the edges after baking, creating a gap for the filling to leak underneath. This tip can also be applied to any square with a fluid filling, such as a lemon square.

Build a Butter Tart Buffet

When I'm hosting a casual holiday get-together such as an open house, I love to set up a butter tart buffet near the coffee and tea.

Many people are particular about their butter tarts: some like them with walnuts or pecans, others insist upon raisins and still others are equally adamant about NO raisins. I've even met people who like chocolate chips or bacon in their butter tarts! A butter tart dessert station caters to all these people.

The buffet begins with a platter of butter tart squares and a series of toppings for guests to choose from. Inevitably, guests pile *all* of the toppings onto their bar!

Here are five steps for a build-your-own butter tart buffet.

1. Bake up a batch of plain Signature Butter Tart Squares (or your favourite plain butter tarts), cut them into individual squares and arrange them on platters.

2. Fill separate small bowls with raisins, walnut pieces, pecans, chocolate chips and cooked crumbled bacon. Don't forget the serving spoons! You can even dress up the traditional fillings: soak the raisins in a little whiskey, toast the walnuts with a little butter and sea salt and make Maple Toasted Pecans (page 321).

3. Cook up some Butter Caramel Sauce (page 316) and place it in a squeeze bottle, or in a bowl with a small spoon, so guests can use it to get their toppings to adhere to their bar.

4. Go for decadence by putting out bowls of whipped cream and/or ice cream for butter tart sundaes.

5. Provide lots of small plates and napkins, and forks for those who might need them.

I remember making a batch of date squares years ago, and while I was assembling the layers Michael came into the kitchen and exclaimed, "Matrimonial chews! My mom made these." I understand now that what I call a date square, Western Canadians call a matrimonial cake or chew. Whatever their name, these are indeed chewy and oat-laden. This version avoids refined sugar, so I see it as a fantastic festive treat with a hint of virtue. Only a little maple syrup adds to the natural sweetness of the dates.

MICHAEL'S FAVOURITE DATE SQUARES

if using
coconut oil

MAKES ONE 8-INCH (20 CM) SQUARE PAN • MAKES 25 SQUARES • PREP: 15 MINUTES • COOK: 40 MINUTES, PLUS CHILLING

MAKE AHEAD
You can store these baked squares (sliced or unsliced) for up to 5 days in an airtight container at room temperature. Or freeze them in an airtight container for up to 1 month and then thaw them on the counter. Once thawed, they will be softer than when they were originally baked.

FILLING
2 cups (300 g) coarsely chopped
    pitted dates
½ cup (125 mL) water
¼ cup (60 mL) pure maple syrup
½ tsp ground cinnamon

CRUMBLE
2 ½ cups (250 g) regular rolled oats
    (not instant) (certified gluten-free,
    if required)
1 cup (150 g) all-purpose flour
½ tsp baking powder
½ tsp ground cinnamon
¾ cup (175 g) unsalted butter or virgin
    coconut oil, melted
⅓ cup (80 mL) pure maple syrup

1. Preheat the oven to 350°F (180°C). Lightly grease an 8-inch (20 cm) square pan and line the bottom and sides with parchment paper.

2. For the filling, place the dates, water, maple syrup and cinnamon in a medium saucepan over medium heat and bring to a simmer. Simmer, uncovered, for 5 minutes and then remove from the heat to cool while you prepare the crumble.

3. For the crumble, stir the oats, flour, baking powder and cinnamon by hand in a large bowl. Stir in the melted butter (or coconut oil for vegans) and maple syrup until the mixture is crumbly.

4. Spoon two-thirds of the crumble into the prepared pan and press in. Spoon the date filling (it's okay if it's still warm) over the crumble base and spread to level it. Cover with the remaining crumble mixture and press down.

5. Bake for about 30 minutes, until the top is golden brown. Let cool in the pan on a wire rack to room temperature.

6. If you made the squares with butter, chill them before slicing (they slice more tidily when chilled); if you made them with coconut oil, slice them once they reach room temperature.

Photo on page 224

HELPFUL HINT
Coconut oil really firms up in the fridge, so if you use it in these squares, avoid chilling them before slicing—they'll set up too firmly. Also, you may find squares made with coconut oil a little softer than those made with butter—use a very sharp knife to cut them nicely.

Remember those old-fashioned bake sale squares made with marshmallows, peanut butter and butterscotch chips? Now add Elvis to the equation, and what do you get? Graceland Squares! This new classic has a chocolate cookie crumb base, plus bacon and banana in the filling (a nod to Elvis's favourite sandwich). You will not be having a "Blue Christmas" if these squares are in your cookie tin!

GRACELAND SQUARES

MAKES ONE 8-INCH (20 CM) SQUARE PAN • MAKES 36 SQUARES •
PREP: 30 MINUTES • COOK: 15 MINUTES, PLUS SETTING

1. Preheat the oven to 350°F (180°C). Lightly grease an 8-inch (20 cm) square pan and line the bottom and sides with parchment paper.

2. For the base, combine the cookie crumbs and melted butter in a small mixing bowl and then press into the prepared pan. Bake for 10 minutes, just to set the crust (you won't see any visible change). While the base is cooling on a wire rack, prepare the topping.

3. For the topping, place the butterscotch chips, peanut butter and butter in a medium saucepan over medium heat and stir until smooth. Remove from the heat and pour into a large mixing bowl to cool for 5 minutes.

4. Stir in the bacon and banana and then add the marshmallows, stirring so they are fully coated. Spread the mixture over the chocolate crumb base and then chill, uncovered, for at least 2 hours to set.

5. Cut the squares when chilled but serve at room temperature.

MAKE AHEAD

You can store these squares in an airtight container at room temperature for up to 5 days, or in the fridge for up to 1 week. Or freeze them, sliced or unsliced but well wrapped, for up to 1 month. Thaw the bars overnight in the fridge before serving.

BASE
1 ½ cups (375 mL) chocolate cookie crumbs
¼ cup (60 g) unsalted butter, melted

TOPPING
1 ¾ cups (300 g) butterscotch chips
1 cup (250 g) pure peanut butter
½ cup (115 g) unsalted butter
4 strips cooked bacon, finely chopped
2 small bananas, or 1 large, small dice
4 cups (200 g) mini marshmallows

> Don't laugh . . . fruitcake *can* be fun! These bars are less like a heavy fruit-cake and more like a lighter hermit bar or other dried fruit bar. I steer clear of candied fruits with added colouring here, and a simple buttercream frosting on top sweetens the whole package.

FUN FRUITCAKE BARS

MAKES ONE 9 × 13-INCH (22.5 × 32.5 CM) PAN • MAKES 48 TO 60 BARS • PREP: 25 MINUTES • COOK: 45 MINUTES, PLUS SETTING

1. Preheat the oven to 350°F (180°C). Grease and line the bottom and sides of a 9 × 13-inch (22.5 × 32.5 cm) baking pan with parchment paper so that the paper comes up the sides.

2. For the bars, beat the butter with the brown sugar in a large mixing bowl using electric beaters, in a stand mixer fitted with a paddle attachment or by hand. Add the eggs 1 at a time, beating well after each addition.

3. In a separate bowl, sift the flour, baking soda, salt, cinnamon and ginger. Add half to the butter mixture and mix until evenly blended. Stir in the apple cider (or juice), followed by the remaining flour mixture.

4. Stir in the raisins, cranberries, apricots, blueberries and pecans until they are fully coated in batter (it will be thick). Spoon into the pre-pared pan and spread to level it.

5. Bake for about 45 minutes, until a skewer inserted in the centre comes out clean. Let cool completely in the pan on a wire rack.

6. For the frosting, beat the butter until smooth using electric beaters or in a stand mixer fitted with the paddle attachment. Add about half of the icing sugar and beat on low speed. Increase the speed to medium-high and beat until fluffy, scraping down the sides of the bowl once or twice. Beat in the cream and vanilla until smooth. Add the remaining icing sugar and beat again on low, then increase to medium-high, until the frosting is fluffy.

7. Spread the frosting over the cooled fruitcake bars and let them sit, uncovered, for 1 hour at room temperature before slicing.

MAKE AHEAD
You can store these fruitcake bars in an airtight container at room temperature for up to 1 week. They stay nice and moist. They also freeze wonderfully well unfrosted (adding the frosting turns them into a squishy mess once thawed). Wrap the unsliced bars well and freeze them for up to 3 months. Thaw at room temperature until soft and then top with the frosting.

BARS
¾ cup (175 g) unsalted butter, at room temperature
1 ¼ cups (250 g) packed light brown sugar
2 large eggs, at room temperature
2 ¼ cups (335 g) all-purpose flour
½ tsp baking soda
½ tsp fine sea salt
½ tsp ground cinnamon
½ tsp ground ginger
½ cup (125 mL) apple cider or juice
1 cup (150 g) raisins (any type)
1 cup (140 g) dried cranberries
½ cup (85 g) chopped dried apricots
½ cup (80 g) dried blueberries
1 cup (100 g) pecan halves or pieces

FROSTING
½ cup (115 g) unsalted butter, at room temperature
3 ¼ cups (420 g) icing sugar, sifted
¼ cup (60 mL) half-and-half cream
1 ½ tsp pure vanilla extract

These bars are a perfect option to replace apple pie as a plated dessert at Thanksgiving or Christmas. The homemade butter caramel sauce inside the bars and on top really adds sparkle.

CARAMEL APPLE BARS

MAKES ONE 8-INCH (20 CM) SQUARE PAN • MAKES 25 TO 36 BARS •
PREP: 25 MINUTES • COOK: 42 MINUTES, PLUS CHILLING

1. Preheat the oven to 350°F (180°C). Grease and line the bottom and sides of an 8-inch (20 cm) square pan with parchment paper.

2. For the base, stir the flour, oats, sugar, cinnamon, ginger and baking powder in a large mixing bowl by hand. Add the melted butter and stir until the mixture is rough and crumbly (like a fruit crisp topping).

3. Firmly press two-thirds of this mixture into the prepared pan and bake for 12 minutes, until browned just a little at the edges. Cool in the pan on a wire rack. Leave the oven on.

4. For the filling, arrange the sliced apples on top of the baked crust (it's okay if it's still warm). Drizzle ½ cup (125 mL) of the warm caramel sauce over the apples, and then top with the remaining crumble mixture, pressing down gently.

5. Bake for 30 minutes, until lightly browned. Let cool in the pan on a wire rack to room temperature.

6. Drizzle the remaining ¼ cup (60 mL) of caramel sauce over the pan and then chill uncovered for at least 2 hours before slicing.

MAKE AHEAD
You can store these bars in the pan, or cut into bars and arranged in a single layer in an airtight container, in the fridge for up to 1 week. Or freeze them (cut or uncut), without the caramel drizzle but well wrapped, for up to 3 months. Thaw the bars overnight in the fridge before finishing them with the caramel drizzle.

BASE
2 cups (300 g) all-purpose flour
1 cup (100 g) regular rolled oats (not instant)
¾ cup (150 g) packed dark brown sugar
1 tsp ground cinnamon
½ tsp ground ginger
½ tsp baking powder
¾ cup (175 g) unsalted butter, melted

FILLING AND ASSEMBLY
3 medium apples, peeled and thinly sliced
¾ cup (175 mL) Butter Caramel Sauce (page 316), warmed, divided

HELPFUL HINT
To serve these bars as a plated dessert, place individual portions on a parchment-lined baking tray and warm them in a 350°F (180°C) oven for about 10 minutes. Arrange them on plates, dollop a scoop of vanilla ice cream on top and drizzle with some warm Butter Caramel Sauce.

Chewy, chocolatey and nutty, these decadent bars are a take on millionaire bars, which have a shortbread base, a dense caramel centre and a chocolate topping.

CHOCOLATE HAZELNUT CARAMEL BARS

MAKES ONE 9 × 13-INCH (22.5 × 32.5 CM) PAN · MAKES 48 BARS ·
PREP: 25 MINUTES, PLUS COOLING · COOK: 25 MINUTES, PLUS SETTING

1. Preheat the oven to 350°F (180°C). Lightly grease a 9 × 13-inch (22.5 × 32.5 cm) pan and line the bottom and sides with parchment paper.

2. For the base, place the flour, icing sugar and cocoa powder in the bowl of a food processor with the hazelnuts and pulse until the nuts are finely ground. Add the butter and pulse until the mixture is rough and crumbly, but it does not need to come together.

3. Press firmly into the prepared pan and bake for 15 minutes. While the base is cooling on a wire rack, prepare the filling.

4. For the filling, place the condensed milk, brown sugar, butter, cream and corn syrup in a medium saucepan over high heat and bring to a boil, stirring constantly with a spatula. Once the mixture reaches a boil, reduce the heat to medium and continue stirring until it reaches 228°F (109°C) on a candy thermometer, about 9 minutes from when it starts to boil. Remove the pan from the heat and stir in the vanilla and salt. Pour over the base and let cool, uncovered, to room temperature, about 2 hours.

5. For the topping, place the chocolate and butter in a metal bowl set over a saucepan filled with 1 inch (2.5 cm) of barely simmering water, stirring until melted and smooth. Pour over the cooled caramel and spread or swirl the pan so that the caramel is coated evenly. Sprinkle the chopped hazelnuts over the chocolate and chill, uncovered, until set, about 2 hours. Slice into individual squares once chilled.

MAKE AHEAD
You can store baked bars in an airtight container at room temperature for 10 days or in the fridge for up to 3 weeks. Do not freeze them, because the caramel layer will liquefy when the bars thaw, making them very soft and messy.

BASE
1 ¼ cups (185 g) all-purpose flour
⅔ cup (90 g) icing sugar
½ cup (60 g) cocoa powder
½ cup (65 g) whole hazelnuts, toasted and peeled
1 cup (225 g) unsalted butter, cold and cut into pieces

FILLING
1 can (10 oz/300 mL) sweetened condensed milk
¾ cup (150 g) packed light brown sugar
¾ cup (175 g) unsalted butter
½ cup (125 mL) whipping cream
½ cup (125 mL) golden corn syrup
1 tsp pure vanilla extract
½ tsp fine sea salt

TOPPING
6 oz (180 g) bittersweet couverture/ baking chocolate, chopped
3 Tbsp (45 g) unsalted butter
⅓ cup (38 g) chopped toasted hazelnuts

CLASSIC CHOCOLATES AND CONFECTIONS

CHRISTMAS TREATS ARE A MUST, whether for gift-giving or for indulging yourself. Making homemade chocolates and other confections is perfectly suited to holiday time, and I love the pride I see on people's faces when they hand out their boxes and bags of candies—a true Santa moment.

Making chocolates and confections takes a little patience, and I separate my candy-making day from my cookie-baking day, since it involves a different process and movement around the kitchen—you'll find you're at your stove more when making candies. So put on your favourite Christmas music, strap on your apron and get your Santa on!

Opposite: Chocolate Barks: Salted Pecan and Dried Cherry Dark Chocolate (page 240); S'mores Milk Chocolate (page 241); Pistachio, Dried Blueberry and Pink Peppercorn White Chocolate (page 242)

CHOCOLATE BARKS

> Barks have really grown in popularity in recent years as a holiday gift and staple sweet nibble. Some people make them by melting chocolate chips, spreading the chocolate on a baking tray, topping with goodies and then letting the chips set up. However, couverture/baking chocolate (page 164) is higher quality and makes a better-looking bark with a rich chocolate flavour and smooth texture. The trick is to temper the chocolate by melting it, cooling it and warming it to specific temperatures so it becomes stable at room temperature, which prevents streaking or dusty bloom. Because dark, milk and white chocolates temper and set at different temperatures, use a candy thermometer for best results.

SALTED PECAN AND DRIED CHERRY DARK CHOCOLATE

MAKES ENOUGH TO ALMOST COVER 1 MEDIUM TO LARGE BAKING TRAY • SERVES 12 TO 16 • PREP: 30 MINUTES, PLUS SETTING • COOK: 6 MINUTES

1. Melt the butter in a medium sauté pan over medium heat and add the pecans and sea salt. Stir until the pecans have toasted, about 6 minutes, then remove from the heat to cool before roughly chopping them.

2. Have a parchment-lined baking tray ready. To temper the chocolate, melt 7 oz (210 g) of it in a metal bowl placed over a saucepan filled with an inch (2.5 cm) of barely simmering water, stirring until it has melted and reaches 113 to 122°F (45 to 50°C). If it gets warmer than this, let it cool to below 113°F (45°C) and re-warm.

3. Remove the bowl from the heat and stir in the remaining 3 oz (90 g) of chocolate to melt it, continuing to stir until the chocolate reaches 82°F (28°C). Return the bowl to the water bath and stir until the chocolate reaches 88 to 90°F (31 to 32°C)—this doesn't take long. The chocolate is ready to use and will set at room temperature with a nice satin finish.

4. Pour the tempered chocolate onto the prepared tray and spread it out evenly to about ¼ inch (0.5 cm) thick.

5. Sprinkle the chocolate with the pecans and cherries. Let the chocolate set up and then pop it in the fridge for 3 to 5 minutes (this final "cure" ensures a perfect set). Break the bark into pieces and store them in an airtight container at room temperature. If gifting, stack the pieces and place in a cellophane bag tied with a ribbon, or layer into a windowed gift box.

MAKE AHEAD

The advantage of tempering your chocolate is that it can be stored, broken into pieces and stacked in an airtight container at room temperature for a few weeks. Keep the container out of direct sunlight, but there is no benefit to freezing it or storing it chilled—which leaves more room in your fridge and freezer for other goodies!

1 Tbsp (15 g) butter
1 cup (100 g) pecan halves
½ tsp coarse or flaked sea salt
10 oz (300 g) bittersweet couverture/baking chocolate, chopped
½ cup (80 g) coarsely chopped dried cherries

MAKES ENOUGH TO ALMOST COVER 1 MEDIUM TO LARGE BAKING TRAY •
SERVES 12 TO 16 • PREP: 30 MINUTES, PLUS SETTING • COOK: 6 MINUTES

10 oz (300 g) milk couverture/baking chocolate, chopped
1 ½ cups (75 g) mini marshmallows
8 to 10 coarsely crumbled graham crackers

1. Have a parchment-lined baking tray ready. To temper the chocolate, melt 7 oz (210 g) of it in a metal bowl placed over a saucepan filled with an inch (2.5 cm) of barely simmering water, stirring until it has melted and reaches 104 to 113°F (40 to 45°C). If it gets warmer than this, let it cool to below 113°F (45°C) and re-warm.

2. Remove the bowl from the heat and stir in the remaining 3 oz (90 g) of chocolate to melt it, continuing to stir until the chocolate reaches 81 to 82°F (27 to 28°C). Return the bowl to the water bath and stir until the chocolate reaches 84 to 86°F (29 to 30°C)—this doesn't take long. The chocolate is ready to use and will set at room temperature with a nice satin finish.

3. Pour the tempered chocolate onto the prepared tray and spread it out evenly to about ¼ inch (0.5 cm) thick.

4. Sprinkle the chocolate with the mini marshmallows and crumbled graham crackers. Let the chocolate set up and then pop it in the fridge for 3 to 5 minutes (this final "cure" ensures a perfect set). Break the bark into pieces and store them in an airtight container at room temperature.

TEMPERING TEMPERATURES FOR CHOCOLATE

	MELTING	COOLING	WARMING
DARK CHOCOLATE	113 to 122°F (45 to 50°C)	82°F (28°C)	88 to 90°F (31 to 32°C)
MILK CHOCOLATE	104 to 113°F (40 to 45°C)	81 to 82°F (27 to 28°C)	84 to 86°F (29 to 30°C)
WHITE CHOCOLATE	104 to 113°F (40 to 45°C)	81 to 82°F (27 to 28°C)	84 to 86°F (29 to 30°C)

PISTACHIO, DRIED BLUEBERRY AND PINK PEPPERCORN WHITE CHOCOLATE

MAKES ENOUGH TO ALMOST COVER 1 MEDIUM TO LARGE BAKING TRAY • SERVES 12 TO 16 • PREP: 30 MINUTES, PLUS SETTING • COOK: 6 MINUTES

1. Have a parchment-lined baking tray ready. To temper the chocolate, melt 7 oz (210 g) of it in a metal bowl placed over a saucepan filled with an inch (2.5 cm) of barely simmering water, stirring until it has melted and reaches 104 to 113°F (40 to 45°C). If it gets warmer than this, let it cool to below 113°F (45°C) and re-warm.

2. Remove the bowl from the heat and stir in the remaining 3 oz (90 g) of chocolate and stir to melt, continuing to stir until the chocolate reaches 81 to 82°F (27 to 28°C). Return the bowl to the water bath and stir until the chocolate reaches 84 to 86°F (29 to 30°C)—this doesn't take long. The chocolate is ready to use and will set at room temperature with a nice satin finish.

3. Pour the tempered chocolate onto the prepared tray and spread it out evenly to about ¼ inch (0.5 cm) thick.

4. Sprinkle the chocolate with the pistachios, dried blueberries and a sprinkling of pink pepper. Let the chocolate set up and then pop it in the fridge for 3 to 5 minutes (this final "cure" ensures a perfect set). Break the bark into pieces and store them in an airtight container at room temperature.

10 oz (300 g) white couverture/ baking chocolate, chopped
½ cup (65 g) coarsely chopped shelled pistachios
½ cup (80 g) dried blueberries
Coarsely ground pink peppercorns

Step 3

Step 4

HELPFUL HINT

Use this chocolate tempering process to make other chocolate confections over the holidays. For example, pour the tempered chocolate into plastic candy molds to make shaped chocolates or dip truffles or almond clusters in the liquid chocolate for extra decadence. Once the chocolate sets up, store the candies in an airtight container at room temperature. They will retain their set and satin shine for weeks.

> These delightful chewy chocolate candies may look like chocolate truffles, but they are quite different. My good friend Amy described them as an upscale, richer Tootsie Roll in taste and texture. In Brazil, they are a year-round staple, served at just about any celebration, or to accent cakes and tortes. Good luck stopping at just one!

BRAZILIAN BRIGADEIROS

MAKES ABOUT 2 DOZEN CANDIES • PREP: 15 MINUTES, PLUS CHILLING •
COOK: 10 MINUTES

1. Grease a small heatproof dish large enough to hold 1 ½ cups (375 mL).

2. Whisk the condensed milk, cocoa powder and butter together in a saucepan over medium heat and bring to a simmer. Whisking constantly, simmer the condensed milk until it reaches 220°F (104°C) on a candy thermometer and begins to thicken and pull away from the bottom of the pan, about 5 minutes.

3. Remove the pan from the heat and whisk in the vanilla and salt. Transfer to the greased dish, cool to room temperature and then chill, uncovered, completely, about 3 hours.

4. Have the sprinkles, chopped pistachios and coconut ready in separate dishes. Line a baking tray with parchment paper.

5. Use a very small ice cream scoop or 2 teaspoons to spoon a truffle-sized portion of the chilled, thickened milk into your hands. Roll it between your palms (greasing them with a little butter helps to prevent sticking) to form a ball, then roll in your choice of sprinkles, pistachios or coconut until fully covered. Set on the baking tray. Repeat with the remaining mixture.

6. Cover the tray and chill until set, at least 2 hours. If gifting, place each brigadeiro into a little paper cup and arrange them in a single layer in a windowed gift box.

MAKE AHEAD
You can store the brigadeiros in an airtight container in the fridge for up to 2 months. Surprisingly, even though sweet, they freeze well for up to 3 months. Thaw them in the fridge overnight before serving chilled, or even enjoy them right out of the freezer!

1 can (10 oz/300 mL) sweetened
 condensed milk
6 Tbsp (45 g) cocoa powder
3 Tbsp (45 g) butter
1 ½ tsp pure vanilla extract
Pinch of fine sea salt
½ cup each (125 mL) chocolate
 sprinkles, chopped pistachios and
 sweetened flaked coconut, for
 rolling

HELPFUL HINT
Just like a chocolate truffle, you can flavour this mixture as it cooks. If I'm rolling the brigadeiros in pistachios, I add the zest of a lime to the saucepan along with the condensed milk, and if I'm rolling them in coconut, I add 1 tsp of rum extract with the vanilla.

> A good maple fudge has a hint of graininess when you first bite into it that suddenly melts away into sweet creaminess with a lingering taste of maple deliciousness.

MAPLE FUDGE

MAKES ONE 8-INCH (20 CM) SQUARE PAN • MAKES 36 TO 48 PIECES •
PREP: 25 MINUTES, PLUS COOLING • COOK: 15 MINUTES, PLUS SETTING

1. Lightly grease an 8-inch (20 cm) square pan and line the bottom and sides with parchment paper.

2. Lightly grease a medium saucepan with butter. Using a wooden spoon, stir both sugars, the cream, butter and maple syrup together in a large saucepan. Bring to a simmer over medium heat, stirring often.

3. Continue to cook the mixture, stirring constantly, until it reaches 240°F (116°C) on a candy thermometer—this takes over 15 minutes from when it reaches the boil – don't be tempted to increase the heat above medium or the sugar will be at a risk of seizing, causing it to crystallize. Remove the pan from the heat and stir in the vanilla.

4. Let the pan sit, without stirring, until the mixture cools to 110°F (43°C)—this can take 30 minutes to over 1 hour.

5. Using electric beaters or a stand mixer fitted with a paddle attachment, beat the cooled mixture on medium-high speed until it becomes lighter in colour and begins to thicken, about 3 minutes (it will appear grainy). Immediately scrape the fudge into the prepared pan and spread quickly to level it.

6. Let set at room temperature, uncovered, for at least 2 hours before cutting into portions. If gifting, stack the fudge in a cellophane bag tied with ribbon or pack into a little gift box or tin.

MAKE AHEAD

You can store the fudge in an airtight container at room temperature for up to 2 weeks. Do not freeze, as the fudge will become sticky once it thaws.

1 ½ cups (300 g) packed light brown sugar
½ cup (100 g) granulated sugar
1 cup (250 mL) whipping cream
½ cup (115 g) unsalted butter, plus extra for greasing
⅓ cup (80 mL) pure maple syrup
1 tsp pure vanilla extract

Swiss Praline Almonds (page 251); Maple Fudge

Panforte is a fruitcake from Siena, Tuscany. It is more candy-like than cake, which is why I've included it in this chapter. A honey-and-sugar syrup is cooked and poured over the fruits, then baked a little. Bite-sized pieces are sweet, spicy and immensely satisfying. When you buy panforte in Italy, it is wrapped in paper, so when giving it as a holiday gift, wrap it in parchment paper and tie it with ribbon or twine for a wonderfully appealing look.

HAZELNUT ORANGE PANFORTE

MAKES ONE 9-INCH (23 CM) PAN · MAKES 36 PIECES · PREP: 20 MINUTES · COOK: 1 HOUR, PLUS COOLING

1. Preheat the oven to 300°F (150°C). Grease a 9-inch (23 cm) springform pan and line the bottom and sides with parchment paper.

2. Sift the flour, cinnamon, cloves and salt into a large heatproof mixing bowl. Add the hazelnuts, prunes, figs, raisins, candied peel and orange zest and stir well so that the pieces of dried fruit do not stick together.

3. Place the sugar and honey in a medium saucepan over medium-high heat and bring to a full simmer, stirring occasionally. Continue cooking until it reaches 240°F (116°C) on a candy thermometer.

4. Pour this syrup over the nut mixture and quickly stir everything together with a wooden spoon or silicone spatula until the fruit and nuts are completely coated and the flour is no longer visible. Scrape into the prepared pan (it will start cooling and setting quickly), wet your hands and press the mixture into an even layer in the pan.

5. Bake the panforte for about 1 hour, until it is bubbling just a little and has browned at the edges. Let cool completely in the pan on a wire rack before removing from the pan (this can take over 3 hours).

6. Cut the cooled panforte into bite-sized pieces, or, if gifting, wrap it whole in parchment paper.

MAKE AHEAD

You can store baked panforte in an airtight container at room temperature for 4 months. Do not freeze it, as the sugar and honey will cause the panforte to become soft and sticky when it thaws.

⅔ cup (100 g) all-purpose flour
1 tsp ground cinnamon
½ tsp ground cloves
¼ tsp fine sea salt
2 cups (270 g) whole toasted hazelnuts, skinned (see page 165)
1 cup (180 g) quartered pitted prunes
1 cup (180 g) quartered dried figs
1 cup (150 g) raisins
⅓ cup (50 g) diced Candied Orange Peel (page 318), or store-bought
Finely grated zest of 1 orange
¾ cup (150 g) granulated sugar
⅔ cup (200 g) honey

> These peppermint marshmallows are divine as a topper to a mug of
> Virtuously Rich Hot Chocolate (page 15) or as a wrapped holiday gift. You
> will need a snowflake-shaped cookie cutter (or make the marshmallows in an
> 8-inch/20 cm pan and cut them into squares instead).

SNOWFLAKE MARSHMALLOWS

MAKES 16 TO 24 MARSHMALLOWS · PREP: 15 MINUTES, PLUS SETTING · COOK: 4 MINUTES

1. Lightly grease a 9 × 13-inch (22.5 × 32.5 cm) pan and line the bottom and sides with parchment paper. Using a paper towel, lightly grease the parchment with vegetable oil.

2. Stir 6 Tbsp (90 mL) of the cold water, the gelatin and meringue powder in a large bowl or the bowl of a stand mixer fitted with the whip attachment and set aside.

3. Place the remaining 4 Tbsp (60 mL) of water, the sugar and corn syrup in a medium saucepan over high heat and bring to a boil. Boil, uncovered and without stirring, until the mixture reaches 240°F (116°C) on a candy thermometer.

4. With the mixer running at high speed, *carefully* pour the hot sugar mixture down the inside of the bowl of gelatin and whip until tripled in volume and cooled, about 5 minutes. Whip in the vanilla bean paste (or extract) and the peppermint extract.

5. Scrape the marshmallow into the prepared pan and spread to level it. Dust the top of the marshmallow generously with cornstarch and let set, uncovered at room temperature, for at least 2 hours.

6. Invert the marshmallow from the pan onto a cutting board, peel away and discard the parchment paper and dust the top generously with icing sugar. Dip your snowflake cookie cutter in cornstarch and cut out individual marshmallows. If gifting, wrap a few marshmallows in a cellophane bag tied with ribbon—they pair very nicely with my Virtuously Rich Hot Chocolate mix (page 15) and a mug!

MAKE AHEAD

You can store the marshmallows in a single layer in an airtight container at room temperature for up to 2 weeks.

10 Tbsp (150 mL) cold water, divided
2 Tbsp (14 g) unflavoured gelatin powder
2 tsp meringue powder
1 cup (200 g) granulated sugar
½ cup (125 mL) white corn syrup
2 tsp vanilla bean paste or pure vanilla extract
½ tsp peppermint extract
Cornstarch, for dusting
Icing sugar, for dusting

HELPFUL HINT

If you are using a cookie cutter to make individual shapes, you will have scraps of leftover marshmallow. Place them in a small saucepan over medium-low heat until melted, then pour the mixture into a parchment-lined and greased 8-inch (20 cm) pan to set for another 2 hours. Cut into more marshmallow shapes.

This sweet treat is one of my favourites to make at holiday time. The almonds are coated in a thin layer of caramelized sugar, cooled and then simply tossed in cocoa powder. The resulting contrast between the hint of sweet and the hint of chocolate is perfectly balanced, which is why I often find myself reaching for a nibble again and again. A lovely confection on their own, these almonds can also be coarsely chopped and sprinkled onto ice cream or a dessert like the Chocolate and Irish Cream Marquise (page 303).

SWISS PRALINE ALMONDS

MAKES ABOUT 1 ½ CUPS (375 ML) · PREP: 15 MINUTES · COOK: 10 MINUTES, PLUS COOLING

MAKE AHEAD
You can store these almonds in an airtight container at room temperature for up to 2 months. That sheer layer of caramelized sugar really does preserve them. There is no advantage to freezing them.

3 Tbsp (45 mL) water
1 tsp lemon juice
½ cup (100 g) granulated sugar
1 ½ cups (240 g) whole blanched (but untoasted), peeled almonds
About ¼ cup (30 g) cocoa powder (certified vegan, if needed)

1. Have a parchment-lined baking tray ready. Place the water and lemon juice in a large saucepan, add the sugar and bring to a boil over high heat without stirring. Let the mixture continue to boil until it reaches 240°F (116°C) on a candy thermometer, about 10 minutes.

2. Stir in the almonds all at once and immediately reduce the heat to medium. Keep stirring the almonds. First the sugar will crystallize and turn white and granular—that is expected. Keep stirring.

3. Gradually the sugar will liquefy again and turn a light amber colour. Once the sugar has fully liquefied again, spoon the toasted almonds onto the baking tray, working quickly to separate them as much as possible. Let cool to room temperature and then toss in cocoa powder. If gifting, pack the almonds into a jar or cellophane bag tied with ribbon. Package separately from other treats since the cocoa might transfer a dust.

Photo on page 247

251
—
CLASSIC
CHOCOLATES
AND
CONFECTIONS

ADD SPARKLE
For dragée almonds, toss the praline almonds in 4 oz (120 g) of tempered dark couverture/baking chocolate (see Chocolate Barks, page 240, for instructions), let them set up on a tray and then toss them in the cocoa powder.

FESTIVE PIES AND TARTS

THE BIGGER THE PARTY you have, the more desserts you can make! A good pie or tart is a staple at Thanksgiving and Christmas, and if you are baking for a crowd, you'll want an assortment of dessert styles, so a balance of pie, tart, cake and other desserts is important.

I love making pies and tarts—they require multiple techniques for the combination of pastry crust, creamy filling (or more than one filling!) and topping. They are immensely enjoyable to present, to serve and to eat, not just at holiday time, but year-round.

> When I make a mincemeat pie, I usually grate a little apple into the filling to keep it from being too dense and sweet. In these little pies, the apple is more dominant, making it a cross between an apple pie and a mincemeat pie.

APPLE MINCEMEAT MINI PIES

MAKES SIX 4-INCH (10 CM) PIES • SERVES 12 • PREP: 20 MINUTES • COOK: 40 MINUTES, PLUS COOLING

1. Preheat the oven to 375°F (190°C). Place six 4-inch (10 cm) pie plates on a parchment-lined baking tray and grease lightly.

2. Place the grated apples, raisins, currants, dried cherries, maple syrup, melted butter, brandy (or orange liqueur or apple cider), candied ginger and cloves in a mixing bowl, stir together and set aside.

3. Cut the first cylinder of dough into 6 evenly sized pieces. Roll out each piece on a lightly floured surface to just under ¼ inch (0.5 cm) thick and then line the inside of each pie plate. Spoon the apple mincemeat filling into the pie shells, pressing it in gently and spooning any residual syrup from the bowl over the fruit.

4. Cut the second piece of pastry into 6 pieces and roll to the same thickness. Cut out circles large enough to cover the filling and overlap the outer edge of the bottom pastry circle and cut a small hole in the centre of each. Trim and pinch together the edges of the top and bottom pastry circles, creating a fluted pattern.

5. Brush the tops of the pies with the egg wash, sprinkle with a little turbinado sugar and bake for about 40 minutes, until the pastry is a rich golden brown.

6. Let the pies cool completely in the pie plates placed on a rack, about 30 minutes. The whole pies look beautiful arranged on a serving platter, straight out of their pie plates.

MAKE AHEAD

You can store the baked pies in an air-tight container at room temperature for up to 4 days, refrigerated for 1 week or in the freezer for up to 1 month.

2 medium tart apples, such as Granny Smith, Mutsu, Spy or Spartan, peeled and coarsely grated

1 cup (150 g) raisins

½ cup (80 g) currants

½ cup (80 g) dried cherries

⅓ cup (80 mL) pure maple syrup

3 Tbsp (45 g) unsalted butter, melted

3 Tbsp (45 mL) brandy, orange liqueur or apple cider

2 Tbsp (20 g) finely diced candied ginger

¼ tsp ground cloves

1 recipe Basic Pie Dough (page 315), shaped into 2 cylinders and chilled for 2 hours

1 egg whisked with 2 Tbsp (30 mL) water, for egg wash

Turbinado sugar, for sprinkling

HELPFUL HINT

To bake a single, full-sized pie, use a 9-inch (23 cm) glass pie plate. Line the bottom with the first piece of dough, spoon all of the filling on top and then roll out the second piece of dough to cover it. Use a sharp knife to pierce a few vents in the pastry so steam can escape. Brush the top crust with egg wash and bake for 50 to 60 minutes, until the pastry is evenly browned.

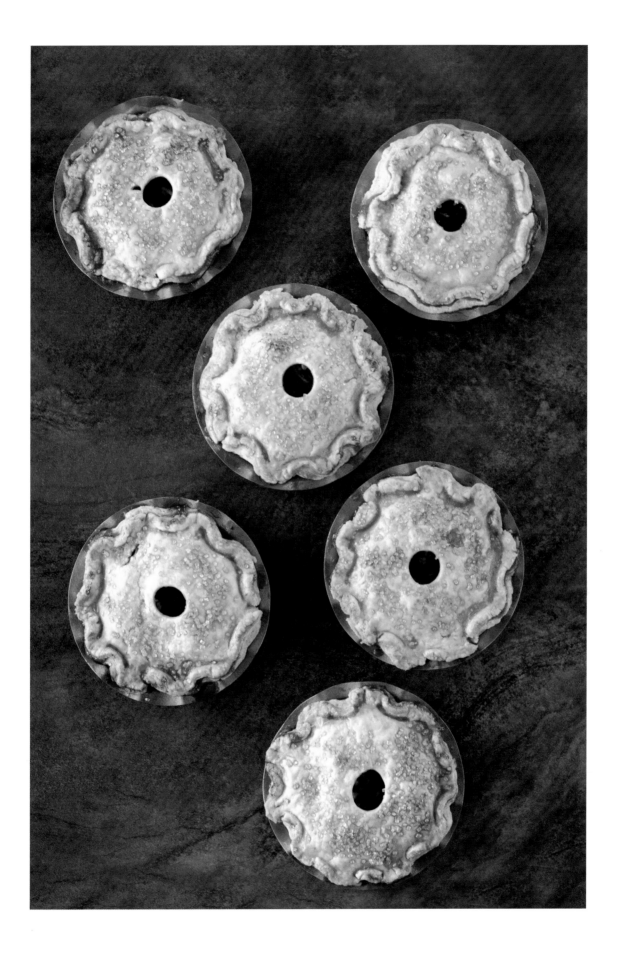

This pie is so named because it is a classic pumpkin pie that has undergone a transformation. A chocolate crust holds a pumpkin cheesecake layer topped with a pumpkin pie filling. The result is a grand two-tiered pumpkin dessert that feeds twice as many people as a regular pumpkin pie. Start this pie the day before you plan to serve it so it has time to set up overnight.

CINDERELLA PUMPKIN PIE

MAKES 1 VERY LARGE, 9-INCH (23 CM PIE) • SERVES 16 •
PREP: 40 MINUTES, PLUS CHILLING • COOK: 100 MINUTES

1. Preheat the oven to 350°F (180°C) and grease a 9-inch (23 cm) springform pan.

2. For the crust, stir the cookie crumbs with the brown sugar and cinnamon and then stir in the melted butter until evenly combined. Press into the bottom and all the way up the sides of the pan. Bake for 10 minutes (no change will be noticeable). Let cool on a wire rack while you make the filling. Leave the oven on.

3. For the cheesecake layer, beat the cream cheese until smooth (by hand is easy enough) and then beat in the sugar, cinnamon, cloves and nutmeg. Switch to a whisk and whisk in the egg, followed by the pumpkin purée.

4. Scrape the batter into the cooled crust and bake for 30 minutes, until the cheesecake no longer jiggles in the centre. While it bakes, prepare the pumpkin pie layer.

Recipe continues ▶

MAKE AHEAD
You can make this pie a full day ahead of serving. Store it, uncovered, in the springform pan in the fridge overnight. Once the pie has been sliced, press a little plastic wrap or parchment paper onto the cut edges and refrigerate for up to 3 days.

CRUST
2 ¾ cups (390 g) chocolate cookie crumbs
2 Tbsp (25 g) packed light brown sugar
½ tsp ground cinnamon
½ cup (115 g) unsalted butter, melted

CHEESECAKE LAYER
1 pkg (8 oz/250 g) cream cheese, at room temperature
⅓ cup (70 g) granulated sugar
1 tsp ground cinnamon
¼ tsp ground cloves
¼ tsp ground nutmeg
1 large egg, at room temperature
½ cup (125 mL) pure pumpkin purée

PUMPKIN PIE LAYER
2 cups (500 mL) pure pumpkin purée
½ cup (100 g) packed light brown sugar
½ cup (100 g) granulated sugar
1 tsp ground cinnamon
¼ tsp ground cloves
¼ tsp ground nutmeg
3 large eggs, at room temperature
1 cup (250 mL) whipping cream
Sweetened whipped cream, for décor (optional)

5. Whisk the pumpkin purée with both sugars and then whisk in the cinnamon, cloves and nutmeg. Whisk in the eggs and then the 1 cup (250 mL) whipping cream. Once the cheesecake layer has baked for 30 minutes, remove the pan from the oven and gently pour the pumpkin pie filling over the cheesecake—it will fill the pan right to the top.

6. Return the pan to the oven and bake for 50 to 60 minutes more, until only the centre of the pie shows signs of jiggling. Let cool in the pan on a wire rack to room temperature, up to 4 hours. Chill the cooled pie, uncovered, in the fridge overnight to set the filling.

7. If you wish to decorate the pie, remove it from the pan and carefully slide it onto a cake stand or a platter. Scoop the whipped cream into a piping bag fitted with a plain or star tip and pipe a crown just around the top of the pie or simply dollop the whipped cream in the centre. Chill until ready to serve.

HELPFUL HINTS

To make a classic pumpkin pie from this recipe, line a 9-inch (23 cm) glass pie plate with ½ recipe of Basic Pie Dough (page 315) and trim and crimp the edges. Prepare the pumpkin pie layer as above, pour it into the pie shell and bake for about 50 minutes at 350°F (180°C), until only the centre of the pie shows signs of jiggling. Cool and then chill completely, uncovered, before serving.

Store-bought pure pumpkin purée works well in this pie. If you'd like to make your own, purchase pie pumpkins, which weigh about 2 lb (900 g) each and will yield about 1 ½ cups (375 mL). (Jack-o'-lantern pumpkins are too stringy and watery for baking.) Cut the pumpkins in half, scoop out the seeds, pierce the skins with a knife or fork and place face down on baking trays. Bake at 350°F (180°C) for 30 to 40 minutes, cool and then peel off the skin and purée the pumpkin until smooth. Pumpkin purée can be packed in resealable bags or airtight containers and frozen for up to 3 months. Thaw overnight in the fridge before using in recipes.

I adore this tart when I'm craving a chocolate dessert. The chocolate pastry shell holds a pomegranate jelly layer hidden under a silky chocolate ganache. The sprinkling of fresh pomegranate seeds on top tantalizingly hints at the hidden layer underneath.

POMEGRANATE CHOCOLATE TART

MAKES ONE 9-INCH (23 CM) TART • SERVES 10 TO 12 •
PREP: 45 MINUTES, PLUS CHILLING • COOK: 35 MINUTES, PLUS COOLING

MAKE AHEAD

You can store the baked tart in the fridge, uncovered, for up to 3 days. Once it's been sliced, cover it to prevent the cut edges from drying out. Or to save time, make the pastry dough ahead of time, wrap it in plastic and freeze for up to 3 months. Thaw overnight in the fridge before rolling.

CRUST

½ cup (115 g) unsalted butter
½ cup (65 g) icing sugar, sifted
3 large egg yolks
1 cup (130 g) cake and pastry flour
⅓ cup (40 g) cocoa powder
½ tsp fine sea salt

POMEGRANATE JELLY

½ cup (125 mL) pomegranate juice
⅔ cup (140 g) granulated sugar
⅓ cup (80 mL) white corn syrup
3 Tbsp (45 mL) liquid pectin

CHOCOLATE GANACHE AND ASSEMBLY

4 oz (120 g) bittersweet couverture/
    baking chocolate, chopped
¼ cup (60 mL) whipping cream
¼ cup (60 g) unsalted butter, cut into
    pieces
2 Tbsp (25 g) granulated sugar
¼ cup (60 mL) pomegranate juice, at
    room temperature
1 large egg, at room temperature
1 tsp pure vanilla extract
Fresh pomegranate seeds and
    chopped pistachios, for garnish

1. For the crust, beat the butter and icing sugar in a large mixing bowl with electric beaters, in the bowl of a stand mixer fitted with the paddle attachment or by hand until fluffy. Beat in the egg yolks 1 at a time, beating well after each addition (scraping down the bowl if needed).

2. Sift in the flour, cocoa powder and salt. Mix on low speed until combined (the dough will be very soft). Scrape the dough onto a piece of plastic wrap, cover and press into a disc. Chill for at least 2 hours before rolling.

3. Have ready a 9-inch (23 cm) fluted tart pan with a removable bottom. Knead the dough once or twice on a lightly floured work surface to soften it, then roll it out to a circle just under ¼ inch (0.5 cm) thick.

4. Lift the dough carefully into the tart pan, pressing it into the corners and trimming away any excess. Dock the pastry with a fork (to prevent air bubbles) and chill the tart shell, uncovered, for at least 20 minutes.

5. Preheat the oven to 350°F (180°C). Place the chilled tart shell on a baking tray and bake for about 18 minutes, until the pastry has an even, dull finish. Let cool completely in the pan on a wire rack while you prepare the pomegranate jelly.

6. For the pomegranate jelly, place the pomegranate juice, sugar and corn syrup in a medium saucepan and whisk together. Bring the mixture to a full boil over high heat (this takes about a minute) and then reduce the heat to medium-high to prevent boiling over. Cook, stirring occasionally, until it reaches 225°F (107°C) on a candy thermometer, about 3 minutes. Remove from the heat and immediately whisk in the pectin. Pour into the cooled tart shell right away and let cool at room temperature to set, about 1 hour.

Recipe continues ▶

7. For the chocolate ganache, preheat the oven to 325°F (160°C). Place the chopped chocolate in a heatproof bowl.

8. Place the cream and butter in a small saucepan over medium heat and bring to just below a simmer. When the cream starts to boil, remove it from the heat and pour it over the chocolate. Let sit for about 30 seconds and then whisk until the chocolate is fully melted and the ganache is smooth. Vigorously whisk in the sugar and the pomegranate juice, followed by the egg and vanilla.

9. Pour the ganache over the jelly layer and bake for 10 minutes (the filling will still be jiggly). Let cool in the pan on a wire rack to room temperature and then chill, uncovered, for at least 2 hours to set the ganache.

10. Sprinkle the top of the tart with pomegranate seeds and chopped pistachios before serving.

HOLIDAY HINT
Not fond of pomegranate, or don't have access to it? This tart is delectable with the same quantities of strained raspberry purée in place of the pomegranate juice in the jelly, and coffee in place of the juice in the ganache. Top it with fresh raspberries, and you've got another holiday-happy treat.

This colourful dessert is refreshing after a rich meal. Since citrus fruits are at their peak around holiday time, you can count on an intense and sweet fruit flavour.

CITRUS MASCARPONE AND PISTACHIO TART

MAKES ONE 12 × 4-INCH (30 × 10 CM) TART · SERVES 8 TO 10 ·
PREP: 30 MINUTES, PLUS CHILLING · COOK: 20 MINUTES

1. Have ready a 12 × 4-inch (30 × 10 cm) rectangular fluted pan with a removable bottom.

2. On a lightly floured surface, roll out the dough to a rectangle about ¼ inch (0.5 cm) thick. Line the tart pan with the dough, pressing it in and trimming away the excess. Dock the pastry with a fork (to prevent air bubbles) and chill, uncovered, for 30 minutes.

3. Preheat the oven to 325°F (160°C). Place the chilled tart shell on a baking tray and bake for about 20 minutes, until lightly browned at the edges. Let cool completely on a wire rack before filling.

4. To make the filling, beat the mascarpone by hand to soften it a little and then stir in the sour cream (or yogurt), icing sugar, orange zest, vanilla and brandy (or orange liqueur). Spoon into the cooled tart shell, spread evenly and level the top.

5. Use a serrated knife to trim the top and bottom from each orange and the grapefruit, and then cut away and discard the rest of the peel, including the white pith. Using a paring knife, gently segment the fruit and separate the flesh from the white membrane. Try to keep each segment whole. Place the flesh in a bowl and discard the membranes. Arrange the citrus segments over the mascarpone filling, alternating colours.

6. Heat the apple jelly (or apricot jam) in a small saucepan over medium-high heat, stirring until melted. Use a pastry brush to brush the citrus segments with the melted jam (to seal them and add shine). Sprinkle with the chopped pistachios and chill, uncovered, for at least an hour before serving.

MAKE AHEAD
You can bake the tart shell and mix the cream filling a full day ahead, but assemble the tart the day you wish to serve it, up to 6 hours ahead of serving. Store it in the fridge, uncovered, until serving time.

½ recipe Vínarterta Linzer Cookie dough (page 216), shaped into a disc, at room temperature
1 cup (235 g) mascarpone cheese
½ cup (125 mL) sour cream or plain Greek yogurt
⅓ cup (45 g) icing sugar
2 tsp finely grated orange zest
1 tsp vanilla bean paste or pure vanilla extract
2 Tbsp (30 mL) brandy or orange liqueur
2 blood oranges (or Cara oranges)
1 large navel orange
1 large pink grapefruit
½ cup (125 mL) apple jelly or apricot jam
2 Tbsp (15 g) chopped shelled pistachios

HELPFUL HINT
If you don't have a rectangular pan, use a 9-inch (23 cm) round tart pan with a removable bottom. And if blood oranges aren't available, use a mix of tangerines or mandarins (2 of each of these for each blood orange).

CELEBRATORY CENTREPIECE CAKES

A FANCY CAKE announces that there's a celebration, no matter the season. All of these cakes meet that expectation: they look stunning when brought to the table, and taste just as good as (or better than) they look.

For the holidays, I like to make classics like plum pudding and trifle (which is a cake assembled and served in a glass bowl), and also introduce some fresh takes on classics, like my spin on Mont Blanc Torte or a Bûche de Noël, to create new traditions. It's been a pleasure to make the classics over the years and to create new ones especially for this book, and it's my hope that you will now take the same pleasure in sharing the sweet side of the holidays with those you love.

Opposite: Lime Chiffon Cake (page 275)

Set a Stunning Dessert Table

If you are a devoted holiday baker like me, it's hard to contemplate serving just one dessert. Or perhaps you have a crowd coming over, so you need to offer a selection of sweet treats. Well, it's showtime! An arrangement of desserts seems natural for a flow-through occasion such as an open house, but I also enjoy setting up a smaller version when I'm having friends over, or for after the big family holiday dinner when we want to push back our chairs and stretch before we take on dessert.

Here are a few tips to keep in mind:

Pick a selection of desserts that balance flavour, colour and texture (see below for some sample menus or read Build a Butter Tart Buffet, page 228).

Play with heights: a trifle bowl or a tiered cake stands high, whereas tarts are elegant down low.

Intermingle grand desserts with a few plates of simpler cookies and squares, and even fresh fruits.

Keep plenty of serving utensils handy.

Label each dessert with a list of ingredients for guests with dietary preferences or allergies.

Decorate the dessert table with ornaments, flowers or other festive décor, but stay away from lit tea lights or candles to prevent the possibility of fire.

CASUAL SWEETS AND TREATS
(FOR 10 TO 24 PEOPLE)

- Classic Spritz Cookies, page 200
- Chocolate Crinkle Cookies, page 209
- Carrot Cake Sandwich Cookies, page 214
- Caramel Apple Bars, page 234
- Graceland Squares, page 230
- Chocolate Barks, page 240
- Maple Fudge, page 246
- Chocolate-Glazed Baked Pumpkin Doughnuts, page 301
- Honey Buttermilk Panna Cotta Verrines with Passionfruit, page 304
- Sticky Toffee Puddings (cut into two-bite portions), page 310

A GRAND SWEET TABLE
(FOR 24 TO 60 PEOPLE)

- Raspberry and Apricot Jam Kolacky, page 210
- Eggnog Buttercream Sandwich Cookies, page 213
- Decorated Speculoos and Vanilla Bean Sugar Cut-Out Cookies, pages 196 and 195
- Candy Cane, Eggnog and Chocolate Orange Macarons, page 219
- Snowflake Marshmallows, page 250
- Cinderella Pumpkin Pie, page 256
- Lime Chiffon Cake with Raspberry Swiss Meringue Buttercream, page 275
- Flourless Chocolate Mont Blanc Torte, page 277
- Light Pineapple Coconut Fruitcake with Fondant, page 281
- Gingerbread White Chocolate Mousse Cake, page 286
- Earl Grey Tiramisu Trifle, page 289
- Festive Red Berry Compote, page 320

Gingerbread White Chocolate Mousse Cake (page 286); A Dickens of a Plum Pudding (page 295); assorted cookies (pages 193–221); Festive Macarons (page 219)

PECAN BUTTER TART CHEESECAKE

MAKES ONE 9-INCH (23 CM) CHEESECAKE · SERVES 16 TO 20 ·
PREP: 30 MINUTES · COOK: 1 HOUR, PLUS CHILLING

1. Preheat the oven to 300°F (150°C). Have the cooled butter tart base at hand in its springform pan.

2. For the cheesecake filling, beat the cream cheese in a bowl using electric beaters, or in a stand mixer fitted with the paddle attachment, on high speed until fluffy. Add the brown sugar and beat well on high speed until dissolved, stopping to scrape down the bowl occasionally.

3. Add the maple syrup and beat again on high speed, scraping the bowl. Add the sour cream and vanilla and beat again on high until smooth. This is the final step to ensure there are no lumps in the mixture, so scrape the bowl well.

4. Reduce the speed to medium-low and add the eggs 1 at a time and then the yolk, beating well after each addition (and yes, scraping down the bowl). Stir in the pecan pieces by hand. Pour over the cooled butter tart base.

5. Bake for about 1 hour, until the cheesecake jiggles in the centre but is set around the outside. (It will still look a little shiny on the surface at the centre.) Let cool in the pan on a wire rack for 10 minutes.

6. Carefully run a palette knife around the inside edge of the pan (this will prevent cracks developing as the cheesecake cools). Once the cake has cooled to room temperature (check by touching the bottom of the pan, not the sides), chill the cheesecake, uncovered, for at least 6 hours, or overnight.

7. To serve the cake, run a palette knife around the inside of the pan again and then loosen and remove the springform ring. Run your palette knife under the base of the cheesecake to loosen it from the bottom of the pan. Carefully slide the cake onto a serving plate.

MAKE AHEAD
You can store the baked but undecorated cheesecake in its pan, well wrapped, in the fridge for up to 4 days. It can be frozen, undecorated and well wrapped, for up to 3 months. Thaw the cake in the fridge overnight before decorating and serving.

BASE
1 recipe Signature Butter Tart Squares (page 227), made with 1 cup (100 g) pecan halves or pieces and baked in a well-greased 9-inch (23 cm) round springform pan, at room temperature

CHEESECAKE FILLING
2 pkgs (each 8 oz/250 g) cream cheese, at room temperature
½ cup (100 g) packed light brown sugar
¼ cup (60 mL) pure maple syrup
½ cup (125 mL) sour cream
2 tsp pure vanilla extract
2 large eggs
1 large egg yolk
½ cup (50 g) lightly toasted pecan pieces

ADD SPARKLE
To decorate the cheesecake, you can top it simply with sweetened whipped cream or sweeten it up even more by adding a few pieces of Maple Fudge (page 246) and Maple Toasted Pecans (page 321) as a garnish.

A Yule log, or bûche de Noël, is a festive classic, and it comes in any
number of flavours. This version will remind you of lemon meringue pie,
with its lemon sponge cake filled with a rich lemon curd and covered
with a sweet, fluffy meringue.

LEMON MERINGUE BÛCHE DE NOËL

Lemon Curd

SERVES 12 TO 16 • PREP: 1 HOUR, PLUS CHILLING • COOK: 25 MINUTES

MAKE AHEAD

You can store the lemon curd in an airtight container in the fridge for up to 3
days. Bake and assemble the cake no
more than 1 day before serving.

LEMON CURD

¼ cup (60 mL) lemon juice
⅓ cup (70 g) granulated sugar
Finely grated zest of 2 lemons
2 large eggs
2 Tbsp (30 mL) full-fat sour cream
½ cup + 2 Tbsp (145 g) cool unsalted
  butter, cut into pieces

CAKE

4 large eggs, separated and at room
  temperature
½ cup (100 g) granulated sugar,
  divided
Finely grated zest of 1 lemon
2 Tbsp (16 g) icing sugar, plus extra
  for dusting the warm cake
⅔ cup (85 g) cake and pastry flour

MERINGUE

3 large egg whites
9 Tbsp (110 g) granulated sugar

1. For the lemon curd, whisk the lemon juice, sugar, lemon zest and
   eggs together in a metal bowl placed over a saucepan filled with
   2 inches (5 cm) of gently simmering water. Whisk constantly (but
   not vigorously) until the mixture thickens, about 9 minutes.

2. Remove the bowl from the heat and whisk in the sour cream. Strain
   the mixture through a fine-mesh sieve into a container tall enough to
   fit an immersion blender (such as a mason jar) and let cool for
   30 minutes.

3. Add the butter pieces all at once and blend until smooth.
   (Alternatively, combine the butter and curd in a blender.) Cover and
   chill for at least 4 hours, until set.

4. For the cake, preheat the oven to 375°F (190°C). Line the bottom of
   a 10 × 15-inch (25 × 37 cm) jelly roll pan with parchment paper and
   leave the sides ungreased.

5. Whisk the egg yolks with ¼ cup (50 g) of the sugar and the lemon
   zest in a metal bowl placed over a saucepan filled with 2 inches
   (5 cm) of gently simmering water, whisking vigorously until the mixture becomes pale and thick, about 4 minutes. Set aside.

6. In a small dish, stir together the remaining ¼ cup (50 g) of granulated sugar and the icing sugar. Using electric beaters or a stand
   mixer fitted with the whip attachment, whip the egg whites on high
   speed until foamy. With the mixer running, gradually pour in the
   sugar and continue to whip until the whites hold a medium peak.

Recipe continues ▶

HELPFUL HINT

Lemon curd is a good staple item to fill tarts or to serve with fresh fruit as a great last-minute dessert. Luckily, this
recipe makes more than you will need to fill the bûche de Noël. You can store leftovers in an airtight container in
the fridge for up to 3 weeks. Small jars of homemade lemon curd make great holiday gifts, too.

7. Fold one-third of the whipped egg whites into the egg yolk mixture. Sift the flour over this and gently fold it in, followed by the remaining egg whites.

8. Spread the batter evenly in the prepared pan and bake for about 10 minutes, until it springs back when gently pressed.

9. Within 5 minutes of removing the cake from the oven, dust the surface with icing sugar and run a palette knife around the inside edge of the pan to loosen the cake.

10. Cover the cake with a clean tea towel. Wearing pot holders, grasp the edges of the pan and the edges of the tea towel and flip the pan over onto a cutting board. Peel away and discard the parchment paper.

11. Dust this second side with icing sugar.

12. Starting at a short end, roll up the bûche and the towel and let them sit like this until cooled.

Step 10

Step 11

Step 12

13. To assemble the cake, gently unroll the cooled sponge cake and remove the towel. Spread an even layer of the lemon curd over the surface of the cake and roll it back up. Place the cake on your serving platter and chill, uncovered, while you prepare the meringue.

14. For the meringue, whisk the egg whites and sugar in a metal bowl placed over a saucepan filled with 2 inches (5 cm) of gently simmering water, whisking constantly until the mixture reaches 160°F (71°C) on a candy thermometer.

15. Using electric beaters, or transferring the mixture to the bowl of a stand mixer fitted with the whip attachment, whip the egg whites until they are thick and glossy and hold a stiff peak when the beaters are lifted. Use the meringue immediately.

16. Spread the meringue over the cake to cover it completely.

17. Use a butane kitchen torch to toast the meringue lightly, or leave as is (since the meringue is cooked, it will hold its shape). Chill the cake until ready to serve.

Step 16

Step 17

> It's not often that I fully commit to a favourite dessert, since I love playing with new ideas, but this one will be on my holiday table for many years to come. It has a fluffy texture, a rich but not overly sweet frosting and a combination of flavours that is truly a crowd-pleaser.

LIME CHIFFON CAKE WITH RASPBERRY SWISS MERINGUE BUTTERCREAM

MAKES ONE 10-INCH (25 CM) LAYER CAKE • SERVES 16 • PREP: 45 MINUTES • COOK: 75 MINUTES

MAKE AHEAD

You can bake the cake up to 2 days ahead and store it, unfrosted and well wrapped, at room temperature. The fully assembled cake can be refrigerated for a further 1 to 2 days. Add the berry garnish no more than 4 hours before serving, otherwise the sugar on the berries will dissolve.

CAKE

7 large eggs, separated and at room
　temperature
3 large egg whites, at room
　temperature
2 tsp cream of tartar
1 ½ cups (300 g) granulated sugar,
　divided
2 ¼ cups (290 g) cake and pastry flour
2 tsp baking powder
½ tsp fine sea salt
Finely grated zest of 3 limes
¾ cup (175 mL) lime juice
½ cup (125 mL) vegetable oil

BUTTERCREAM

6 large egg whites
1 ⅔ cups (240 g) granulated sugar
1 ⅔ cups (365 g) unsalted butter, at
　room temperature, cut into pieces
⅓ cup (80 mL) unstrained raspberry
　purée, made from frozen and
　thawed raspberries
1 Tbsp (15 mL) fresh lime juice
2 tsp pure vanilla extract
1 ½ cups (255 g) fresh raspberries
Granulated sugar, for garnish
Fresh mint leaves, for garnish

1. Preheat the oven to 325°F (160°C). Have ready an ungreased 10-inch (25 cm) angel food cake pan.

2. For the cake, place the 10 egg whites in a large mixing bowl, or in the bowl of a stand mixer fitted with the whip attachment. Add the cream of tartar and whip on high speed until foamy. With the mixer still running, add ¼ cup (50 g) of the sugar and continue to whip until medium peaks form when the beaters are lifted. Set aside.

3. Sift the flour, the remaining 1 ¼ cups (250 g) of sugar, baking powder and salt into a mixing bowl (if using a stand mixer, you do not need to wash the bowl or whip attachment after whipping the egg whites). Add the lime zest, lime juice, oil and the 7 egg yolks. Whip on medium-low speed for 1 minute and then increase the speed to medium-high, whipping for about 2 minutes, until the batter is smooth.

4. Fold the whipped whites into the batter in 2 additions (using a whisk allows you to fold easily without deflating the whipped whites).

5. Pour the batter into the tube pan and bake for about 1 hour, until the centre springs back when gently pressed. Cool the cake in the pan, either upside down on a wire rack or, if the pan has "feet," directly on the counter.

6. To make the buttercream, place the egg whites and sugar in a metal bowl and set it over a saucepan filled with 2 inches (5 cm) of gently simmering water. Whisk constantly (but not vigorously) until the mixture reaches 150°F (65°C) on a candy thermometer, about 6 minutes.

7. Use electric beaters or transfer the mixture to the bowl of a stand mixer fitted with the whip attachment and whip on high speed until the meringue has cooled to room temperature (it will hold a stiff peak by then).

Recipe continues ▶

8. With the mixer running on high speed, add the butter a few pieces at a time. At first the meringue will hold its volume, then the buttercream will deflate a little and become very creamy yet fluffy looking. Beat in the raspberry purée, lime juice and vanilla. Set aside.

9. When the cake has cooled and you're ready to assemble it, run a palette knife around the inside edge of the cake pan. Insert a skewer down the inside of the centre hole in a few places, just to loosen the cake a bit. Tap out the cake onto the counter (you may have to tap it quite hard, but it will come out intact).

Step 10

10. To assemble the cake, use a serrated knife to slice it horizontally into 3 equal layers. Place the bottom third of the cake on a platter or a cake stand and spread the top of it with buttercream. Use a small palette knife to reach into the centre hole and spread buttercream on the inside ring.

11. Set the middle layer on top. Spread buttercream in the centre hole and spread a little buttercream on the edges of both layers of cake. Make sure it is well covered.

12. Spread some buttercream on top of the middle layer of cake and then add the top layer, pressing gently to ensure the cake is level.

13. Spread some buttercream around the edges of the centre hole and then cover the top and sides of the cake completely. Chill the cake for about an hour to set the buttercream, uncovered, until ready to serve.

14. To garnish the cake, make sure the raspberries are dry and at room temperature. Dip half of the raspberries into granulated sugar in a small bowl, shaking off any excess—the sugar will stick to the berries and look like a light coating of frosting. Alternate dusted and undusted berries in a circle on top of the cake, and insert a few mint leaves so the arrangement has the appearance of a wreath.

Step 13

HELPFUL HINT

Use the buttercream at room temperature. When frosting the cake, it's easiest to spread buttercream inside the centre hole at each layer with a small palette knife, rather than trying to do all 3 layers together once the cake is fully assembled.

Mont Blanc Torte, named after the tallest mountain in the European Alps, typically has a meringue base, a cream element and a topping of piped chestnut purée that looks like vermicelli pasta. I've adapted this classic, adding a flourless chocolate torte as the base, but still respecting the chestnut cream and meringue elements.

FLOURLESS CHOCOLATE MONT BLANC TORTE

GF

MAKES ONE 10-INCH (25 CM) TORTE · SERVES 16 ·
PREP: 1 HOUR, PLUS CHILLING · COOK: 135 MINUTES

MAKE AHEAD

You can bake the cake and the meringue a day ahead of serving. Store the cake in the pan in the fridge, uncovered, overnight; loosely cover the baking tray of meringue and leave at room temperature.

FLOURLESS CHOCOLATE CAKE
1 ¼ cups (285 g) unsalted butter, cut into pieces
9 oz (270 g) dark couverture/baking chocolate, cut into pieces
10 large eggs, separated and at room temperature
1 ½ cups (300 g) granulated sugar
2 tsp pure vanilla extract
½ cup (60 g) Dutch process cocoa powder
½ cup (125 mL) full-fat sour cream

MERINGUE CRUMBLE
2 large egg whites, at room temperature
½ cup (100 g) granulated sugar

CHESTNUT CREAM
¾ cup (175 g) canned unsweetened chestnut purée
6 Tbsp (75 g) granulated sugar
½ cup (125 mL) full-fat sour cream (14 to 18%)
2 Tbsp (30 mL) brandy
1 tsp pure vanilla extract
½ cup (125 mL) whipping cream

CHESTNUT VERMICELLI
2 cups (475 g) canned unsweetened chestnut purée
1 tsp pure vanilla extract
¾ cup (100 g) icing sugar, sifted
Splash of brandy, if needed

1. Preheat the oven to 300°F (150°C). Grease a 10-inch (25 cm) springform pan and line the bottom and sides with parchment paper.

2. For the cake, place the butter and chocolate in a metal bowl and set it over a saucepan with an inch (2.5 cm) of barely simmering water, stirring gently until everything has melted and is smooth. Set aside (but the chocolate can be used while still warm).

3. Using electric beaters, or in a stand mixer fitted with the whip attachment, whip the egg whites on high speed until frothy. With the mixer running, slowly add ½ cup (100 g) of the sugar and continue whipping until the whites hold a soft peak when the beaters are lifted. Set aside.

4. Whip the egg yolks, the remaining 1 cup (200 g) of sugar and the vanilla on high speed until the mixture has doubled in volume and is pale and thick, about 4 minutes. Whisk in the melted chocolate by hand.

5. Sift the cocoa powder over the egg yolk mixture and use a whisk to stir it in. Whisk in the sour cream. Fold in the egg whites in 2 additions, almost completely folding in the first before adding

Recipe continues ▶

the second. Scrape the batter into the prepared pan and bake for about 75 minutes, until the top puffs up like a soufflé, cracks a bit and sounds a bit like a drum when tapped.

6. Let cool completely to room temperature in the pan on a wire rack (the cake will fall in the centre), then chill, uncovered, in the pan for at least 2 hours, so that it sets up and is easy to remove from the pan.

7. For the meringue crumble, reduce the oven temperature to 275°F (135°C) and line a baking tray with parchment paper.

8. Using electric beaters or in a stand mixer fitted with the whip attachment, whip the egg whites on high speed until foamy. With the mixer running, slowly pour in the sugar, continuing to whip on high until the egg whites hold a stiff peak when the beaters are lifted. Spoon the meringue into a piping bag fitted with a ½-inch (1 cm) plain tip and pipe lengths (they don't need to be equal) of meringue onto the baking tray.

9. Bake for 40 to 60 minutes, cracking open the oven door a little if you notice the meringues begin to colour within the first 20 minutes (a hint of browning by the end is OK—it matches the look of the assembled torte). The cooking time will depend on the ambient humidity and temperature. Let cool on the baking tray on a wire rack.

10. For the chestnut cream, scoop the chestnut purée into a bowl and smooth it out by hand with a spatula. Beat in the sugar until well combined, then whisk in the sour cream, brandy and vanilla.

11. In a separate bowl, whip the whipping cream on high speed until it forms a soft peak when the beaters are lifted and then fold it into the chestnut mixture. Cover the bowl and chill while you prepare the vermicelli.

12. For the chestnut vermicelli, scoop the chestnut purée into a bowl and smooth it out by hand using a spatula. Stir in the vanilla. Stir in the icing sugar, ¼ cup (32 g) at a time, until the mixture becomes a thick paste that holds its shape but is soft enough to pipe. If it seems a bit stiff, add a splash of brandy. Spoon into a piping bag fitted with a small plain tip, less than ¼ inch (4 mm to 0.5 cm). Keep at room temperature until ready to use.

13. To assemble the cake, release it from the pan, peel away and discard the parchment paper and set the cake on a platter or cake stand. Dollop the chestnut cream on top of the cake, filling the centre where the cake has fallen and spreading to level it. Hold the piping bag full of chestnut vermicelli icing about 2 inches (5 cm) above the torte and squeeze out the purée, letting it wiggle and squiggle into vermicelli as you cover the chestnut cream. Chill the cake, uncovered, for at least 2 hours to set.

14. Immediately before serving, break up the meringue and pile the crumbled pieces high on top of the chilled torte.

HELPFUL HINT

I associate chestnuts with coziness, comfort and the holiday season, especially when I hear someone singing "chestnuts roasting on an open fire." Look for fresh chestnuts and canned unsweetened chestnut purée at stores that stock European ingredients. Can sizes vary, so if you have extra, mix it with a touch of sour cream to garnish Leek, Potato and Celeriac Soup (page 88) or stir into your morning oatmeal.

This fruitcake is not just light in colour, as some fruitcake aficionados prefer, but also light in texture. Instead of serving small pieces along with cookies, cut this cake into slices and present them as an elegant plated dessert.

LIGHT PINEAPPLE COCONUT FRUITCAKE WITH FONDANT

MAKES ONE 9-INCH (23 CM) CAKE • SERVES 16 TO 20 • PREP: 30 MINUTES •
COOK: 60 MINUTES, PLUS SETTING

MAKE AHEAD

Fruitcake is a great make-ahead recipe. You can store the decorated cake, well wrapped, at room temperature for up to 10 days. Or tightly wrap the baked fruitcake without the fondant and freeze it for up to 3 months. Thaw the cake overnight at room temperature before covering it with the fondant.

1 cup (150 g) golden raisins
1 cup (100 g) sweetened flaked coconut
3 Tbsp (30 g) finely diced candied ginger
1 cup (250 mL) well-drained crushed pineapple (about one 14 oz/396 mL can)
¼ cup (60 mL) sweet vermouth or Sherry (or pineapple juice)
Finely grated zest of 1 lime
Zest of 1 lemon
2 tsp pure vanilla extract
1 ⅓ cups (200 g) all-purpose flour
¾ cup (150 g) granulated sugar
1 ½ tsp baking powder
½ tsp fine sea salt
¼ tsp ground nutmeg
¼ tsp ground allspice
6 Tbsp (90 g) unsalted butter, at room temperature and cut into pieces
3 large eggs, at room temperature
10 oz (300 g) white rolling fondant
Icing sugar, for rolling

1. Preheat the oven to 325°F (160°C). Lightly grease a 9-inch (23 cm) round springform pan and line the bottom and sides with parchment paper.

2. Place the raisins, coconut and candied ginger in a bowl with the crushed pineapple, sweet vermouth (or Sherry or pineapple juice), lime and lemon zests and vanilla. Mix together, then set aside to macerate, stirring occasionally, while you prepare the cake batter.

3. Sift the flour, granulated sugar, baking powder, salt, nutmeg and all-spice into a large mixing bowl or the bowl of a stand mixer fitted with the paddle attachment. Add the butter and beat (using electric beaters if not a stand mixer) on medium-low speed until no large bits of butter are visible, about 2 minutes. Break the eggs into a dish, whisk lightly and then add to the flour mixture, mixing on medium-low again, until combined.

4. Stir in the macerated fruits mixture (including any liquids) by hand until it is evenly blended (the batter will be quite liquid). Scrape into the prepared pan and bake for 50 to 60 minutes, until a skewer inserted in the centre comes out clean. Let cool completely in the pan on a wire rack.

5. To decorate the fruitcake, remove it from the pan, peel away and discard the parchment paper and place the cake on a platter.

6. Knead the fondant to soften it a little and, using icing sugar to prevent sticking, roll it into a circle about 10 inches (25 cm) across.

Recipe continues ▶

7. Roll the fondant around your rolling pin and gently unroll it over the cake, pressing it gently to conform to the shape of the cake. (Alternatively, for a fondant topper that leaves the sides of the cake exposed, place the base of your springform pan on the fondant, use a knife to cut out a circle, and slide the fondant onto the springform base and then gently off the base onto the top of the fruitcake.) Trim any extra fondant from the base of the cake.

8. If desired, use cookie cutters to cut out fondant shapes or patterns and arrange them on top of the cake.

9. Before serving, let the cake sit for 1 hour to allow the fondant to dry.

HELPFUL HINTS
This is not an overly boozy fruitcake. To make it more intensely "spirited," brush it with an additional ¼ cup (60 mL) of Sherry or even rum as it cools. For a spirit-free cake, replace the Sherry in the recipe with the same volume of pineapple juice from the can.

Although fresh pineapple might seem a tastier choice for this recipe, I get a more consistent result with canned. The amount of moisture in the pineapple can change the texture of your baked cake, and the moisture content of canned pineapple varies less than with fresh.

This dark fruitcake is as much like a rich, moist chocolate cake as it is a fruitcake. The orange flavour really comes through—and with the chocolate, it's one of my top holiday flavour combinations. Be sure to start this recipe at least the day before you plan to serve it, as the fruit needs to macerate overnight.

CHOCOLATE ORANGE BUNDT FRUITCAKE

MAKES ONE 10-CUP (2.5 L) BUNDT CAKE • SERVES 24 TO 30 • PREP: 30 MINUTES, PLUS RESTING • COOK: 3 ½ HOURS, PLUS SETTING

MAKE AHEAD

You can bake this fruitcake weeks or months ahead of time and freeze it, well wrapped, without the ganache glaze. Thaw the cake overnight at room temperature and then prepare the glaze the day you wish to serve it. Leftovers can be wrapped and stored at room temperature for up to a week (no need to refrigerate).

FRUIT BASE

1 ½ cups (225 g) raisins
1 ½ cups (200 g) dried cranberries
1 cup (175 g) chopped dried apricots
1 cup (160 g) dried cherries
1 cup (150 g) chopped pitted dates
½ cup (85 g) diced Candied Orange Peel (page 318), or store-bought
1 navel orange
½ cup (125 mL) brandy
½ cup (125 mL) orange liqueur

GANACHE GLAZE

4 oz (120 g) chopped bittersweet couverture/ baking chocolate
2 Tbsp (30 g) unsalted butter, cut into pieces
1 Tbsp (15 mL) white corn syrup
1 Tbsp (15 mL) orange liqueur
Silver, white or other coloured dragée candies, for décor

CAKE

1 cup (225 g) unsalted butter, at room temperature
1 cup (200 g) packed dark brown sugar
4 large eggs, at room temperature
2 oz (60 g) chopped bittersweet couverture/ baking chocolate, melted (warm is OK)
1 ⅓ cups (200 g) all-purpose flour
⅓ cup (40 g) Dutch process cocoa powder
1 tsp baking powder
½ cup (50 g) walnut pieces
½ cup (85 g) semisweet chocolate chips

1. The day before you plan to bake the fruitcake, prepare the fruit base. Place the raisins, cranberries, apricots, cherries, dates and candied orange peel in a large mixing bowl and stir to combine. Cut the navel orange into quarters (do not peel), remove any seeds and purée the entire fruit in a blender or food processor (skin and pulp). Measure ½ cup (125 mL) of the purée into the bowl of fruits (add any leftovers to a smoothie or whisk it into a salad dressing), add the brandy and orange liqueur and stir to combine. Cover the bowl with plastic wrap and let sit overnight on the counter.

2. Preheat the oven to 300°F (150°C) and grease a 10-cup (2.5 L) Bundt pan.

3. For the cake, beat the butter and brown sugar together on medium-high speed in a large mixing bowl with electric beaters, or in the bowl of a stand mixer fitted with the paddle attachment, until light and fluffy, about 2 minutes.

4. Add the eggs 1 at a time, beating well after each addition (the mixture may not seem smooth, but that is OK). Beat in the melted chocolate until smooth.

Recipe continues ▶

5. In a separate bowl, sift the flour, cocoa powder and baking powder. Add all at once to the butter mixture and mix on medium-low speed until evenly combined.

6. Stir in the walnut and chocolate chips by hand. Add the fruit in 2 additions, stirring by hand after each addition, until all of the fruit is covered in batter.

7. Spoon the batter into the prepared pan and spread it level. Cut a circle of parchment paper and cut a hole in the centre, trimming it so that it fits directly on the surface of the batter.

8. Bake for 3 to 3 ½ hours, until a skewer inserted in the centre of the cake comes out clean. Let cool in the pan on a wire rack for 30 minutes, and then turn out onto the rack to cool completely.

9. For the ganache glaze, stir the chocolate, butter and corn syrup in a bowl placed over a saucepan filled with an inch (2.5 cm) of barely simmering water until it is smooth. Remove from the heat and stir in the orange liqueur. Let cool to room temperature.

10. Place the fruitcake on a platter and pour the ganache over the top, letting it drip down the sides—the ganache will not completely cover the cake.

11. Sprinkle a few dragée candies on the ganache before it sets. Let the cake sit for 1 hour at room temperature before serving.

Step 10

Step 11

I love a good gingerbread cake, but on its own, it doesn't always get the attention it deserves. This grand dessert is composed of two gingerbread cake layers completely surrounded by a white chocolate mousse and decorated with a few speculoos cookies. The result is a gingerbread cake with a definite "wow" factor.

GINGERBREAD WHITE CHOCOLATE MOUSSE CAKE

MAKES ONE 9-INCH (23 CM) CAKE · SERVES 12 TO 16 ·
PREP: 45 MINUTES, PLUS CHILLING · COOK: 30 MINUTES

1. Preheat the oven to 350°F (180°C). Grease two 8-inch (20 cm) round cake pans and line the bottoms with parchment paper. Dust the sides of the pans with flour, tapping out any excess.

2. For the cake, whisk together the oil, both sugars, egg, egg yolk and ginger by hand.

3. In a separate bowl, sift the flour, baking powder, cinnamon, cloves, allspice and nutmeg. Add to the oil mixture and whisk until blended.

4. In a third bowl, whisk the ginger beer (or ginger ale or club soda), molasses, maple syrup and baking soda. The mixture will be frothy. Add to the batter and beat vigorously until smooth—the batter will be very liquid.

5. Pour the batter into the prepared pans and bake for about 30 minutes, until a skewer inserted in the centre comes out clean. Let cool in the pans on a wire rack for 30 minutes, and then turn out onto the wire rack to cool completely, keeping the parchment on them.

6. For the mousse, have the white chocolate ready in the bowl of a food processor or a blender.

MAKE AHEAD

You can store the baked gingerbread cake layers, each well wrapped, at room temperature for 2 days, or freeze them for up to 3 months. Thaw them at room temperature before you prepare the mousse. If you prefer to get a bit further ahead, store the baked and assembled cake in its springform pan for up to 2 days in the fridge, or even freeze it in the pan, well wrapped, for up to 1 month. Thaw it overnight in the fridge before unmolding and decorating.

CAKE
⅓ cup (80 mL) vegetable oil
¼ cup (50 g) granulated sugar
¼ cup (50 g) packed dark brown sugar
1 large egg
1 egg yolk
1 Tbsp (6 g) finely grated fresh ginger
1¼ cups (185 g) all-purpose flour
1 tsp baking powder
½ tsp ground cinnamon, plus more for dusting the cake
¼ tsp ground cloves
¼ tsp ground allspice
¼ tsp ground nutmeg
½ cup (125 mL) ginger beer, ginger ale or sparkling apple cider
¼ cup (65 g) fancy molasses
¼ cup (60 mL) pure maple syrup
½ tsp baking soda

16 to 24 Speculoos Cut-Out Cookies (page 196), cut into small diamond shapes and baked without the royal icing filling, for garnish (optional)

MOUSSE
10 oz (300 g) chopped white couverture/baking chocolate
¼ cup (60 mL) cold water
1 Tbsp (7 g) unflavoured gelatin powder
2 cups (500 mL) whipping cream, divided

Recipe continues ▶

7. Place the cold water in a small dish and sprinkle the gelatin on top, stirring and then letting it sit for 1 minute. Heat ¾ cup (175 mL) of the cream in a small saucepan over medium heat until it just begins to simmer. Remove the pan from the heat and stir in the gelatin until it dissolves.

8. Pour the hot cream over the white chocolate and blend until smooth, about 30 seconds. Transfer the white chocolate cream to a bowl to cool almost to room temperature, about 30 minutes. (If it sets up, reheat to soften it again for a smooth mousse.)

9. Whip the remaining 1 ¼ cups (310 mL) of cream using electric beaters or a stand mixer fitted with the whip attachment on high speed until it holds a soft peak when the beaters are lifted.

10. Fold half of the whipped cream into the white chocolate mixture using a whisk (it might deflate a little) and then fold in the remaining cream, using a spatula toward the end. The mousse will be pourable.

Step 10

11. To assemble, first peel away and discard the parchment from the baked cake layers and set the cakes aside. Lightly grease a 9-inch (23 cm) springform pan and line the bottom and sides with parchment paper. A large pan is used, so that the mousse can completely surround the cake layers. Pour two-thirds of the mousse into the pan (you are assembling this upside down, so the mousse goes in first.) Gently set 1 cake layer on top, pressing it gently so that the mousse just comes up the sides of the cake (but the cake should not touch the bottom of the pan).

12. Pour the remaining mousse over the bottom cake layer and set the second cake layer on top, again pressing gently so the mousse just comes up the sides of the cake (the cake layers should not touch). Loosely cover and chill the cake for at least 4 hours.

Step 12

13. To decorate and serve, remove the springform ring from the cake and peel away and discard the parchment from the sides of the mousse cake. Place a platter over the top of the cake (really the bottom) and carefully invert both the cake and the platter together. Remove the springform pan base and peel away and discard the parchment.

14. Sprinkle the top of the cake with a little cinnamon or arrange the speculoos cookies in a pattern. Chill until ready to slice and serve.

HELPFUL HINT

If you're looking for a nice, simple gingerbread cake to serve with just a dollop of whipped cream, bake this cake in a greased 9 × 13-inch (22.5 × 32.5 cm) pan for about 40 minutes, until a skewer inserted in the centre comes out clean. Once cooled, cut the cake into squares and serve.

This elegant trifle combines layers of Genoise (sponge cake) and cream like a tiramisu, but with a twist. Instead of coffee, Earl Grey tea is the lead flavour, giving this dessert a milder, more delicate character. Madeira is the base spirit, and steeping it with the tea allows its flavour to infuse each component of the trifle evenly. Don't be put off by the number of parts to this recipe. Each step is relatively simple, and you and your guests will be impressed by the end result. It is perfect for a dessert buffet, as it can sit out on a dessert table for an hour or two.

EARL GREY TIRAMISU TRIFLE

MAKES ONE 10-CUP (2.5 L) TRIFLE • SERVES 16 TO 20 •
PREP: 1 HOUR, PLUS CHILLING • COOK: 1 HOUR

MAKE AHEAD

You can store the baked sponge cake, well wrapped in plastic, at room temperature for up to 3 days, or freeze it for up to 1 month. Thaw it completely at room temperature before using. If you can, assemble the whole trifle a day ahead of serving and chill it to allow the flavours and textures to meld overnight.

SPONGE CAKE

6 large eggs, at room temperature
1 cup (200 g) granulated sugar
1 Tbsp (15 mL) lemon juice
1 tsp finely grated lemon zest
1 cup (150 g) all-purpose flour
¼ tsp fine sea salt
2 Tbsp (30 g) unsalted butter, melted
1 tsp pure vanilla extract

STEEPED MADEIRA

½ cup (125 mL) Madeira
2 Earl Grey tea bags
3 strips lemon peel (peeled using a vegetable peeler)
1 Tbsp (15 mL) pure vanilla extract

SYRUP

½ cup (125 mL) strongly brewed hot Earl Grey tea
⅓ cup (70 g) granulated sugar

CREAM

2 cups (500 mL) whipping cream
2 Tbsp (30 mL) instant skim milk powder
2 Tbsp (25 g) granulated sugar

FILLING

1 pkg (1 lb/450 g) mascarpone cheese
5 large egg yolks
⅓ cup (70 g) granulated sugar
1 oz (30 g) milk couverture/baking chocolate, chopped

ASSEMBLY

1 cup (250 mL) apricot jam, stirred to soften
Milk couverture/baking chocolate, for grating

1. Preheat the oven to 325°F (160°C). Line the bottom of a 9-inch (23 cm) springform pan with parchment paper, but do not grease the pan.

2. For the sponge cake, whip the eggs and sugar with electric beaters, or in a stand mixer fitted with the whip attachment, on high speed until they are almost white and more than triple in volume and hold a ribbon when the beaters are lifted, about 8 minutes. Reduce the speed to medium and mix in the lemon juice and zest.

3. Sift the flour and salt into a bowl. With the mixer still running on medium speed, add the flour to the egg mixture in a quick, steady stream. Spoon about 1 cup (250 mL) of the batter into a bowl (the bowl from the flour works), and stir in the melted butter and vanilla. Return this mixture to the bowl of batter and stir until blended.

Recipe continues ▶

4. Pour the batter into the prepared pan and bake for about 40 minutes, until the centre of the cake springs back when gently pressed. Let cool completely in the pan on a wire rack.

5. For the steeped Madeira, place the Madeira, tea bags and lemon peel in a small saucepan over low heat, let it warm through and then steep over the heat for about 15 minutes, to extract the flavour. Discard the tea bags and lemon peel, stir in the vanilla and set aside to cool.

6. For the syrup, whisk the hot tea with the sugar in a bowl until the sugar dissolves. Stir in 3 Tbsp (45 mL) of the steeped Madeira and set aside.

7. For the cream, whip the cream with the skim milk powder using electric beaters or a stand mixer fitted with the whip attachment on high speed until the cream holds a soft peak when the beaters are lifted. Stir in the sugar and 2 Tbsp (30 mL) of the steeped Madeira. Chill, uncovered, until ready to assemble.

8. For the filling, beat the mascarpone gently by hand with a spatula to soften it. Fold one-quarter of the whipped cream into the mascarpone with a whisk (it might deflate a little) and then fold in another quarter of the whipped cream. It may take some vigorous folding, depending on the brand of the mascarpone and how firm or soft it is. Set aside.

9. Place the egg yolks, sugar and the remaining 5 Tbsp (75 mL) of the steeped Madeira in a metal bowl and place over a saucepan filled with 2 inches (5 cm) of simmering water on medium heat, whisking constantly until the mixture has more than doubled in volume and holds a "ribbon" on the surface when the whisk is lifted.

10. Remove from the heat and add the chocolate, whisking until melted. Whisk in one-third of the mascarpone cream until smooth (again, if might deflate a little) and then fold in the remaining mascarpone cream. Set aside or cover and chill until ready to assemble.

11. To assemble, have ready a 10-cup (2.5 L) trifle bowl. Slice the sponge cake horizontally into 3 layers. Place 1 layer in the bottom of the trifle bowl (trimming it to fit, if needed), brush one-third of the syrup over the sponge cake and top with one-third of the filling, spreading it evenly. Dollop teaspoonfuls of jam overtop but do not spread it. Repeat with the 2 remaining cake layers, syrup, filling and jam.

12. Top the trifle with the remaining whipped cream, levelling the top, and garnish with a little grating of milk chocolate. Chill, uncovered, for at least 4 hours before serving.

Sometimes, the holiday meal calls for a true classic. This recipe has everything you would expect from a proper English trifle: cake, custard cream, fruit and Sherry. It will satisfy even the most ardent Christmas traditionalist.

CLASSIC ENGLISH FRUIT AND CREAM TRIFLE

MAKES ONE 10-CUP (2.5 L) TRIFLE • SERVES 16 TO 20 •
PREP: 1 HOUR, PLUS CHILLING • COOK: 30 MINUTES

MAKE AHEAD

The flavour and texture of trifle improve if it is assembled a day ahead. You can prepare the cake and the pastry cream ahead of time. Store the baked sponge cake, well wrapped in plastic, at room temperature for up to 3 days, or freeze it for up to a month. Thaw it completely at room temperature before using. Prepare the pastry cream up to 2 days ahead and chill it in an airtight container in the fridge. Cover and refrigerate leftover trifle for up to 3 days.

PASTRY CREAM

¼ cup (60 g) unsalted butter, cut into
    pieces
2 cups (500 mL) 2% milk
1 vanilla bean or 1 Tbsp (15 mL) vanilla bean
    paste
6 large egg yolks
6 Tbsp (75 g) granulated sugar
¼ cup (30 g) cornstarch

CREAM AND FRUIT LAYERS

1 ½ cups (375 mL) whipping cream,
    divided
2 Tbsp (25 g) granulated sugar
1 tsp pure vanilla extract
4 cups (680 g) assorted fresh berries
    (raspberries, blueberries, blackberries,
    sliced strawberries)
⅔ cup (160 mL) berry jam

1. For the pastry cream, place the butter in a heatproof bowl and set a fine-mesh sieve on top.

2. Heat the milk with the scraped seeds of the vanilla bean (or vanilla bean paste) in a saucepan over medium heat until just below a simmer.

3. In another heatproof bowl, whisk together the egg yolks, sugar and cornstarch. Gradually whisk the hot milk into the egg mixture and then return it all to the pot. Whisk constantly (switching to a spatula now and again, to get into the corners) until thickened and glossy, about 2 minutes.

4. Immediately pour the milk mixture through the sieve over the butter, whisking it through if needed, then remove the sieve. Stir the milk into the butter until the butter melts and the mixture is fully combined. Place a piece of plastic wrap directly over the surface of the pastry cream, let it cool to room temperature and then chill for at least 2 hours.

5. For the cream and fruit layers, whip the cream using electric beaters, or a stand mixer fitted with the whip attachment, on high speed until the cream holds a soft peak when the beaters are lifted. Gently fold one-third of the whipped cream into the chilled pastry cream with a spatula. Fold the sugar and vanilla into the remaining whipped cream. Chill until needed.

6. In a separate bowl, toss the berries gently with the jam.

ASSEMBLY
1 baked Sponge Cake (page 289)
⅓ cup (80 mL) cream Sherry
¼ cup (30 g) toasted sliced almonds

7. To assemble, have ready a 10-cup (2.5 L) glass bowl. Cut the cake horizontally into 3 to 4 layers, depending on the depth of your bowl.

8. Place 1 cake layer in the bottom of the bowl and sprinkle or brush generously with a third or a quarter of the Sherry, followed by a third or a quarter of the pastry cream (depending on the number of cake layers). It's easiest to dollop the pastry cream over the cake and spread it out to level it. Spoon a third or a quarter of the berries over the cream. Repeat with the remaining cake, Sherry, pastry cream and berries.

9. Top the trifle with the reserved whipped cream and sprinkle with toasted almonds. Chill, uncovered, until ready to serve.

HELPFUL HINT

For a family-friendly version of this trifle, simply omit the Sherry. It will slightly change the flavour but not the moistness of the cake.

Participating in a public reading of Charles Dickens's *A Christmas Carol* is one of my holiday traditions. For me, the most memorable sections of this classic tale are the food scenes. In stave 3 of the novella, the Ghost of Christmas Present brings the miserly Ebenezer Scrooge to his underpaid clerk Bob Cratchit's home, where the family is preparing their Christmas feast. Mrs. Cratchit is wearing her well-worn dress "but brave in ribbons," Master Peter is diving into the pan of potatoes and the two littlest children are imagining a roasted goose so intensely that they can smell the onions and sage with it and the bird being brought to the table "hissing hot" to be enjoyed by all. But the masterpiece everyone is waiting for is the pudding . . . and I love the holiday stress that shows in Mrs. Cratchit's doubts about it not being done enough or it breaking while being turned out after steaming or being stolen while the family was merry with the goose . . . Yet, "in half a minute Mrs. Cratchit entered—flushed, but smiling proudly—with the pudding, like a speckled cannonball, so hard and firm, blazing in half of half-a-quartern of ignited brandy, and bedight with Christmas holly tuck into the top. Oh, a wonderful pudding!"

A DICKENS OF A PLUM PUDDING

MAKES ONE 8-CUP (2 L) PUDDING • SERVES 12 TO 14 • PREP: 20 MINUTES • COOK: 4 HOURS

MAKE AHEAD

You can store the baked pudding in its mold in the fridge for up to 3 days. Before serving, fill the stockpot with 3 inches (7.5 cm) water, set the mold on a metal cookie cutter and steam until warmed through, about 40 minutes. The pudding can also be made and frozen, well wrapped, out of the pan, for up to 3 months. Thaw it overnight in the fridge and then reheat in the pan, as above.

1 cup (160 g) dried currants
1 cup (150 g) raisins
1 cup (100 g) walnut pieces
½ cup (85 g) homemade
  diced Candied Orange Peel
  (page 318), or store-bought
2 tsp ground cinnamon
1 tsp fine sea salt
1 tsp ground cloves
1 tsp ground nutmeg
½ tsp ground allspice
½ cup (125 mL) brandy or dry
  Sherry

5 large eggs
1 cup (200 g) granulated sugar
1 cup (250 mL) 2% milk
2 cups (300 g) all-purpose flour
2 cups (260 g) dry breadcrumbs
1 cup (225 g) unsalted butter,
  melted
1 tsp baking soda
1 recipe Honey Crème Anglaise
  (page 317)

1. Lightly grease an 8-cup (2 L) steam pudding mold (a curved metal or ceramic mold with a lid). Have ready a large stockpot filled with 3 inches (7.5 cm) of water and a metal cookie cutter about 3 inches (7.5 cm) in size, as well as the metal ring from the lid of a mason jar, or a small wire rack that will fit inside the stockpot.

2. Toss the currants, raisins, walnuts, candied peel, cinnamon, salt, cloves, nutmeg and allspice together. Stir in the brandy (or Sherry) and let sit while preparing the pudding batter.

3. Whisk the eggs with the sugar in a large bowl, then whisk in the milk. Sift in the flour and whisk well to combine. Stir in the breadcrumbs followed by the melted butter. Stir in the macerated fruits and nuts (including any soaking liquid).

—
CELEBRATORY
CENTREPIECE
CAKES

Recipe continues ▶

4. Stir the baking soda in a small dish with 1 Tbsp (15 mL) of warm water. Add this mixture to the batter quickly, stirring until just combined, and then scrape the batter into the prepared pudding mold and secure the lid.

5. Bring the stockpot of water to a gentle simmer over medium heat. Set the cookie cutter (or mason jar lid or wire rack) in the bottom of the saucepan and place the pudding mold on top of the ring (this prevents it from touching the bottom of the saucepan and possibly burning). The water should only come halfway up the sides of the pan.

6. Cover the stockpot with a lid and steam the pudding for 4 hours, checking periodically to be sure the water level remains the same. Add hot water as needed to keep the level constant and adjust the temperature, if required, to keep it at a very gentle simmer.

7. Remove the pudding from the pot, remove the lid and let the pudding cool for 1 hour on a wire rack.

8. To serve, turn out the pudding onto a serving platter. Serve warm or at room temperature with the crème anglaise.

HELPFUL HINTS

A pudding mold really is recommended here. I have tried making pudding in ceramic and metal pans that have been covered and wrapped with parchment paper and aluminum foil, but I find that too often water seeps in—and you don't want to be like Mrs. Cratchit, stressing over your pudding.

Omit the brandy and use apple cider or apple juice in the same measure for a family-friendly version of this pudding.

PLATED PUDDINGS AND OTHER ELEGANT DESSERTS

NOT EVERY DESSERT falls into the pie, tart or cake category. An individually baked or chilled dessert can be just as stunning, and each person at the table feels special because they have their own personal dessert. In some instances, you may enjoy taking the time to carefully plate the dessert (like dressing up a slice of Marquise with a sauce); in other cases (like the Panna Cotta) the vessel in which the dessert is prepared is plating enough—just a cocktail napkin and a plate underneath do the trick.

Opposite: Chocolate and Irish Cream Marquise (page 303)

When I was a kid, homemade doughnuts were always something special. These baked ones are a little more virtuous than their fried counterparts, and they make a great treat after shovelling snow or while gathering around the TV for a movie night during the holidays. They are also a delight to serve like petits fours, with coffee or tea after a special meal.

CHOCOLATE-GLAZED BAKED PUMPKIN DOUGHNUTS

MAKES 18 LARGE DOUGHNUTS OR 6 DOZEN MINI DOUGHNUTS •
PREP: 25 MINUTES • COOK: 25 MINUTES, PLUS SETTING

MAKE AHEAD

You can store baked and glazed doughnuts in an airtight container at room temperature for up to 3 days. Or freeze them, unglazed but well wrapped, for up to 3 months. Thaw them completely at room temperature before glazing.

DOUGHNUTS

1 cup (250 mL) pure pumpkin purée
½ cup (100 g) granulated sugar
½ cup (100 g) packed light brown sugar
½ cup (125 mL) full-fat sour cream
½ cup (115 g) unsalted butter, melted (warm is OK)
2 large eggs
1 tsp pure vanilla extract
2 cups (300 g) all-purpose flour
2 tsp baking powder
1 tsp ground cinnamon
1 tsp ground ginger
½ tsp ground nutmeg
½ tsp fine sea salt

CHOCOLATE GLAZE

6 oz (180 g) bittersweet couverture/baking chocolate, chopped
6 Tbsp (90 g) unsalted butter, cut into pieces
1 Tbsp (15 mL) white or golden corn syrup

1. Preheat the oven to 350°F (180°C) for regular-sized doughnuts or 325°F (160°C) for mini doughnuts. Lightly grease your doughnut pans.

2. For the doughnuts, whisk the pumpkin purée, both sugars, sour cream, melted butter, eggs and vanilla in a large mixing bowl until evenly combined.

3. In a separate bowl, sift the flour, baking powder, cinnamon, ginger, nutmeg and salt and add all at once to the pumpkin mixture. Whisk until the batter is evenly combined and there are no visible lumps.

4. Spoon the batter into a piping bag fitted with a large plain tip (or a medium plain tip for mini doughnuts) and pipe it into the prepared pans.

Recipe continues ▶

301
—
PLATED
PUDDINGS
AND OTHER
ELEGANT
DESSERTS

HELPFUL HINT

To get a proper doughnut shape, you do need to use doughnut pans. They look like muffin pans except they have a raised bit in the centre of each cavity that creates the hole in the middle. If you don't have a doughnut pan, make these as muffins—you will get 18 regular muffins from the recipe and the bake time will be just 5 minutes longer (or 3-4 minutes shorter if you'd like to make mini muffins).

5. Bake for about 20 minutes for regular doughnuts (15 minutes for minis), until the doughnuts spring back when gently pressed. Turn them out onto a wire rack to cool completely.

6. For the glaze, place the chocolate, butter and corn syrup in a metal bowl and set it over a saucepan filled with an inch (2.5 cm) of barely simmering water, stirring gently with a spatula. When the glaze has melted, remove from the heat and use immediately.

7. Dip the tops of the doughnuts into the glaze, place glazed side up on a wire rack or a baking tray and let set for 1 hour before eating.

Step 5

Step 7

> A marquise is denser than a mousse but fluffier than a chocolate truffle. It is typically poured into a loaf pan or mold and chilled before being sliced into portions.

CHOCOLATE AND IRISH CREAM MARQUISE

MAKES ABOUT 2 CUPS (500 ML) · SERVES 8 ·
PREP: 20 MINUTES, PLUS CHILLING · COOK: 10 MINUTES

MAKE AHEAD

You can store the marquise, well wrapped, in the fridge for up to 4 days before serving, or freeze it in its pan for up to 1 month. Thaw it overnight in the fridge before serving.

8 oz (240 g) semisweet couverture/ baking chocolate, chopped

½ cup + 6 Tbsp (215 mL) whipping cream, divided

½ cup (125 mL) 2% milk

2 large egg yolks

2 Tbsp (25 g) granulated sugar

¼ cup (60 mL) Irish cream liqueur

6 Tbsp (90 g) cold unsalted butter, cut into pieces

Fresh berries or Festive Red Berry Compote (page 320), for garnish

1. Line the bottom and sides of a small loaf pan, terrine or another mold that can hold 2 cups (500 mL) with parchment paper or plastic wrap.

2. Place the chopped chocolate in the bowl of a food processor or blender.

3. Place the ½ cup (125 mL) of cream and the milk in a small saucepan over medium heat and bring to a simmer.

4. Whisk the egg yolks and sugar together in a heatproof bowl. Pour the hot milk into the egg yolk mixture a little at a time. Return the entire mixture to the saucepan and stir with a wooden spoon until it coats the back of the spoon, about 2 minutes.

5. Pour the custard into the food processor or blender and blend with the chocolate until melted and smooth. Blend in the Irish cream. Let the custard cool for 10 minutes, and then blend in the butter until smooth. Transfer to a bowl to cool to room temperature, about 20 minutes.

6. Whisk the remaining 6 Tbsp (90 mL) of cream by hand (since it's such a small amount, this won't take long) until it holds a soft peak. Use a spatula to quickly fold the whipped cream into the chocolate mixture (it might deflate a little).

7. Scrape into the prepared pan, cover with plastic wrap and chill for at least 4 hours before serving.

8. To serve, carefully turn out the marquise onto a serving platter and discard the parchment (or plastic wrap). Using a hot, dry knife, cut individual slices and arrange them on plates. Garnish with a few berries or a spoonful of Festive Red Berry Compote.

Photo on page 298

303
—
PLATED
PUDDINGS
AND OTHER
ELEGANT
DESSERTS

ADD SPARKLE

If you have a terrine mold in the shape of a semi-circle or a triangle, feel free to use it.

These eggless custards are simple to make and not as heavy as many holiday treats, and they're garnished with passionfruit, which are at their peak during this season and make a lovely aromatic topping. *Verrines* just means small glass containers, so choose the size and shape that works best for your menu.

HONEY BUTTERMILK PANNA COTTA VERRINES WITH PASSIONFRUIT

SERVES 6 AS A FULL DESSERT, 18 AS A MINI DESSERT •
PREP: 15 MINUTES, PLUS CHILLING • COOK: 5 MINUTES

1. Pour the milk into a small dish and sprinkle the gelatin on top. Stir and set aside.

2. Place the cream, honey and vanilla in a medium saucepan over medium heat and whisk until warm but not simmering, about 4 minutes. Remove the pan from the heat and whisk in the softened gelatin. Let cool for about 15 minutes and then whisk in the buttermilk. Divide evenly among serving glasses and chill uncovered until set, at least 4 hours.

3. To serve, cut each passionfruit in half and spoon out the flesh into a small dish. Place a little on top of each chilled dessert. Garnish with mint leaves.

MAKE AHEAD
You can store the baked panna cottas in the fridge for up to 2 days (once set, they can be wrapped).

¼ cup (60 mL) cold 2% milk
1 Tbsp (7 g) unflavoured gelatin
    powder
1 ½ cups (375 mL) whipping cream
¼ cup (75 g) honey
1 tsp pure vanilla extract
1 cup (250 mL) buttermilk
2 ripe passionfruit
Mint leaves, for garnish

HELPFUL HINT
When buying passionfruit, look for fruit that is developing a wrinkle on its skin—this tells you the fruit is ripe. If the skin seems taut, let the passionfruit ripen on the counter for a few days.

> *Pouding chômeur* means "poor man's pudding" and it originated in Quebec during the Great Depression. While we consider maple syrup a decadent ingredient now, at that time, it was the local sweetener and granulated sugar was the decadent, inaccessible ingredient. If you've never tried this dessert, you are in for a treat: it's a scone-like batter with a syrup poured over it, and as the pudding bakes, it rises and the syrup cooks and thickens underneath. It's like a French-Canadian version of sticky toffee pudding. Here I've added diced apples, which meld with the syrup, giving these puddings an apple pie character.

INDIVIDUAL APPLE POUDINGS CHÔMEUR

SERVES 8 • PREP: 15 MINUTES • COOK: 30 MINUTES

MAKE AHEAD

These pudding cakes really are best served right after baking. If you must make them ahead, store them well wrapped and chilled. Reheat them in a 300°F (150°C) oven for about 20 minutes, but be prepared for some of the sauce to get absorbed into the cake.

PUDDING CAKES

2 medium apples, peeled and diced
1 ½ cups (225 g) all-purpose flour
½ cup (100 g) granulated sugar
1 ½ tsp baking powder
Pinch of fine sea salt
½ cup (115 g) cold unsalted butter, cut into pieces
1 cup (250 mL) 2% milk

SAUCE

¾ cup (175 mL) pure maple syrup
¾ cup (150 g) packed light brown sugar
⅓ cup (80 mL) water
¼ cup (60 g) unsalted butter
1 tsp pure vanilla extract

1. Preheat the oven to 350°F (180°C). Lightly grease eight 5 oz (150 mL) ramekins or other ovenproof dishes and place them on a baking tray.

2. For the pudding cakes, divide the diced apples evenly among the dishes.

3. Sift the flour, sugar, baking powder and salt into a large mixing bowl. Add the butter and use a pastry cutter or your fingertips to work it into the flour until you have a rough, crumbly mixture (small bits of butter may be visible, but that is OK). Add the milk and stir just until the mixture comes together—it will be sloppy. Spoon into the prepared ramekins.

4. For the sauce, place the maple syrup, brown sugar, water, butter and vanilla in a medium saucepan over high heat and bring to a boil, stirring occasionally. Once it reaches a rolling boil, remove from the heat and ladle the syrup over the cake in the ramekins. It will seem like a lot of syrup, but half will bake into the cake and half will thicken into a sauce at the bottom . . . magic!

5. Bake for about 30 minutes, until a skewer inserted in the centre of a pudding comes out clean. Transfer the ramekins to a rack to cool for about 15 minutes before serving (that syrup is hot!).

307
—
PLATED
PUDDINGS
AND OTHER
ELEGANT
DESSERTS

HELPFUL HINT
If you are a pouding chômeur purist, you can omit the apples.

I love a good bread pudding in the winter (in fact, I can't recall ever having bread pudding in warm weather—it seems somehow wrong). If you've been gifted a large panettone and don't know what to do with it, you'll love this recipe. And if you've made my homemade Panettone (page 182) and have any leftovers, this is the recipe for you.

PANETTONE BREAD PUDDINGS

SERVES 6 · PREP: 15 MINUTES · COOK: 50 MINUTES, PLUS CHILLING

1. Preheat the oven to 350°F (180°C). Grease six 5 oz (150 mL) ramekins and place them in a roasting pan.

2. Place the panettone cubes in a large mixing bowl. In a separate bowl, whisk together the eggs and egg yolks and then whisk in the milk, sugar and vanilla. Pour this over the panettone and stir well. Let it sit for about 15 minutes, stirring once or twice, so the bread can absorb some of the liquid.

3. Ladle the bread and liquid into the ramekins. Sprinkle the tops with cinnamon sugar. Pour boiling water into the roasting pan, so that the water comes halfway up the sides of the ramekins.

4. Bake, uncovered, for about 50 minutes, until the bread puddings puff up, turn golden brown and spring back when gently pressed in the centre. Let the ramekins cool in the pan for 15 minutes, then transfer to a wire rack to cool for about 30 minutes before serving. To serve cold, chill uncovered for at least 3 hours after cooling.

MAKE AHEAD

You can refrigerate the baked bread puddings in their ramekins, well wrapped, for up to 2 days. Serve cold, or re-warm the puddings, covered, in a 325°F (160°C) oven for about 20 minutes.

Unsalted butter, for greasing ramekins
6 cups (300 g) diced day-old Panettone (page 182), crusts removed
2 large eggs
2 large egg yolks
2 ½ cups (625 mL) 2% milk
¾ cup (150 g) granulated sugar
2 tsp pure vanilla extract
Cinnamon sugar, for sprinkling

ADD SPARKLE

I'm perfectly content to enjoy bread pudding on its own, but you can serve it with warm Butter Caramel Sauce (page 316), Festive Red Berry Compote (page 320) or Honey Crème Anglaise (page 317) on the side.

> This sticky toffee pudding recipe is baked in a pan and cut into squares like a gingerbread cake. It is moist and delicious and super simple to make. It's also one of my mom's favourite desserts, so you know that this warm wintry classic is on my table during the holidays.

STICKY TOFFEE PUDDINGS

MAKES ONE 8-INCH (20 CM) SQUARE PAN • SERVES 12 •
PREP: 15 MINUTES, PLUS COOLING • COOK: 30 MINUTES

1. Preheat the oven to 350°F (180°C) and grease an 8-inch (20 cm) square metal or ceramic pan. Line the bottom and sides of the pan with parchment paper if you plan on portioning and plating in the kitchen before serving.

2. Place the dates in a large heatproof bowl and pour the boiling water over them. Stir in the baking soda and set aside until lukewarm.

3. Cream the butter and sugar together by hand in a large mixing bowl—the mixture will be sandy, not smooth or creamy. Add the eggs 1 at a time, beating well after each addition. Sift in the flour, baking powder, salt and cloves and stir to combine.

4. Add the date mixture (including all of the water) and stir well—the batter will be very pale and liquid. Pour into the prepared pan and bake for about 30 minutes, until a skewer inserted in the centre comes out clean. Let cool for at least 15 minutes on a wire rack before serving.

5. To serve, cut the pudding cake into individual squares and serve warm, topped with the toffee sauce, or pool the sauce on the plate and place the pudding on top.

MAKE AHEAD
You can store the baked pudding cake in the pan, well wrapped, at room temperature for up to 3 days. Warm it in a 300°F (150°C) oven for 15 minutes (or microwave individual slices) to heat through before serving. The toffee sauce can also be made ahead, chilled in a bowl or jar and gently warmed over medium heat just before serving.

2 cups (300 g) chopped pitted dates
1 cup (250 mL) boiling water
¾ tsp baking soda
¼ cup (60 g) unsalted butter, at room temperature
¾ cup (150 g) granulated sugar
2 large eggs, at room temperature
1 ¼ cups (185 g) all-purpose flour
1 ½ tsp baking powder
¼ tsp fine sea salt
Pinch of ground cloves
1 recipe Warm Toffee Sauce (page 317)

ADD SPARKLE
To serve this fragrant and appealing dessert at the table, bake it in an 8-cup (2 L) capacity ceramic dish. Pour the warm toffee sauce into a pitcher and let guests drizzle it over their pudding.

These light steamed puddings are citrusy and moist. They are a nice option for a casual supper, and can easily be made ahead and reheated as needed.

CRANBERRY ORANGE STEAMED PUDDINGS

SERVES 6 • PREP: 15 MINUTES • COOK: 30 MINUTES, PLUS COOLING

1. Preheat the oven to 350°F (180°C). Grease six 5 oz (150 mL) ramekins and sprinkle them with a coating of granulated sugar, tapping out any excess. Place the ramekins in a roasting pan with sides higher than the ramekins.

2. Beat the butter, sugar and orange zest by hand until smooth. Add the eggs 1 at a time, blending well after each addition, and then beat in the egg yolk, orange juice and vanilla.

3. Sift in the flour, baking powder and salt and stir until evenly combined. Stir in the cranberries. Spoon the batter into the ramekins and level it off.

4. Pour boiling water into the roasting pan to reach halfway up the ramekins. Cover the pan with aluminum foil (or a lid, if available) and bake for about 30 minutes, until the tops of the puddings spring back when gently pressed.

5. Using a tea towel or canning tongs, transfer the ramekins to a wire rack to cool for at least 20 minutes before serving.

6. To serve, unmold the puddings from the ramekins by inverting them onto individual plates. Serve with Honey Crème Anglaise.

MAKE AHEAD

You can refrigerate these cooled baked puddings in the ramekins, wrapped in plastic, for up to 3 days. Before serving, let them sit at room temperature for 1 hour, then reheat in a covered water bath for 20 minutes at 300°F (150°C), or in the microwave for 30 to 45 seconds.

¾ cup (150 g) granulated sugar, plus more for sprinkling
½ cup (115 g) unsalted butter, at room temperature
Zest of 1 orange
2 large eggs, at room temperature
1 large egg yolk
2 Tbsp (30 mL) orange juice
1 tsp pure vanilla extract
1 ⅓ cups (200 g) all-purpose flour
1 tsp baking powder
Pinch of fine sea salt
½ cup (70 g) dried cranberries
1 recipe Honey Crème Anglaise (page 317), chilled

SWEET SUPPORTING ACTS

This is my go-to pie dough for both savoury and sweet pie-making the whole year through. I always make an extra batch at holiday time and keep it in the freezer, just in case.

BASIC PIE DOUGH

MAKES ENOUGH FOR ONE 9-INCH (23 CM) DOUBLE-CRUST PIE · PREP: 10 MINUTES, PLUS CHILLING

MAKE AHEAD
You can refrigerate the dough, well wrapped, for up to 2 days, or freeze it for up to 3 months. Thaw overnight in the fridge before rolling.

2 ½ cups (375 g) all-purpose flour
1 Tbsp (12 g) granulated sugar
1 tsp fine sea salt
3 Tbsp (45 mL) vegetable oil
1 cup (225 g) cool unsalted butter, cut into pieces (does not have to be ice cold)
¼ cup (60 mL) cool water
2 tsp white vinegar or lemon juice

1. Combine the flour, sugar and salt in a large mixing bowl. Add the oil and blend in using a pastry cutter, electric beaters or a mixer fitted with the paddle attachment, until the flour looks evenly crumbly in texture.

2. Add the butter and cut in until the dough is rough and crumbly but small pieces of butter are still visible.

3. Place the water and vinegar (or lemon juice) in a small bowl, stir together and then add all at once to the flour mixture, mixing just until the dough comes together. Shape it into 2 discs, wrap well and chill until firm, at least 1 hour.

HELPFUL HINT
For a vegan version of this pie dough, replace the 1 cup (225 g) of butter with ¾ cup (180 g) of virgin coconut oil and increase the cool water to 7 Tbsp (105 mL). Do not chill the dough (the coconut oil sets up too firmly when chilled). Instead, let it rest, wrapped, at room temperature for at least 2 hours before rolling. (You can also freeze this dough, and thaw it, just like the regular recipe.)

Regular caramel is finished with cream, but this super-rich version is finished with a combination of cream and butter. It is wonderfully gooey at room temperature, making it great for that perfect drizzle or drip over a slice of cake, a steamed pudding or a bowl of ice cream.

BUTTER CARAMEL SAUCE

MAKES ABOUT 1 ½ CUPS (375 ML) · PREP: 5 MINUTES · COOK: 6 MINUTES

1. Place the water and lemon juice in a medium saucepan and then add the sugar (do not stir). Bring to a full boil on high heat and continue to boil, without stirring, until the sugar becomes amber, about 4 minutes from when it begins to boil. As the sugar cooks, occasionally brush the sides of the saucepan with water to keep the saucepan clean (this prevents the sugar from crystallizing).

2. Remove the saucepan from the heat. Carefully whisk in the cream, and then whisk in the butter until melted.

3. Whisk in the vanilla and salt and set aside to cool for at least an hour. Serve warm (it can be reheated, if needed). To store, cool to room temperature before chilling in an airtight container or jar (see note below). If gifting, pack the fluid caramel into little jars, then let set in the fridge before labelling with a "serve by" date along with heating instructions.

MAKE AHEAD

You can refrigerate the caramel sauce in an airtight container until the expiry date on the cream you used to make it. To use, reheat the sauce over medium-low heat until fluid, or microwave on high for 10-second intervals, stirring until the sauce is pourable.

3 Tbsp (45 mL) water
2 tsp lemon juice
1 cup (200 g) granulated sugar
½ cup (125 mL) whipping cream
½ cup (115 g) unsalted butter, cut in pieces
1 tsp pure vanilla extract
1 tsp fine sea salt

HELPFUL HINT

I store all of my holiday sauces in labelled and dated mason jars so that I can see the contents. In these jars they can go from fridge to table, and with the metal lid off, can go right into the microwave for reheating, if need be.

This is the quintessential sauce to serve with Sticky Toffee Puddings (page 310) or A Dickens of a Plum Pudding (page 295). This is quicker and simpler to make than caramel sauce, so in a pinch you can serve this sauce over ice cream for a last-minute dessert.

WARM TOFFEE SAUCE

MAKES ABOUT 1 ½ CUPS (375 ML) • PREP: 5 MINUTES • COOK: 5 MINUTES

MAKE AHEAD
You can refrigerate this sauce in an air-tight container until the expiry date on the cream you used to make it. To use, reheat the sauce in a small saucepan over medium heat or microwave until fluid.

1 cup (250 mL) whipping cream
1 cup (200 g) packed demerara or
    dark brown sugar
2 Tbsp (37 g) honey
¼ cup (60 mL) whiskey or brandy

1. Place the cream, demerara (or brown) sugar and honey in a small saucepan over medium heat and bring to a boil, whisking occasionally. Reduce the heat to medium and simmer for 2 minutes, whisking occasionally, to thicken a little.

2. Whisk in the whiskey (or brandy) and simmer for 1 minute more, while still whisking. Serve the sauce warm.

I love to serve a custard sauce like this one with fruit desserts such as Cranberry Orange Steamed Puddings (page 312), or as an alternative to toffee sauce with Sticky Toffee Puddings (page 310). Or with just about anything chocolate.

HONEY CRÈME ANGLAISE

MAKES ABOUT 1 CUP (250 ML) • PREP: 10 MINUTES • COOK: 7 MINUTES

1. Place the cream in a small saucepan over medium heat and bring to just below a simmer.

2. Whisk the egg yolks and honey together in a small heatproof bowl. Whisking constantly, ladle up to half of the hot cream into the egg yolk mixture a little at a time.

3. Return the entire mixture to the saucepan, reduce the heat to medium-low and stir with a wooden spoon until the sauce coats the back of the spoon, about 3 minutes.

4. Pour the sauce through a fine-mesh sieve into a clean bowl and let cool to room temperature. Chill the sauce for at least an hour before serving.

MAKE AHEAD
You can refrigerate crème anglaise in an airtight container for up to 4 days.

1 cup (250 mL) half-and-half cream
2 large egg yolks
2 Tbsp (37 g) honey

CANDIED ORANGE PEEL

MAKES ABOUT 2 CUPS (500 ML) · PREP: 10 MINUTES · COOK: 20 MINUTES

1. Using a paring knife or an orange peeler, score the peel of the oranges without cutting into the flesh. Start by making 2 circular scores, 1 around the top and bottom of each fruit, and then 4 or 5 vertically to connect the round scores. Peel away the skin of the fruit, including the white pith, carefully and then cut into ¼-inch (0.5 cm) strips. (Reserve the flesh for salads or smoothies.)

2. Bring a small saucepan of water to a boil over high heat and drop in the citrus peel. Simmer for 1 minute, then strain, discarding the water.

3. Refill the saucepan with 1 ½ cups (375 mL) of fresh water and add the sugar. Bring to a simmer over medium-high heat, and then add the citrus peel. Simmer gently, uncovered, for about 20 minutes—the peel will look slightly, but not completely, translucent. Remove the saucepan from the heat and let the peel cool in the syrup to room temperature.

4. Pour the cooled peel and syrup into an airtight container and chill until ready to use. If gifting, pack the candied peel in its syrup in a mason jar, with a tag saying to refrigerate.

MAKE AHEAD
You can refrigerate the candied peel in the syrup in an airtight container for up to 3 months. If the peel or syrup begins to crystallize, warm it over low heat until the crystals dissolve, and then cool and chill again.

3 large navel oranges, well washed
1 ½ cups (300 g) granulated sugar

HELPFUL HINT
I love having candied orange peel on hand around holiday time, but if you are a fan of candied lemon peel, you can prepare this recipe using lemons instead. It will work in place of the candied orange peel in any of my recipes in this book.

Top left: Candied Orange Peel (page 318); *bottom right:* Festive Red Berry Compote (page 320)

This fruit compote smells like Christmas as it simmers—the aroma of pears, cranberries and raspberries melding with orange zest and spices is better than any scented candle you could buy. Best of all, this compote has many uses, making it a true holiday fixture and a wonderful gift. Serve it as a sauce with the Pomegranate Chocolate Tart (page 259) or the Chocolate and Irish Cream Marquise (page 303) or as a topping for pancakes or waffles. It works well with savoury dishes too: bake it on top of a wheel of Brie and serve with crackers.

FESTIVE RED BERRY COMPOTE

MAKES ABOUT 2 CUPS (500 ML) • PREP: 10 MINUTES • COOK: 20 MINUTES

1. Place the fruit, sugar, zest and spices in a saucepan and bring to a simmer over medium heat, stirring occasionally. Simmer gently, uncovered and stirring occasionally, until the pears are translucent, 15 to 20 minutes. Let the compote cool in the pan to room temperature.

2. Scoop the cooled compote into an airtight container and chill until ready to use.

Photo on page 319

MAKE AHEAD
You can refrigerate cooled compote in an airtight container for up to 3 weeks.

1 cup (110 g) frozen cranberries
1 cup (170 g) frozen raspberries
1 pear, peeled and cut into a small dice
½ cup (100 g) granulated sugar
2 tsp finely grated orange zest
½ tsp ground cinnamon
¼ tsp ground ginger
¼ tsp ground cloves

HELPFUL HINTS

Double the recipe for gift-giving, and add a label to the jars to let recipients know that the compote should be refrigerated and used within 3 weeks. (This recipe is suitable for canning, if you prefer to store it at room temperature in the pantry. Be sure to thoroughly sterilize the jars and lids in boiling water and follow safe canning procedures. You will need to leave ¼ inch (0.5 cm) of headspace at the top of each jar and boil the filled jars for 10 minutes.)

To take this compote from nice to a little naughty, add a splash (or more) of Grand Marnier to it after you take it off the heat.

These pecans are a perfect holiday add-on for dressing up a cake (or Pecan Butter Tart Cheesecake, page 268), sprinkling on a simple bowl of ice cream or stirring into your morning yogurt. They look stunning on a cheese plate and, packed in a jar, make an easy gift that will be well appreciated.

MAPLE TOASTED PECANS

GF
Ve

MAKES 2 CUPS (200 G) • PREP: 5 MINUTES • COOK: 15 MINUTES

MAKE AHEAD
You can store these pecans in a glass jar or airtight container at room temperature for up to 2 months.

2 cups (200 g) pecan halves
¼ cup (60 mL) pure maple syrup
Black pepper (optional)

1. Preheat the oven to 350°F (180°C) and line a baking tray with parchment paper.

2. Place the pecan halves in a bowl with the maple syrup and black pepper (if using) and toss well. Spread the mixture in an even layer on the baking tray.

3. Bake for about 15 minutes, stirring once or twice, until the pecans darken a little bit. Let cool completely on the tray on a wire rack. If gifting, pack the pecans into cellophane bags, sealable windowed bags or mason jars tied with ribbon.

Photo on page 228

HELPFUL HINT
The black pepper adds a nice little kick that balances the sweetness of the pecans, making them perfect for savoury dishes too. Sprinkle them over your favourite salads or soups.

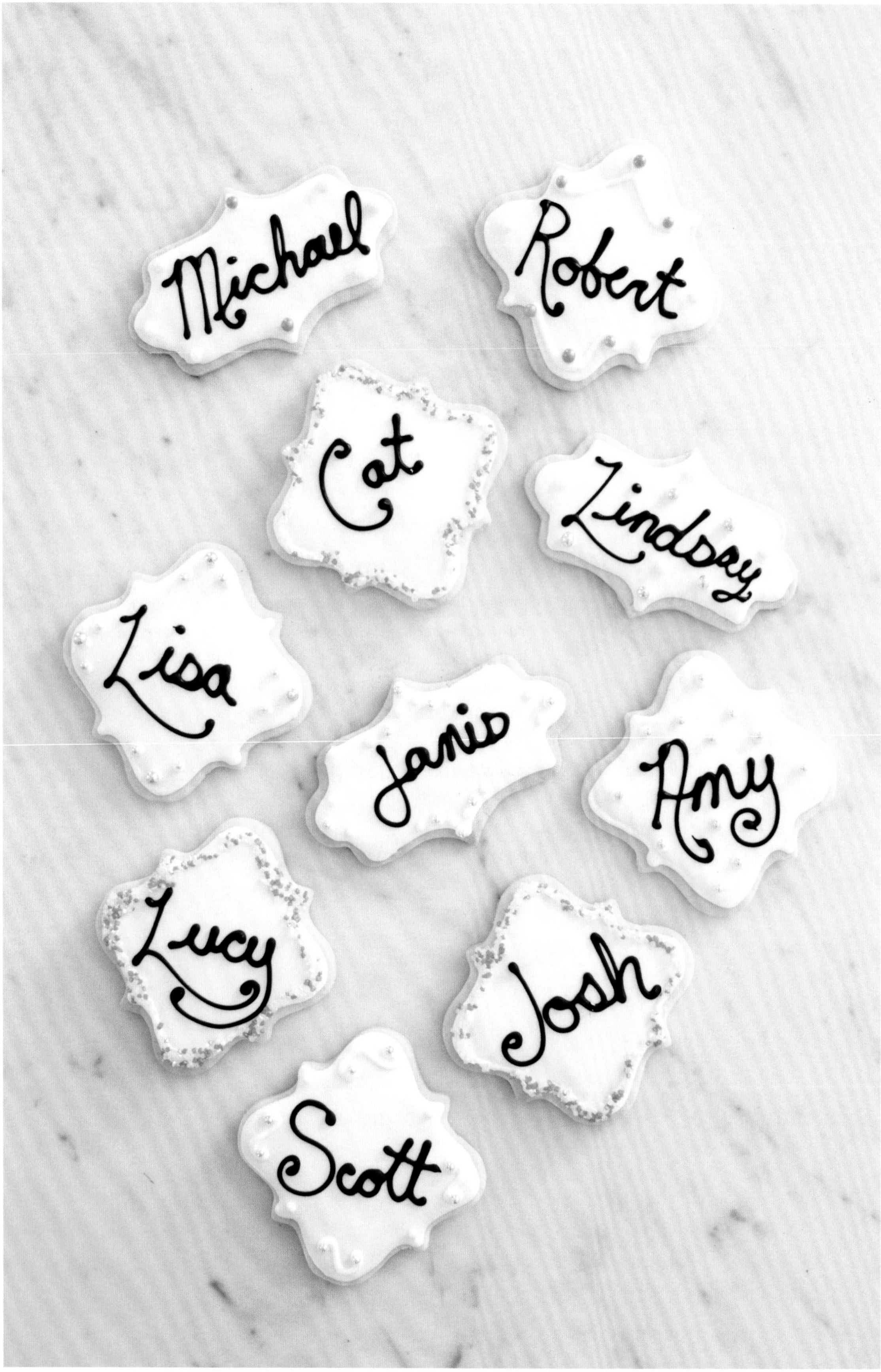
Michael
Robert
Cat
Lindsay
Lisa
Janis
Amy
Lucy
Josh
Scott

Acknowledgements

⌘

The journey of putting this cookbook together has been a truly joyful one and came to be because of the people I get to work with every day. The holiday season is all about sharing, and in the spirit of this season there are so many people with whom I need to share my appreciation.

Robert McCullough deserves first thanks for convincing me that this book was inside of me. My dearest Michael, you are my constant support and encourager, and I love you. My friends, including Mike and Tina Papp, and family who taste-tested everything in its various stages, you all deserve my thanks for your patience. Lisa Rollo tests, reviews and styles with festive fervour, and we constantly laugh through every step. Amy Pelley's grace and ease when testing and baking are always valued, especially on testing and photo days.

Photo days truly sparkled due to the vision and gift of photographer Janis Nicolay and stylist Catherine Therrien—and now I have two new, good friends to add to my Christmas list. And thank you to the Fairmont Jasper Park Lodge, especially Robin Linden, for inviting Michael and me to be a part of Christmas in November every year. We eagerly look forward to the trek to the Rockies to surround ourselves with crackling fireplaces, icy lakes, delicious treats and inspiring decor by Marna as well as Cory Christopher.

I consider Lucy Kenward a friend now because of the trust and respect we have built together through our conversations throughout the editing process, and Lesley Cameron was a valuable influence in the copyediting. Lindsay Paterson is a voice of reason in all of my Christmas chaos, and Scott Richardson and Rachel Cooper translated my festive spirit into gorgeous graphics. Josh Glover and the entire team at Penguin Random House Canada who are a part of putting this book into your hands also deserve my thanks.

Because of these people, in the true holiday spirit of the holiday season, I can now share this book with you, dear reader.

A Note to My British Readers

I know you'll be pleased to see that all of the recipes in this book include weighted measurements alongside the imperial to make your life simpler! I'm also including below a list of some of the terminology I believe is different in the UK than in North America. Here are the equivalents or appropriate substitutions to keep you cooking with confidence.

Canadian	British
All-purpose flour	Plain flour
Apple cider	Non-alcoholic, fresh-pressed apple juice
Arugula	Rocket
Bok choy	Pak choi
Bread flour	Strong white bread flour
Chex or Crispix	Similar to Shreddies and Frosted Shredded Wheat, or use more of the other two cereals in my snack mix (see page 50), or your own favourite
Chocolate: dark	Plain chocolate
Chocolate: semisweet or bittersweet	Dark or plain chocolate
Chocolate: unsweetened	Plain chocolate, 85% cocoa or higher
Cilantro and coriander	In North America, cilantro is the fresh herb and coriander is the dried version
Corn syrup	Golden syrup
Cornstarch	Corn flour
Food colouring paste	Food colour gel
Graham cracker crumbs	Digestive biscuit crumbs
Grainy mustard	Wholegrain mustard
Green onions	Scallions or spring onions
Milk: 2%	Semi-skimmed milk
Old Bay seasoning	If you can't find Old Bay, try a mix of celery salt, black pepper, crushed red pepper flakes, and paprika
Plain yogurt	Natural yoghurt
Red bell peppers	Red peppers
Sour cream	Soured cream or crème fraîche
Whipping cream	Double cream
White corn syrup	Light corn syrup
Whole wheat flour	Wholemeal flour
Zucchini	Courgette

Index